THE WAR PROFITEERS

Richard F. Kaufman

THE WAR PROFITEERS

THE BOBBS-MERRILL COMPANY, INC.
Indianapolis • New York

The Bobbs-Merrill Company, Inc.
A Subsidiary of Howard W. Sams & Co., Inc.
Publishers / Indianapolis Kansas City New York

To the memory of Robert M. Ockene

TABLE OF CONTENTS

TABLES

ACKNOWLEDGMENTS

This book was made possible by the foresight of Robert M. Ockene and the assistance of many friends and concerned citizens in the Department of Defense. The dedication to the public interest of elected representatives like Congressman Henry B. Gonzalez and Senator William Proxmire was a constant source of inspiration. A special note of thanks goes to my wife, Catharine, who typed most of the manuscript, helped with the editing, and made the many months of research and writing worthwhile.

INTRODUCTION

This book is a study of the way profits are taken from military spending—especially in the procurement of major weapons systems, who profits, and whether standards can be used to measure gains as reasonable or unreasonable. The close of the Second World War brought the end of what might be termed the classical era of war and peace, when wars had a beginning and an end and war profiteering rose and fell accordingly. The advent of the Cold War changed all that. The federal government has spent money for military purposes at wartime levels since 1951 and will continue to do so for the foreseeable future; the amounts spent during the wars in Korea and Indochina (née Vietnam) represent only peak expenditures from a wartime base. The nature of war profiteering has also changed, for it no longer depends upon a shooting war to flourish.

The Cold War imposed permanent mobilization on the United States and transformed the defense industry and the weapons procurement divisions of the Department of Defense into influential economic and political forces, insulated for the first time from the violent fluctuations of sudden mobilization followed by sudden demobilization. Among the advantages to those with major roles to play in the modern military establishment were opportunities for private wealth, career advancement, and corporate and bureaucratic expansion, provided the defense budget was kept high and allowed to rise steadily.

The difficulties that had been encountered by defense contractors prior to the Second World War, stigmatized as "merchants of death" by a press and public indignant over the scandals that followed the First World War, were largely avoided in the 1950s and 1960s. But war profiteering was not eliminated; it was institutionalized. For one thing, the decision was made, first by the Air Force, later by the Army and Navy, to shift most research out of the government and into the private sector. The rise of the defense industry and the government's reliance, to a greater degree than ever before, upon defense contractors for its weapons needs accompanied the decline of government in-house laboratories, arsenals and shipyards. At the same time, the traditional dividing line between government and industry was all but obliterated as high-ranking military and civilian officials shuttled back and forth between posts in the Pentagon and the defense community, creating blatant conflicts of interest which were ignored or glossed over.

Second, defense contractors learned to make large amounts, in some cases the largest amounts, of their profits practically indetectable by old-fashioned auditing methods. Much, if not most, of the profits from defense contracts are hidden in ways not apparent from an examination of a firm's profit and loss statement.

Third, the various government agencies charged with responsibilities for scrutinizing defense spending and monitoring profits accommodated themselves to the political reality of forces more powerful in the military establishment. Lax and sloppy enforcement of government regulations and contractual provisions, preferential treatment of the giant contractors, unconcern with the economic consequences of military spending, and intimidation of persons within the system who disagreed with such policies became the order of the day. The Bureau of the Budget, the Renegotiation Board, the General Accounting Office and other agencies, as well as Congress, granted so many exemptions and privileges to the military and its contractors that control over and public accountability for defense spending were gradually lost. This problem became so serious that in many cases even the service branches were unable to control critical aspects of their own weapons programs including costs, technical performance, and delivery schedules.

Finally, both wings of the military establishment launched a massive public relations and propaganda campaign to preserve and enhance the favorable image projected by them during the Second World War, to keep alive the fear of international communism, to win public and congressional support for higher defense budgets, to promote individual new weapons programs, and to sell the advantages of the contract system. The military-industrial "partnership" was heralded as a model of efficiency and effectiveness, and those who questioned it from outside were branded as kooks, Commie sympathizers, unilateral disarmers, or worse.

Thus, through the skillful use of Cold War fears, political and economic pressure, and Madison Avenue marketing techniques, the military establishment was able to secure for itself a firm grip on a disproportionate share of federal budgets and national resources. The success of its strategy is underlined by the fact that in 1969 and 1970, as the war in Indochina was being wound down (according to the Administration) with the gradual withdrawal of U.S. troops, and amid congressional demands for defense reductions, the debate in Washington centered around the question of whether to cut back expenditures from $75–80 billion annually to $70–75 billion annually; and the President asserted that his $73.2 billion budget request for national defense for fiscal year 1971 demonstrated a shift in national priorities and the transition from a wartime to a peacetime economy. After a rise in military outlays of almost seventy percent since 1965, federal decisionmakers were considering reductions of ten percent at most, and taking advance credit for the prospective cuts. But there can be no real shift in priorities until the defense budget is rolled back to a peacetime standard, and it will be recalled that $47 billion was spent for defense in 1965, a figure that seemed extravagant to many at the time.

Although defense profits in the age of permanent mobilization are characteristically concealed in one way or another, instances of the traditional kinds of profiteering are occasionally revealed. The details of a few are brought to light each year or so by the U.S. Tax Court adjudicating disputes between the Renegotiation Board and defense contractors. The Board itself reports determinations of about $40 million (including voluntary refunds) of excess profits each year, and in 1970 it announced a fifty percent increase in profit determinations over the prior year and the highest amount since 1960. Occasionally, the Justice Department enforces the seldom enforced laws prohibiting fraud and kickbacks on government contracts. Such a case, involving the procurement of rocket launchers used on aircraft in the war in Indochina, ended in convictions and prison sentences for the contractors in 1970.

The Pentagon began doing business with Chromcraft Corporation, a manufacturer of chrome furniture, in 1957 when the firm won an Air Force contract for rocket launchers. Its performance was so poor that early samples were rejected by the Air Force as unacceptable, and the number of units to be produced under the contract was reduced from 34,000 to fewer than 21,000. As a result, however, Chromcraft increased the unit price by one-third and collected cancellation costs of $133,000. In the early 1960s the Navy, which had originally developed this weapon, awarded the first of a new series of rocket launcher contracts to Chromcraft, impressed no doubt with the company's adroit financial management, if nothing else. The Army followed suit and soon Chromcraft was the sole-source producer of 2.75-inch rocket launchers for all the armed services.

In 1965 the firm merged with Alsco, Inc. By then, Chromcraft/Alsco had refined its highly profitable, although troublesome, technique of delivering defective products, then hiking the price and collecting cancellation costs for cutbacks. It began subcontracting out almost the entire job of making and assembling the rocket launchers. One subcontractor, an independent and honest manufacturer, did most of the actual work. Another, Western Molded Fibre Products, Inc., did a little of the work but performed the most lucrative service. It charged Chromcraft/Alsco for phony billings received from a dummy chemical corporation in Europe. Chromcraft/Alsco then shipped the finished rocket launchers to the Pentagon along with the padded costs supported by the phony billings. The difference between what Chromcraft/Alsco paid for legitimate services rendered and the inflated costs charged to the government was excess profit, about $4 million of which ended up in a Swiss bank account opened by the contractor to avoid disclosure.

The scheme was uncovered when a private accountant, going over the books of Western Molded, noticed the enormous invoices for chemicals but no inventory. The suspicious information was passed along to the Navy and FBI in 1967. Undeterred by the evidence of irregularities produced by the investigation that ensued, the military continued buying rocket launchers from Chromcraft/Alsco. In 1968 a federal grand jury indicted the company, its president and three others, charging a conspiracy to defraud the government, falsification of cost data, diversion of funds through a dummy corporation, and illegal kickbacks. After the indictments were issued, the Navy placed additional orders with the contractor.

The Navy defended its actions on the grounds that the rocket launchers were urgently needed in Vietnam and that Chromcraft/Alsco was the only available producer. This was true, as a result of the shortsighted and quite common policies pursued by the Navy. For years it dealt exclusively with that contractor, negotiating with it on a sole-source basis, refusing to allow others to bid for the work, and effectively stifling competition. Although the law requires advertised bidding whenever practicable, in the years 1961–1969 Navy officials used one of the built-in exceptions to make numerous determinations that advertising for bids, meaning competition, was not practicable, usually finding that "public exigency" required that there be no delay. The Army did the same, and in 1968 the Army and the Navy told a congressional committee that they were fully satisfied with the contractor's performance and the prices it was charging. Yet, in the same year the Army placed a limitation on the use of its launcher, namely, that it should not be fired over the heads of friendly troops for fear of converting them into friendly casualties. One year later, after the disclosures were made, the Navy finally solicited bids from others for a new rocket launcher contract. Forty companies responded and two submitted prices below Chromcraft/Alsco's. Later that year the Army's price was also lowered when it sought and easily obtained competition.

One of the most clouded aspects of the case was the part played by the Navy. As early as 1963 a low-echelon Navy auditor warned that actual costs could not be obtained from Chromcraft's accounting system. A similar warning was repeated in 1965, and in that year the General Accounting Office audited the contractor, found several discrepancies, and urged that "the Navy make a thorough review of Navy contracting at Chromcraft." Nothing was done by the Navy's top brass to follow up any of these reports, and were it not for the private accountant reporting what he discovered when he audited Western Molded, the Navy might still be buying rocket launchers from the same contractor. It is also notable that neither the Navy auditors nor the Renegotiation Board uncovered the scheme; nor did the General Accounting Office pursue the matter further than making recommendations to the Navy. The government's decision to accept the defendants' guilty pleas was unfortunate, because it prevented a trial on the evidence by which more details of the case might have been revealed and brought to the attention of the public.

The fact that the contractor in the Chromcraft case was convicted of violating the law was unusual. The fact that questionable accounting practices coupled with lax government contract administration were used to hide excess profits in padded costs was not unusual. More typical are the problems of major weapons purchases involving multihundred-million- and multibillion-dollar contracts with one or more of the giant aerospace contractors. Here the sheer magnitude of the money involved and the relationship between the partners of the military-industrial establishment make it unnecessary for criminal laws to be broken. If the enormous flow of funds required to finance the major weapons programs is kept up through wartime defense budgets, the profitability of government business is assured even without illegal acts, although the laws and the regulations may be bent somewhat. High profits are assured for the giant contractors most of the time in two ways: formally through profits allowable under the contract, which may or may not be excessive, and informally through the profits that are hidden in such things as padded costs, the use of government-owned equipment for commercial activities, the cash flow advantages of progress payments, the privilege of making late delivery of products that do not meet original specifications, bail-outs and get-well devices for contractors with cost overruns, executive salaries and fringe benefits, and the personal career opportunities for those who oscillate between the Pentagon and the defense industry and who operate within those two powerful publicly supported institutions. The excess military profits taken by the few are costs imposed upon everyone, and eventually, if the profits and the defense outlays that support them are large enough and sustained for a long enough time, the political structure and the economy will be seriously and irreparably altered. So long as military spending is kept at wartime levels and so long as the present contract system is used to meet military requirements, the problem of profiteering will remain and grow worse.

THE WAR PROFITEERS

Chapter One

WAR PROFITEERING IN AMERICAN HISTORY

Profiteering during war is a recurrent phenomenon that can be traced back to the earliest civilizations—and as one surveys the historical evidence there is a temptation to conclude that profiteering, like poverty, will always be with us. There is a difference, however, between the kind of profiteering customarily referred to and what is found to be the practice today. The difference lies in the nature of the military establishment, its relationship to industry, and the level of military spending.

In the past profiteering has been a sometime thing. War created a sudden transformation of society, causing traumatic shifts in the economic and political systems. To gear up for armed conflict it was necessary to enlarge the Army by conscription and the procurement of weapons and materials. Whatever mobilization measures were taken were temporary, for the duration of the emergency. After the war, conditions would return more or less to normal.

The profit motive and greed being what they are in human nature, it is not surprising to find examples of corruption in high places, overcharging for military supplies, and the taking of exorbitant profits and other advantages in the midst of the disrupted and accelerated conditions of war while the energies of most of the people are concentrated on the fighting. Because of suppression of the evidence, there has been a good deal of ignorance about these practices, and much of our knowledge has come years after the fact through individual research or investigations by various government groups. The work of the Nye Committee of Congress during the 1930s concerning profiteering in World War I was such an investigation. Disclosures of other congressional inquiries conducted during or after each of America's wars dating back to the Revolution have always created a certain amount of anger among the public and indignation within the government at having been so abused. Never again, it would be resolved, and a stream of laws, taxes and regulations has flowed from the wartime scandals. Strangely, few criminal prosecutions or dismissals of government officials have ever resulted from the investigations of profiteering, and the ineffectiveness of antiprofiteering measures has been assured by the near-hysteria accompanying mobilization for renewed warfare and the anxiety of political leaders that a failure to coddle the war industry could result in the failure of the war effort.

Still, the temporariness of war promised a return to peacetime conditions, a reduction of military expenditures, demobilization and the resumption of more normal relations between the government and its contractors. With the advent of the first of the modern advanced weapons systems, the steel-plated warship developed toward the end of the nineteenth century, the possibility of total demobilization began to decline. After World War I the forces in favor of continued government expenditures for the purchase of weapons systems and in favor of a large permanent peacetime military establishment began to gather the strength to overwhelm the older tradition.

The Nye Committee, whose relentless and thorough investigations have not yet been equaled in this area, glimpsed the growing tendency for war profiteering to become institutionalized, a fixed pattern of doing business in war or peace.

THE COLONIAL WARS

Three major stages of profiteering can be identified in the development of America prior to the Revolution: the original conquest by European colonizers, the Intercolonial Wars, and the pre-revolutionary struggle. During the initial period of exploration and conquest, bands of soldiers and later colonists came to subjugate the natives, plunder their cities and ship as much booty to the mother country as could be carried off. It no doubt pleased Christopher Columbus to discover that the American Indian lived in a primitive state unencumbered by techniques to resist the predatory European invaders, as he recorded in his journal:

> They do not bear arms or know them, for I showed them swords and they took them by the blade and cut themselves through ignorance. They have no iron. . . . They should be good servants.[1]

Bernal Diaz, accompanying Hernán Cortés and the conquistadores some years later, articulated their purposes with aristocratic candor: "We came here to serve God and the king, and also to get rich." The Spaniards held on to their newly acquired territory through all of the methods observed by Machiavelli in *The Prince* (written in 1513): by pillaging, by occupation and by administration through local officials and taking tribute.

The Intercolonial Wars lasted three-quarters of a century, until 1762. In this time there were four definable conflicts involving England, France and Spain. The contest was to decide which colonial power would own the North American continent, and, often as not, the combatants reverted to the ancient European forms of looting, pillaging and sacking one another's towns and property in the innumerable battles that were fought. Throughout, skirmishes were fought against the Indians, who clung stubbornly to the idea that their land was theirs.

In this period the colonists began to use taxation to finance the wars and to purchase arms and supplies by contract from private suppliers, and William Pepperell of Maine emerged, in the early 1700s, as the prototype of a kind of New World Renaissance man

---

[1] "The Journal of Christopher Columbus," in Wilcomb E. Washburn (ed.), *The Indian and the White Man* (New York: New York University Press, 1964), p. 5.

who could successfully combine the roles of entrepreneur, military leader and public officeholder. He was a shipbuilder, shipper, naval supplier, merchant, landowner, and colonel in the Massachusetts militia. In 1727 he became a member of the Massachusetts royal council. In 1745, while president of the council, he led an attack against Louisbourg, the French bastion on Cape Breton Island, gateway to the St. Lawrence River, guardian of the Grand Banks fishing grounds, haven for French privateers and a fabulous prize. During the campaign more than a million pounds sterling was taken off captured French vessels alone. Pepperell was knighted, made a baronet, commissioned a colonel in the British army and given a regiment, to be raised in America. In 1747 he built four warships for the British navy and a few years later was commissioned a major-general in the British army and appointed acting governor of Massachusetts.

At the same time the more enduring patterns of profiteering were becoming familiar. Governors and military commanders began to assign the profitable military-supply responsibilities to their friends and relatives, and some took kickbacks. Late delivery, no delivery, and delivery of inferior goods were common and helped decide a number of battles, such as the one near Fort Duquesne (now Pittsburgh) in 1755, fought by the British and French to decide the possession of the rich Ohio Territory. The British force, led by General Edward Braddock and George Washington, was routed in a major disaster. Both men complained bitterly of the high prices, lack of supplies and inferior supplies, although large sums had been spent on military contracts. Corruption in the colonies of France was, if anything, worse. At the close of the Intercolonial Wars, the French, having lost, turned their attention to rumors of official misconduct. An investigation disclosed the fact that high government officials in Canada had sold military supplies intended for the Colonial Army to traders, then repurchased them at higher prices, inflated the costs of gifts to Indians, charged the government for the cost of entertainments and otherwise lined their pockets with public funds.

In the years preceding the Revolution, England extracted as much wealth as possible out of her colonies as part of an overall policy to defray the costs of the Seven Years' War against the French and the expenses of her worldwide empire. Americans viewed English taxes for what they were—imperial tribute—and they refused to pay. Benjamin Franklin plainly accused British officials of profiteering from military expenditures and "useless expeditions," and linked the costs of profiteering with the impropriety of taxing the colonists. He wrote:

That Governors often come to the Colonies merely to make Fortunes, with which they intend to return to Britain, are not always Men of the best abilities and Integrity, have no Estates here, nor any natural Connections with us, that should make them heartily concern'd for our Welfare; and might possibly be sometimes fond of raising and keeping up more Forces than necessary, from the Profits accruing to themselves, and to make Provision for their Friends and Dependents. . . . That compelling the Colonies to pay Money without their Consent would be rather like raising contributions in an Enemy's Country, than taxing of Englishmen for their own publick benefit.[2]

THE REVOLUTION

Just as it had in Colonial times, Yankee ingenuity and business enterprise rose to the challenge of getting rich in war during the Revolution. Americans traded with the enemy, engaged in privateering (a form of legalized piracy) and sold guns and supplies to the Army and Navy. The profit motive provided an irresistible impulse for all but the most radical revolutionaries, with the exception of a few moderates like Washington. A Hessian officer employed by the British wrote from New York City:

Almost open trade is carried on from here with the rebels; at least both sides close one eye. Passionately anxious for gold and silver, they constantly brought us cattle and other provisions from the outset.[3]

Speculation in the privateers became the eighteenth-century counterpart to the stock market. Shares in privateers were widely sold, traded, discounted and used as collateral not only by merchants, but by military officers and government officials as well. Estimates of the numbers engaged in privateering range as high as 90,000, compared to about 100,000 who bore arms in all of the military services combined, including repeated enlistments, and the con-

[2] Letter to William Shirley, in Ralph Ketchum (ed.), *The Political Thought of Benjamin Franklin* (Indianapolis: Bobbs-Merrill, 1965), pp. 98–99.

[3] Robert A. East, *Business Enterprise in the American Revolutionary Era* (New York: Columbia University Press, 1938), p. 180.

tinued demand for seamen created a serious shortage of military and arms-manufacturing manpower.

Although there were some real shortages as a result of the non-importation agreements and the interruptions of warfare, monopoly was chiefly responsible for direct inflation, and the monopolists and their brethren, the engrossers and forestallers, prospered and multiplied. It was a time for speculation and overcharging at anyone's expense, including the soldiers at Valley Forge, who went hungry and frozen while fat merchants reveled in nearby Philadelphia. Profiteers included high government officials such as Samuel Chase, who, acting on the knowledge he gained as a member of Congress from Maryland, tried to corner the market on flour. When this incident was discovered, the Maryland legislature prohibited merchants from representing it in Congress. Virginia passed a similar law.

Some of the revolutionaries took the Revolution seriously as an overthrow of old tyrannies, including the tyranny of economic exploitation, and there was deep resentment among the more radical leaders as well as popular indignation over profiteering because of the shortages and inflation. In response the revolutionary committees and a number of state legislatures and local governments tried to impose price limitations, the first serious effort to control profiteering in America. The controversy surrounding the issue of price-fixing separated the oligarchic from the democratic subversives. In 1776 the New England states agreed upon a series of price and wage controls, ordering prosecution of offenders, with one-half the amount of the fines imposed on profiteers to go to the informer as a bounty. These and other antiprofiteering measures were opposed by merchants such as Nathanael Greene, who happened also to be Quartermaster General of the Army and who denounced them as "founded in public covetousness, a desire to have the property of the few at a less value than the demand will warrant to the owner." Even Washington, who damned the profiteers as "murderers of our cause," was against controls on grounds that they were "inconsistent with the very nature of things."[4] Rampant profiteering by government officials, often acting in secret concert with private contractors, finally erupted in a series of congressional investigations and public scandals. Merchants in public office were mingling the government's

4 Merrill Jensen, *The New Nation* (New York: Random House, 1950), p. 183.

business with their own to a degree far beyond the limits of propriety and legality. Procurement officials had purchased goods for the government from themselves and their business partners, used government vessels and wagons to carry their own goods, seized public property as security for debts incurred by them on behalf of the government, failed to maintain adequate books or records or otherwise account for their activities, and practiced nepotism, favoritism and various other forms of corruption.

Robert Morris was the master profiteer. From his position as chairman of the committees of Congress with authority over finances and government purchasing, and after 1781 as Superintendent of Finance, he was at the hub of innumerable schemes and intricate government-business relationships. Acting for his own personal gain while in office, he exported and imported, fitted out and employed ships, managed specific supplies, used his bank in Paris for government transactions, had his friends appointed to important government posts, awarded contracts to himself and his partners, and saw that his business associates were paid for claims against the depleted public treasury while equally valid ones by others were denied. In 1782 Congress directed him to look into "fraud, negligence, or waste of public property." Instead, he modified contracting procedures by substituting advertised competitive bidding for other methods of procurement—requisitions, commissions and noncompetitive contracts.

In theory newspaper announcements would indicate the day on which sealed bids would be received for a specified contract. The lowest bid complying with the specifications would be accepted. The government would make a small advance with the contract and monthly payments based on vouchers. In practice Morris deviated from his own system by awarding contracts to his friends without going to the bother of advertising for bids.

Morris also engineered what historian Merrill Jensen has termed an "Army-creditor" combination, composed of military officers and merchants who had speculated in government obligations and who had a mutual interest in a strong central government that could assume and pay off the debts contracted during the war. As the war drew to a close, Morris feared the loss of speculative profits and wrote that "a continuance of the War is necessary until our Confederation is more strongly knit, until a sense of the obligations to support it shall be more generally diffused amongst all Ranks of

American Citizens, until we shall acquire the Habit of paying Taxes." Seeing an opportunity to unite the military, who were demanding lifetime pensions as well as back pay, with the merchants, Morris met with fellow nationalists such as Alexander Hamilton and James Wilson and Army officers to decide on how to press their claims. But Washington denounced the dissidents at Newburgh in 1783 and the plot dissolved. Later that year most of the Army was disbanded as the nation demobilized with the end of the war.

THE CIVIL WAR

From the Civil War through World War II popular outrage forced the government to make efforts to control at least the most blatant forms of war profiteering. Statutes requiring competition for military contracts, conflict-of-interest laws, price and wage controls, and excess profit taxes were tried. But in each war the controls were evaded or not fully enforced, and profiteers prospered, as the major congressional investigations during or following the wars demonstrated. There are distinctions of scale and technique spurred by industrialization as we move from the eighteenth- to the nineteenth-century conflicts. The Civil War, for example, used up much more men and materials than had been consumed in previous wars (over 600,000 men were killed), and opportunities for pocketing public moneys were greatly increased.

Few opportunities were missed. Corruption by government officials and contractors was widespread. The Secretary of War, Simon Cameron, was implicated in a number of sordid transactions and was removed from office by President Lincoln after disclosures were made in congressional hearings. The congressional investigation, headed by Representative Charles H. Van Wyck, concluded after extensive testimony was taken:

The government has been the victim of more than one conspiracy, and remarkable combinations have been formed to rob the treasury. The profits from the sale of arms to the government have been enormous, and realized, too, in many instances, even by our own citizens, through a system of brokerage as unprincipled and dishonest, as unfriendly to the success and welfare of the nation, as the plottings of actual treason.[5]

5 Thirty-seventh Congress, second session, House Select Committee to Inquire into the Contracts of the Government, "House Report No. 2," Part 1 (1861), p. 34.

A government commission headed by Colonel Joseph Holt and Robert Dale Owen found in a separate investigation that contractors had adopted the attitude that "the country, as a whole, is a fair subject of plunder." The author of the definitive history of the Union Army wrote that Army contractors handled at least a billion dollars of government money during the war and, by conservative estimate, kept half of it.[6]

A new industrial order was hammered out of the Civil War, composed largely of war profiteers and others who grew rich on government contracts and the requirements of national emergency, and who during the war and its aftermath were able to influence the economic reconstruction. Charles Beard called it the "Second American Revolution," winning for industry the assurance of "an immense national market surrounded by a tariff wall bidding defiance to the competition of Europe." Business tycoons also won banking and investment privileges, land grants, railroad subsidies, and repeal of the moderate wartime income tax. The most important of the nineteenth-century American capitalists acquired their first great fortunes during the war. J. P. Morgan, Philip Armour, Clement Studebaker, John Wanamaker, Cornelius Vanderbilt, and the du Ponts had all been government contractors. Andrew Carnegie got rich speculating in bridge and rail construction while assistant to the Assistant Secretary of War in charge of military transport.

THE NAVAL ARMS RACE AND THE SPANISH-AMERICAN WAR

Although industrial technology began to be applied to the problems of killing men and destroying property during the Civil War (breech-loading rifles, mortars, exploding shells, machine guns, rockets, incendiary weapons, land mines, sea mines, grenades, searchlights, balloons, small ironclad vessels and a submarine were used), not until the Spanish-American War, toward the end of the century, did anything like a modern advanced weapons system come into play—the gigantic, expensive, steel-plated, steam-propelled, heavily armed warship—and not until World War I was it used in large numbers on a sustained basis. The advanced weapons system, requiring large sums of money to support the physical facilities, materials and manpower necessary for its manufacture, as well as long

[6] Fred A. Shannan, *The Organization and Administration of the Union Army, 1861–1865* (Magnolia, Mass.: Peter Smith, 1965), Vol. 1, p. 71.

lead times for planning and coordination so that numerous parts and components can be produced and brought together at the right time, is the symbol of the international arms race, the expensive military budget and the high-powered defense industry that has come to be a hallmark of the twentieth century. From the beginning it has represented an occasion for profiteering. More importantly, the interests ranged around the modern weapons system have created pressures that have permanently altered the private sector, the public sector and the relationship between the two.

Because of exorbitant prices being paid by the government for armor plate for warships, Congress investigated the two sole manufacturers, the Carnegie Steel Company and the Bethlehem Steel Company, in 1896.[7] Bethlehem was charging the Navy more than 200 percent the price being charged to the Russian government for the same armor plate. Both companies denied they were making excessive profits from their United States sales, and Andrew Carnegie himself testified that the only reason he was in the armor-plate business was out of patriotism. When Congress established a fixed price for armor plate both companies refused to sell to the government at the price deemed reasonable by it, and they would not permit the government to inspect their books to determine their profits. Pressed by the requirements of the war, Congress finally gave in and abolished the price limits. The disclosures that Bethlehem and Carnegie were rigging their bids, that naval procurement officers owned or had interests in some of the patents awarded for the processes used by the companies and that naval officers were in the habit of going on leave of absence in order to work temporarily for Navy contractors and then returning to active duty, raised disquieting questions about the way the Navy was procuring its weapons and reinforced the suspicions that the contractors were taking advantage of the government. Neither Congress nor the Executive pursued the matter further.

WORLD WAR I: THE NYE COMMITTEE

In addition to the unprecedented carnage and havoc produced in World War I, profiteering in the traditional sense reached some

[7] Fifty-fourth Congress, second session, Senate Report No. 1453, "Report of Committee on Naval Affairs on Prices of Armor for Vessels of the Navy" (1897).

sort of zenith as military spending climbed to a phenomenal (for the time) $11 billion. There were financial as well as physical killings to be made, and they were executed so mercilessly by the war contractors that a public cry of outrage against them was provoked that reverberated for two decades. On May 27, 1918, President Woodrow Wilson, addressing a joint session of Congress, warned about the heavy war profiteering going on: "There is such profiteering now, and the information with regard to it is available and indisputable." One month later the Federal Trade Commission (FTC) published a brief report entitled "Profiteering," containing evidence of "inordinate greed and barefaced fraud," deceptive accounting practices, artificial price inflation, and huge profits taken by basic industries such as steel, oil and gas.[8] One phenomenon exposed for the first time by the FTC was the practice of paying extraordinary salaries and bonuses to corporate officers of war suppliers. For example, the American Metal Company in 1917 paid salaries and bonuses to four of its officers of over $135,000 each, one other more than $200,000 and another more than $350,000. The contrast with the foot soldier's $1.25 per day was something the average citizen could understand. Because there was still a clear idea of what profiteering was in those days, public consciousness of the practice probably reached an all-time high as disclosures of other investigations were made during and following the war, and even groups such as the American Legion lobbied in behalf of war-profit controls. One popular approach, adopted by the American Legion in its 1922 National Convention, was to demand that materials as well as men be made subject to a universal draft in time of war, thus distributing the burden of armed conflict on capitalist and workingman alike and, hopefully, discouraging war by eliminating profits. The 1924 platforms of the Democratic and Republican parties made similar recommendations. In 1931 General Douglas MacArthur, then Army Chief of Staff, referred to "profiteering by the unscrupulous contractor" in his testimony before the War Policies Commission.[9] In the same hearings Norman Thomas, the Socialist leader, said that the war-profit outrages proved that the profit system does not work under emergency conditions, and he called for a "war against poverty" through

8 Sixty-fifth Congress, second session, "Senate Document No. 248" (1918).

9 Seventy-second Congress, first session, War Policies Commission Hearings, "House Document No. 163" (1931), p. 365.

a planned economy and distribution for use, not profit.[10] "Take the profits out of war" had become a national slogan.

In 1934 the Senate, disturbed by the continued public unrest over war profiteering and allegations about the effects of American business practices on world rearmament, created the Special Committee on Investigation of the Munitions Industry. Its chairman was Senator Gerald P. Nye, a Republican from North Dakota who had previously been chairman of the Senate committee investigating the Teapot Dome naval-oil scandal of the late 1920s. Senators Arthur H. Vandenburg, Walter F. George, Bennett Champ Clark, Homer T. Bone, James P. Pope and W. Warren Barbour were also members of the new committee.

The Nye investigation lasted almost three years and was the first systematic study of the structure of what was then known as the munitions industry, its relations with the military, and the international sale of arms. It disinterred many of the World War I contracts, providing conclusive evidence of how big business performed during the war. It showed that profiteering had been much more extensive than was generally known. The most serious abuses uncovered were in connection with the large Navy contracts. In addition to excessive profits on ship construction, the committee found an absence of real competition and suggested collusion on the part of the shipbuilders in the submission of bids: "If there was no collusion, there was a sympathetic understanding among big companies of each other's desires." And, "If there were no conversations about bidding among them, there was telepathy."[11]

Shipbuilders, the committee reported, bought shipyards from the government for a fraction of their value. In at least one case the sale to the shipbuilder was prearranged before the yard was built. The New York Ship Company allowed the government to construct a yard on the company's land only after the government agreed to give the $14 million facility to the company after the war for $500,000. Newport News paid $2 million for facilities built by the government at a cost of $10 million, and there was evidence that this deal was prearranged also.

The ship contracts themselves were of a cost-plus type, that is,

10 *Ibid.*, pp. 722–27.

11 Seventy-fourth Congress, second session, *Report of the Special Committee on Investigation of the Munitions Industry, U.S. Senate,* 5 volumes (1936). The quotations are from Vol. 5, p. 8.

the government agreed to pay the shipbuilder all of his costs of production plus an additional amount as profit. But contract costs were inflated by questionable charges such as rental payments, which were larger than the plant values of the companies whose facilities were used. For example, in 1918 Bethlehem made "rental payments" of more than $11 million to one of its own subsidiaries, Union Iron Works Company. The net plant value of Union Iron Works that year was only $5 million. The following year Bethlehem paid the same subsidiary $7.5 million for rentals. The effect of such spurious rental payments, of course, was to conceal the contractors' profits and his tax liability. The Navy also allowed wines, liquors, cigars and other entertainment expenses as legitimate costs of ship-building. After the war was over, knowingly exorbitant claims were filed against the government for cancellation costs.

In an updating of part of the old Federal Trade Commission study, the committee further documented the charges that corporate executives and so-called dollar-a-year men made tremendous personal fortunes from war business. In a two-year period Eugene G. Grace, President of Bethlehem, received almost $3 million in bonuses from his company. Another Bethlehem executive, J. W. Powell, left the company to contribute his services to the war effort as head of the Emergency Fleet Corporation, created by Congress to establish a government-owned and -operated merchant marine. While employed by the government he received as a "bonus" from Bethlehem a share in all the profits from the construction of a large number of ships built by the company for the Navy and of all ships built for the Emergency Fleet Corporation. On top of this astonishing conflict of interests, Powell later was a witness in behalf of Bethlehem in a lawsuit against it by the Emergency Fleet Corporation. Bethlehem won the suit and Powell submitted a bill to it for five percent of the amount that the court found due to Bethlehem. The Emergency Fleet Corporation, by the way, had such a reputation for paying exorbitant prices for engines and other equipment that Wilson's Secretary of the Treasury, William G. McAdoo, once complained that the machinery being bought must have been made of silver instead of iron and steel.

The dates on some of the contracts were changed to permit the shipbuilders to report their profits after the repeal of the war taxes, when the rates were much lower, and one company, Newport News, was in the habit of understating its reported income for tax purposes by several hundred percent. For one year the contractor reported his tax liability as $153,000. The revenue agents found profits of $1,664,000, and the case was finally settled for a payment of $1,300,000.

Probably the most significant wartime shipbuilding case of all concerned a series of contracts awarded to several shipbuilders by the Navy for a total of 91 destroyers. The contracts were awarded late in the war, and when it ended, none of the keels of the ships had yet been laid. The logical decision at that point would have been to cancel the contracts. Instead, the Navy permitted the contractors to proceed and ultimately paid out $181 million for the unneeded vessels. The committee tried without much success to discover why the program was not terminated. The contractors could only say that they had a contract, it was not canceled, so they built the ships. Theirs was not to reason why. But in 1933 the Naval Appropriations Committee had raised the same question and received an intriguing response from one of its witnesses, Admiral Pratt, which the Nye Committee quoted in its hearings and its final report. The question was why, since there was no longer a desperate need for destroyers, Navy ship construction was not slowed down.

ADMIRAL PRATT: That seems like a very fair question. I cannot give you a real, practical, definite reason why, but I should say this: That if you start a big machine moving, such as this production is, it takes a certain amount of time before it gets slowed up and working normally; and I should think that that had about as much to do with it as anything. We just got swept into it and, before we could get our breath and stabilize and get together, there we were with our output.[12]

Mobilization for war, especially the purchasing of large weapons systems from private contractors, had become to a certain extent self-perpetuating, and the process once begun was not so easily turned off. The Navy would not lobby for a reduced budget just because the war was ended. The contractors would not offer to go out of the weapons business. Quite the reverse.

Profiteering, in the sense of financial gains from government contracts obtained during the war, had provided the original impetus for the committee's investigation, and throughout, it was on the lookout for evidence of corruption and hard bargaining. As the

12 *Ibid.*, Vol. 5, p. 58.

inquiry proceeded it became clear that there was much more to the problem than could be found on the profit-and-loss statement. There were what the committee called "Gains to Contractors in Addition to Large Profits." These included the absence of risk on government contracts due to cost-plus contracting, whereby the contractor was assured of reimbursement for all costs plus a profit; the advancement of large sums of money to contractors before completion of the contract so that it was unnecessary for them to borrow or use their own funds (a total of $355 million was advanced by the War Department to contractors during the war); and an overgenerous policy toward claims by contractors for payments in addition to those specified in the contract and payments for the cancellation of contracts at the war's end.

As the committee studied these aspects of military procurement, other problems arose, such as the momentum generated by the Navy's ship program so that it could not be stopped even when the war was over. The investigation was thus propelled forward, and it came to focus as much on postwar military-contracting and weapons-industry practices as on the subject of "war profiteering." The results of its inquiry into peacetime problems produced the most disturbing and far-reaching findings.

It was puzzling, for example, to discover that in 1933 the Navy's need for a large number of ships brought about an increase in the prices charged by the private shipbuilders, a fact readily admitted by the shipbuilders. How was it that the government, which was in a dominant position as a buyer of ships and presumably needed them for national security, would subject itself to artificial price increases? The explanation was related more to political pressures than to economic principles. First, the shipbuilders opposed the use of Navy yards for new ship construction despite the fact that the cost of building ships was less in Navy yards than in private yards. The Navy yards at the time were considered excellent "yardsticks" for comparing the costs of private construction with government estimates. One study showed that a cruiser could be built for more than $2 million less in a Navy yard than privately. As a result, corporate officials such as the vice-president of Newport News considered it better "to kill the Navy bill entirely" than to spend any of it in Navy yards.[13] Second, the contractors' opposition to Navy

[13] *Ibid.*, Vol. 5, pp. 8–9.

yards succeeded in making the government dependent upon the private shipbuilders for most of its warships and the abandonment of the Navy's yardsticks. This led to the granting of special favors to the contractors, including the increased prices of 1933 and 1934, and the Navy's opposition to profit limitations in 1934. In return, the committee found, the shipbuilders lobbied in Washington for the Navy's interests. It was able to influence the passage of legislation and the appointment of congressmen to certain committees. The Washington lobbyist for United Drydocks claimed that the price of getting a bill through Congress was $50,000.

The government's dependence upon the war industries generally led the committee to be skeptical of the possibility of eliminating profiteering with regulatory schemes. In addition to the decreasing capability for government production of ships and other war materials, the committee observed that the administration of industrial controls would necessarily be placed "in the hands of men who are industrially trained and sympathetic to industry's contentions." Government officials would be drawn from the businesses they are supposed to regulate. The Bethlehem executive who headed the Emergency Fleet Corporation was only one of many such wartime examples. The then Secretary of War, Patrick J. Hurley, had stated publicly a few years before the committee's investigation that under the War Department's current plan the purchasing of supplies in any future war would be controlled by the industrialists, and it was clear that this was already the case at the time the committee was conducting its hearings. The committee concluded that government antiprofiteering efforts in procurement, price fixing and taxation would be undermined by infiltration from officials of the war industries: "It would be contrary to both their self-interest and their root convictions for them to do anything calculated drastically to curtail these profits."

The committee was able to perceive in the war experience and current practices the relative power of the military and war industries that underlies their formal relationship. It was disturbed over the government's weak bargaining position with respect to a number of contracts then in contention, over the fact that the War Department had already directed its business to a very few contractors and over the likelihood that further concentration of war business would occur in any future war. "Under these circumstances," the committee predicted, "there will be an overwhelming preponderance of bargaining strength on the side of the contractor when the many doubtful points which must be settled by negotiation arise." The military demonstrated little willingness to assist its own contracting officials in contract negotiations, as the War and Navy Departments had practically no information on the costs of war production or on profits, thus making it difficult for contract officers to evaluate proposals and estimates from industry. Nor were there any government agencies that could act as a brake on the accelerating flow of money to the contractors (military spending began rising after 1934). The committee foresaw further weakening of the government's position under the pressures of future wartime conditions and the granting of higher profits and other favorable terms. "Certain contracts will be of such crucial importance to the prosecution of the war that there will be a strong tendency for the Government to modify any previously conceived contracting arrangements if the contractor urges it."

The most sensational disclosures and the most controversial findings concerned the international activities of the munitions makers, as they were then known. Briefly, many of the major weapons suppliers actively sought to sell their wares in foreign countries and with the collaboration of the War and Navy Departments were quite successful. In the process a new arms race was being fueled that, some feared, would lead to a second world war. Sales methods revealed by the committee included bribery of foreign government officials; the use of naval warships and planes for sales-demonstration purposes; the hiring of retired and reserve military officers by arms contractors; and the employment of lobbyists to defeat the goals of disarmament conferences, obtain support for military expenditures in Congress, and oppose recalcitrant congressmen in their campaigns for reelection.

Shipbuilders, aircraft companies, chemical suppliers and small-arms manufacturers beat the international bushes for new markets and sold indiscriminately to foreign governments whether or not they were at peace or at war with one another. The Sino-Japanese War was a great source of business, and in the 1930s companies such as Lockheed Aircraft and Douglas Aircraft were selling planes, Sperry Gyroscope was selling aviation instruments and the du Pont Company was selling explosives to Japan and to Japan's puppet state in Manchuria, Manchukuo, despite the fact that the United States had condemned the Japanese aggression against China and refused to recognize Manchukuo. At the same time, Boeing Aircraft and United Aircraft were selling planes to China. When it was revealed that some of the sales involved the giving of United States military secrets to Japan, military witnesses testified that it is good policy to sell munitions to our potential enemies because (1) "it gives business to this country," and (2) "it gives us the advantage of knowing at least part of what they are buying and what guns it is intended for." Meanwhile, United Aircraft, Sperry Gyroscope, du Pont, the Remington Arms Company and the Electric Boat Company were carrying on a brisk trade with Germany and Italy, and they and numerous other firms were also selling war materials throughout Europe and South America. The committee was particularly disturbed over the role of American firms in the rearming of Germany—a clear violation of the Versailles Treaty.

Much confusion has grown up around what the committee concluded from the evidence it gathered about profiteering and the arms traffic. It did not say that the munitions makers had started World War I or that they were engaged in a conspiracy to begin another in order to boost their profits. In one of its many findings it did suggest a relationship between the unbridled activities of the war industries and the possibilities of war:

> While the evidence before this Committee does not show that wars have been started solely because of the activities of munitions makers and their agents, it is also true that wars rarely have one single cause, and the Committee finds it to be against the peace of the world for selfishly interested organizations to be left free to goad and frighten nations into military activity.[14]

The committee was properly alarmed at what it found. At one point in the hearing the president of the Sperry Gyroscope Company offered to explain why he believed the sale of military hardware abroad served the goals of peace and humanity. He said, among other things, "We believe that the mechanization of warfare is benign in its effect in that it tends toward a condition where the issues of warfare will be decided by the effectiveness of mechanism rather than by the relative ability of the participants to sacrifice human lives."[15] Today such a statement seems ridiculous in view

14 *Ibid.*, Vol. 1, p. 8.
15 *Ibid.*, Vol. 1, p. 59.

of the horrors of the wars that have since transpired and somehow the word "benign" has dropped out of the vocabulary of the present-day military contractor. But even in the 1930s it would have taken a group considerably less sophisticated than a committee of senators to receive those remarks with equanimity or not to question the sanity of the speaker. At the very least they should have been impressed with the dangers inherent in a system that encourages the profit motive to influence weapons policy.

Two basic recommendations emerged from the investigation, each one designed to get at the root of what was found wrong with military procurement and the private manufacture of military weapons. First, the committee advocated government ownership of all facilities necessary to construct all warships, gun forgings, projectiles and armor plate, as well as for the production of powder, rifles, pistols and machine guns. In other words, it recommended nationalization of much of the arms industry, an idea that has recently been revived by John Kenneth Galbraith. It was convinced, as we have seen, of the unenforceability of profit limitations and the fact that other regulations would be easily evaded by the influential munitions makers. It took note of the wartime experience when "the munitions companies insisted throughout on their pound of flesh in the form of high profits for their production, and did not let their patriotism stand in the way of their 'duty as trustees' to the stockholders," and of the pressure they exerted on the services for contracts, for help in foreign sales and in opposition to arms embargoes and other disarmament measures. And it pointed out that the government was already heavily engaged in arms production, manufacturing half of its naval vessels in Navy shipyards and an equal proportion of its guns and ammunition in government arsenals.

The aircraft industry was exempted from this recommendation, "because airplane and engine construction are still rapidly developing arts and in that way different from the somewhat more standard articles for which it is proposed to have the government acquire facilities." The committee was willing to allow this young industry, holding out more promise than performance but in a stage of experimentation and rapid technological advancement, to remain in the hands of a still highly competitive industry.

Second, the committee made a series of recommendations to strengthen the restrictions on shipments of arms and war materials to foreign countries and to forbid military aid to all belligerents. These were intended to slow down the arms race by preventing United States firms from contributing to it by pushing their goods abroad and to maintain our neutrality in the event of war between foreign nations. The Neutrality Act marked an effort to restore the policy of noninvolvement in foreign entanglements followed from George Washington's day until the Spanish-American War. Frustrated and disillusioned by the results of our greatest entanglement to date, World War I, the "war to end wars," Americans were anxious to avoid another, and curbing the munitions makers seemed an obvious step to take.

WORLD WAR II: THE TRUMAN COMMITTEE

Writing in the mid-1950s, former President Harry S Truman, discussing the investigations he headed as a U. S. senator during World War II, damned the earlier work of Senator Nye as "pure demagoguery in the guise of a congressional investigating committee." According to Truman, the Nye Committee "made it appear that the munitions manufacturers had caused World War I," and the Neutrality Act that resulted from the hearings "placed an embargo on arms shipments to the democratic forces in Spain," and "was partly responsible for our losing that country as a potential ally in World War II."[16] This bit of false history is typical of the distortions that surround the Nye investigations.

The Nye Committee did not say, as I have shown, that the munitions makers caused World War I. If one disagrees with the evidence suggesting that the actions of military contractors had something to do with the conditions that led to the war or with the committee's conclusion that it is "against the peace of the world for selfishly interested organizations to be left free to goad and frighten nations into military activity," then the rational thing to do would be to show that the evidence was incorrect or insufficient, or to argue that the committee came to the wrong conclusion. To say that the Nye Committee "made it appear" that the munitions makers caused the war is to imply that it fabricated or twisted the evidence and is an attempt to distort.

[16] Harry S Truman, *Memoirs: Years of Decisions* (Garden City, N.Y.: Doubleday, 1958), pp. 189–90.

Similarly Truman's interpretation of the Neutrality Act is less than an accurate one. The act (prohibiting exports of arms, munitions or implements of war to nations at war) was passed in 1935 and extended and amended in succeeding years. Its first use was during the Italian invasion of Ethiopia, and its application ran against the aggressor, Italy, since Ethiopia had no transportation facilities or funds to import goods, and therefore only Italy was prevented from buying United States weapons, a fact acknowledged at the time by the Roosevelt administration. Unfortunately, the act had a loophole. There was nothing in the law making it illegal to export raw materials to belligerents, even though intended for war production, and American business proceeded to supply Italy with oil, copper and scrap metal despite President Roosevelt's appeal for a "moral embargo" and his denunciation of the profiteering in Italian trade. But at least the arms industry was prevented from giving direct assistance to Fascist Italy.

The following year civil war broke out in Spain as General Francisco Franco, supported by the army and with the aid of Hitler and Mussolini, made his move to overthrow the government. The Neutrality Act as originally passed did not apply to civil wars and undoubtedly would have allowed sales of arms to the Spanish government. It was Roosevelt who recommended, in late 1936, that the act be extended to apply to the Spanish civil war, and a bill to do so was sent to Congress by the White House and enacted in early 1937. The new provision prohibited exports of arms to any foreign state involved in civil strife upon a finding by the President that the export of arms to it "would threaten or endanger the peace of the United States." Roosevelt made such a finding for the war in Spain, although it is hard to see on what grounds, and the embargo was on. This was a dubious form of neutrality, for the amendment changed the relationship that then existed between the United States and Spain, and in view of the fact that Germany and Italy were already aiding Franco, it amounted to a great victory for the rebels. Thus it was through the initiative of the President that the United States chose to wash its hands of the totalitarian power play against the liberal government of Spain. To blame the Nye Committee's investigation of profiteering for this strange sequence of events is a gross distortion.

In setting up the Special Committee to Investigate the National Defense Program in 1941, Truman, who was then a senator, was determined to avoid what he called the "misdirected" efforts of the

Nye Committee. But many of the disclosures of Truman's investigations fulfilled the prophecies of the Nye reports.

"We found," states Truman, "that the Navy was extremely liberal with the private shipbuilders."[17] In fact, nine shipbuilding companies in the first year of the war were entitled to receive fees, plus possible bonuses, exceeding the amount of their net worth on December 31, 1939. In one case fees plus bonuses exceeded by almost 800 percent the firm's average annual net profits and in other cases by 20 to 40 times. The amounts, Truman concluded, were excessive. Profits for repairs and ship-conversion work "were found to be even more staggering." The old cost-plus contract was now prohibited, but "huge fixed fees were offered by the government in much the same way that Santa Claus passes out gifts at a church Christmas party."[18]

A Navy spokesman testified that it was almost impossible to compare private with naval-yard costs of construction because of inadequate Navy accounting methods. One report was entitled "Concerning Faking of Inspections of Steel Plate by Carnegie-Illinois Steel Corporation,"[19] and severely criticized that subsidiary of U. S. Steel for supplying naval and merchant ships with defective steel plate. The committee accused contractors of inflating advertising expenditures and condemned the Curtiss-Wright Corporation for its advertising costs, most of which the government had to pay, as well as for misleading advertising. The Navy was criticized for condoning the misleading advertising.[20] The Curtiss-Wright investigation, probably the most publicized of all the Truman hearings, involved the production of defective aircraft engines, excessive production costs and mismanagement.

But an important distinction needs to be made between the Nye and Truman investigations. The Nye Committee attempted to take a comprehensive view of arms production and military-industrial relations, to dig up evidence of profiteering during a war that had ended 15 years earlier, as well as contemporary peacetime practices, to expose the influence of contractors and lobby groups such as the Navy League on military and foreign policy and to retard a

17 *Ibid.*, p. 178.
18 *Ibid.*, p. 171.
19 Seventy-eighth Congress, first session, "Senate Report No. 10," Part 7.
20 *Ibid.*, pp. 15–16.

worldwide arms race that seemed destined to end in war. Only one of Truman's objectives was the same as Nye's—to curtail profiteering. Truman's prime motivation was to help win the war in progress. Truman's focus was therefore different from Nye's, who was operating in a time of peace threatened by a future war. For this reason Truman was as concerned with efficient mobilization and increasing production as he was with profiteering and corrupt practices. In Truman's words,

> The idea of the committee was to conduct the investigation of the defense effort simultaneously with the war program in order that mistakes could be remedied before irretrievable damage was done. We were interested in doing a surgeon's job to cure, not in performing an autopsy to find out why the patient died.[21]

Thus the bulk of the Truman investigations was into the problems of mobilization, of war-material production such as aluminum, rubber and magnesium, the conversion program, gasoline rationing, merchant shipping, farm machinery and equipment, and manpower. Investigations like the Curtiss-Wright case were relatively infrequent.

After Truman left the committee in 1944 to run as Franklin Roosevelt's Vice-President, the committee continued its work for several years and made its final report in 1948.

In the demobilization following the war, military expenditures were sharply reduced. But in a few years, with the advent of the Cold War, expenditures for defense rose sharply and the problem of "war" profits took on a new aspect. For the first time the United States was faced with the maintenance of a huge military force in a period of peace. When the Hoover Commission studied the defense establishment, it learned, to its amazement, that the military departments were requesting more than $30 billion for defense in fiscal year 1950. At the time of their report, 1949, defense expenditures were about $15 billion per year, approximately a third of the total federal budget. The Hoover Commission said of the new military request:

> Such a budget would be justifiable only if the nation were actually involved in warfare. It would require a sharp reduction in production for

21 Truman, *op. cit.*, p. 167.

civilian consumption, precipitate the need for controls over the economy, and enormously increase inflationary pressures. It reflects a lack of realistic understanding by the three military departments of the economic and social factors of national security.

But the military would soon be asking for and receiving much more.

Chapter Two

THE END OF DEMOBILIZATION

Following World War II, military spending was cut back drastically for a few years and then, as the Cold War settled over East and West, began climbing. In the peak wartime year of 1945, military outlays totaled $80.5 billion.[1] Three years later a postwar low of $11.9 billion was reached. Though this reduction constituted only a flirtation with demobilization, it threw the defense industry into a panic.

Before World War II, military spending had never reached $2 billion per year and did not exceed $1 billion until the late 1930s. With the outbreak of the Korean War in 1950 military spending leaped forward, reaching $44 billion in 1953. Afterward, it receded somewhat, but the post-Korean low was much higher than any of the pre-Korean years, just as military spending after World War II was never so low as during the previous prewar period.

[1] Figures for annual outlays are taken from *Statistical Appendix to Annual Report of the Secretary of the Treasury on the State of the Finances, for the Fiscal Year Ended June 30, 1968,* pp. 8–17.

The United States' failure to demobilize fully after World War II was something of a historical discontinuity. The pattern had always been high military expenditures during wartime followed by rapid cutbacks in spending and troops, approximating peacetime levels. After the last two wars, however, the military-spending and military-personnel floors were left at "peacetime" levels that would have previously been considered mad—even when inflation is taken into consideration—although spending and troop numbers tended to creep upward with each of the earlier wars. Following World War II, demobilization in the traditional sense became an old-fashioned and outdated idea. We have had no true demobilization since the post-World War I era.

The traditional concern for war profiteering also seems to have become a thing of the past. No hue and cry was made after World War II to expose the profiteers. There was no demand for new measures to "take the profits out of war," at least not to the extent that could still be heard only ten years earlier. Yet enormous profits had been made during the war. Why then did profiteering decline as a popular issue? For one reason, with military spending on a permanent wartime basis there was no longer the startling contrast between peace and war economies, between "normal" and abnormal government spending and government contracting activities, and between accustomed and unaccustomed defense production and corporate growth. It was no longer easy to measure "wartime" profiteering. Mobilization for war became the norm.

In addition, an institutional accommodation between government and industry was accomplished, creating the belief that war profiteering had been brought under control, excepting isolated and insignificant cases. The government declared, in effect, that (1) it had established the necessary machinery to eliminate almost all profiteering, and (2) whatever excessive profits were made on defense contracts would be recaptured and violators of the law punished. In making these assurances the government was able to point to regulatory agencies such as the Renegotiation Board, to "watchdogs" such as the Government Accounting Office (GAO), to statutory controls, and to administrative regulations and contractual provisions enforced by the Department of Defense. Industry, at the same time, made its peace with the government, if not its *mea culpa* for past sins, disavowed any desire for unreasonable profits and enlisted in the defense-industry "team" and, more recently, the space-industry "team." The public, unable to comprehend the meaning of billion-dollar programs, terrified by the possibility of nuclear war, awed by the complexity of modern defense systems and denied access to military secrets, for the most part went along.

Occasional congressional investigations and reports of the General Accounting Office in the 1950s and early 1960s did produce disturbing evidence of excessive profits on defense contracts. Hearings in 1956 by a House Armed Services subcommittee headed by Representative F. Edward Hébert into aircraft production and profits revealed before-tax profits on net worth for the years 1952 through 1955 of from 47 to 74 percent for government airframe contractors such as Boeing, Lockheed and North American Aviation. Republic Aviation made 142 percent in 1952 and Northrop Aircraft made 92 percent in 1955. In addition, enormous "indirect" charges on defense contracts—that is, unspecified costs of overhead as opposed to direct charges for items like labor and material—gave rise to suspicions of hidden profits buried in the maze of contractor accounting practices. In 1959 and 1960 the General Accounting Office, under Comptroller General Joseph Campbell, reported gross overcharges and fraudulent practices in defense contracting. In one case, involving the production of radar systems by General Electric, GAO attributed a $3,408,800 overcharge on a $19,528,300 contract to the "use of estimated costs in excess of costs known to GE or which GE could reasonably expect to incur in performance."

Numerous similar GAO reports of excessive costs, unreasonably high profits, failure to solicit competition, interest-free use of government funds and rent-free use of government property were issued on defense contracts with Westinghouse, General Motors, Philco, Bell Helicopter, McDonnell Aircraft, Avco, Lockheed and other military contractors.[2]

LYNDON B. JOHNSON DISCOVERS
THE MISSILE GAP

There have always been advocates for a large peacetime standing army. The reasons they succeeded for the first time in the post-World War II period will perhaps never be altogether clear. No doubt the atomic bomb and other breakthroughs in warfare tech-

---

[2] Summaries of the GAO reports are collected in Eighty-sixth Congress, second session, House Committee on Armed Services, "Hearings Pursuant to Section 4, Public Law 86-89," pp. 64–70.

nology played an important part. After Hiroshima the atavistic fear that one's enemy might invent a "secret weapon" so powerful it could annihilate the country in a stroke became quite real. In addition there was "The Red Menace in the East." Still, the new weapons were bound to be acquired by other nations, despite the secrecy fetish, and the real question was, How much defense is enough? The tragedy is that this question was not fairly addressed at that time, and has not been until very recently. The postwar fears of communism and the Soviet Union, intensified to the point of national hysteria by McCarthyism, together with the brooding omnipresence of atomic war, allowed only one kind of military question to be raised: Why not spend more?

There were many throughout the nation in business and government who were advocating a greater defense budget; there always had been. In the past the major and often the decisive obstacle to such demands was to be found in the Congress. But this time the congressional leadership got behind the demands. The most important of the leaders of Congress urging higher defense spending was Lyndon B. Johnson.

As a young congressman from Texas, Johnson had been a member of the House Naval Affairs Committee and during World War II chairman of a special investigating committee on the progress of the war, the House counterpart of the Truman Committee, though not nearly so well publicized. After the war Congressman Johnson became, in the words of Rowland Evans and Robert Novak, a "noisy advocate" of high military budgets and especially a large Air Force. Evans and Novak speculate on Johnson's reasons:

> Almost overnight, a vast new industry—the aircraft industry—sprang up, with unlimited demands on the federal dollar. Because of successive engineering advances, the new aircraft industry promised to become one of the most important and profitable in the country. Ferocious competition for military contracts quickly built up political pressures of explosive potential, and in the center of this competition was the State of Texas.[3]

In the 1940s the aircraft industry grew up in Texas and came to rival oil and gas in economic importance and political clout.

In 1948 Johnson was elected to the Senate. His first committee assignment was to the Armed Services Committee. In 1950 a few

---

[3] Rowland Evans and Robert Novak, *Lyndon B. Johnson: The Exercise of Power* (New York: New American Library, 1966), pp. 16–17.

days after the commitment of U.S. troops to Korea, Johnson persuaded the chairman of the Armed Services Committee, Richard Russell, to set up a Defense Preparedness Subcommittee to investigate the conduct of the Korean War, with Johnson as subcommittee chairman. Within a few months Johnson was denouncing the Truman administration for not adequately mobilizing for war, and by 1952 the Johnson Committee was bombarding Truman with demands for sharp increases in air power.

In a June 1952 report, based characteristically on secret testimony not made public because of "security considerations," the committee stated somberly that "the question of an adequate air defense for these United States is a question of life or death for ourselves and our institutions" and warned of "the possible extinction of our way of life" unless there is a "doubling and redoubling of our efforts to fortify ourselves." The committee also chided the Defense Department for poor planning and failing to meet the aircraft production schedules of the Joint Chiefs of Staff, stating:

Aircraft and engine manufacturers told us that when the schedules were originally prepared they were promised sufficient supplies of Government-furnished tools and components. For various reasons, these never materialized. As a consequence, schedules were not met.[4]

In future years there would be no shortage of government-owned property and equipment in the hands of contractors.

Throughout that election year Johnson kept up a drumfire attack against the Truman administration for not mobilizing fast enough and for failing to meet the Air Force's expectations for an enlarged Air Force. Yet Air Force outlays had increased from $1.7 billion in 1949 to $12.8 billion in 1952 and had doubled over the year before; and total defense spending had increased from $13.4 billion in 1950 to $40.5 billion in 1952.

In March the Preparedness Subcommittee had been critical of the limited production of tanks, guns and ammunition as well as aircraft.[5] In August it bemoaned the "too hasty demobilization that followed World War II," the United States' failure to heed the "Cold War call-to-arms" and the fact that "America has lost the right to claim unquestioned mastery of the air." Once again air-

---

[4] Eighty-second Congress, second session, "39th Report of the Senate Preparedness Investigating Subcommittee," p. 4.

[5] Eighty-second Congress, second session, "Annual Report of the Senate Preparedness Investigating Subcommittee," pp. 12–13.

craft production was condemned for being too slow, but the committee took care to relieve the aircraft industry of any blame. The fault was the government's failure to meet the industry's requirements: firm contracts, plant expansion, government-furnished equipment, more money for research and development, and most significantly, "continuity of operation." Of course, interruptions in military production, which unfortunately slacked off after every war, were the bane of the defense industry.

One of the principal thrusts of the August report was promotion of a greater Air Force. The committee formally recommended that:

1. The Secretary of Defense or the President appoint a full-time production "czar" to meet minimum air power requirements.

2. The Secretary of Defense appoint a committee to reassess air strategy and research and development procedures.

3. The Secretary of Defense report to the Preparedness Subcommittee on his program for plant expansion.

4. The Aircraft Advisory Committee to the Munitions Board present recommendations to Congress *"to maintain the aircraft industry in a healthy state in periods of peace as well as in periods of defense mobilization"* (emphasis added). The committee also recommended that contractor "incentives" be increased.[6]

In the late 1950s, in the midst of the crisis atmosphere generated after the successful launching of Sputnik (1957), Johnson became chairman of the new Committee on Aeronautical and Space Sciences. He could now speak as majority leader and chairman of two important committees, and from these bases of political influence he renewed his efforts in behalf of higher defense spending, especially for missiles and strategic bombers, as well as space spending. Both committees held extensive hearings over the next three years in which leading advocates of stepped-up military and space spending were called to testify and encouraged to belittle administration efforts. One of the favorite complaints of the Joint Chiefs of Staff was that the Bureau of the Budget's conservative approach to government expenditures was impairing new programs such as those for intercontinental ballistic missiles, nuclear aircraft carriers, the B-70 bomber and the nuclear-powered airplane.

The culmination was the 1960 hearings on "Missiles, Space, and Other Major Defense Matters," a military all-star show held jointly

---

6 Eighty-second Congress, second session, "43rd Report of the Senate Preparedness Investigating Subcommittee," pp. 19–20.

by the Preparedness Subcommittee and the Aeronautical and Space Sciences Committee. After hearing from all the Joint Chiefs plus other military experts, Johnson's grand finale was to deliver to Eisenhower's Secretary of Defense, Thomas S. Gates, who was about to give the last day's testimony, a litany of military requests and an indictment of administration failures. Among the charges leveled was the existence of "the missile gap."[7] The charge, which later turned out to be false, became an important part of the Kennedy-Johnson campaign. The litany became a military shopping list.

Although there were other congressional advocates of high defense spending and greater air power during the 1950s, none pumped for those objectives so long, so hard, or so effectively as Senator Johnson. He helped to elevate the Air Force to a preeminent position among the service branches, which meant the purchase of large numbers of new-generation aircraft and missiles, and more significantly, to stabilize the defense industry by eliminating the boom-and-bust cycle in defense expenditures. His recommendations that defense contractors be given a more favorable position were all translated into official policy, particularly the step-up in the furnishing of government-owned property and the increase in military and space research and development programs.

As President, he helped engineer the greatest Pentagon raid on the treasury since World War II. Among other results was a gigantic defense-industry boom for his home state, Texas. In 1964 military procurement in Texas totaled $224 million. In 1967 procurement shot up to $1.25 billion, and Texas rose from eleventh- to second-largest recipient of defense outlays. When he abdicated in 1968, in the midst of the war in Indochina, military spending had reached a "peacetime" high. He rode the tiger of military spending into the White House, but it rode him out.

A PROFILE OF THE DEFENSE BUDGET

President Eisenhower's concern over the dangers of military spending was not born during the days he had to consider what to say in his farewell address, when he gifted the nation with the phrase "military-industrial complex." As early as 1956 he expressed

7 Eighty-sixth Congress, second session, Hearings Before the Senate Preparedness Investigating Subcommittee, "Missiles, Space, and Other Major Defense Matters," p. 438.

his fear that someday a President would be in office who would not know how to cut the spending requests of the military services. In 1957 and 1958 he tried to prevent the useless expenditure of millions of dollars on the mythical bomber gap. Later he tried to head off the orgy of military spending he knew would follow the false charges of a missile gap. More importantly, he understood the basic principle that no civilized nation intent on peace had ever been—or should be—at full military strength at the time of an outbreak of war. What he tried to resist was the illusory quest for "absolute security" and the pressures that would, in his words, "turn the United States into an armed camp." [8]

It was this vision which moved Eisenhower to attempt to open the door on the skeleton in the closet. In 1960, when he tried to articulate the nature of the specter, the defense budget was about $44 billion. When Lyndon B. Johnson left office in 1968, it was nearing $80 billion. War profiteering had been transformed into an American institution, accepted as a legitimate cost of permanent mobilization.

1. Total Defense Expenditures

To comprehend the new meaning of profiteering one must know something about the defense budget, the defense industry, and the way they interact. The total amount of federal outlays in 1969 for military and nonmilitary purposes was $184.5 billion. How much went for defense? This question is not so easy to answer as one might think, mainly because it is government policy to create confusion over the federal budget. There is no way for anyone to learn how much money is spent for military purposes by simply reading the budget document. Military outlays of the Department of Defense were $77.9 billion in 1969.[9] But if we add the expenditures of other agencies which were intended for purposes of defense, the total would be much higher. For example, military-assistance funds spent by the Department of State amounted to $685 million. Expenditures by the Atomic Energy Commission, almost entirely for military purposes, were $2.5 billion. The costs of stockpiling ma-

[8] Dwight D. Eisenhower, *Mandate for Change, 1953–1956* (Garden City, N.Y.: Doubleday), p. 454.

[9] Figures for defense outlays are from *The Budget of the United States Government, Fiscal Year 1971.*

terials deemed essential for reasons of national security, of the selective service system and of other minor defense-related activities total about $120 million. The outlays mentioned thus far bring the defense bill to $81.2 billion. Even the federal government formally recognizes this much.

Now consider some items that are not recognized as essentially for defense purposes. The cost of veterans' programs is largely the cost of old wars and old defense programs. Veterans' pensions, compensation and insurance cost $7.6 billion in 1969. The interest on the national debt, most of which was borrowed in order to finance World War II, amounted to $15.8 billion and is another cost of old wars. The space program is closely intertwined with defense, primarily in the advancement of missile technology and the potential use of space and space platforms for military purposes. It cost $4.2 billion in 1969. Federal maritime subsidies, justified on the grounds that a healthy maritime industry is essential to national security,

TABLE 1.*   **The Federal Program by Function**

Summary of Budget Outlays

(IN MILLIONS OF DOLLARS)

Function	Outlays 1969 actual
National defense	81,240
International affairs and finance	3,785
Space research and technology	4,247
Agriculture and rural development	6,221
Natural resources	2,129
Commerce and transportation	7,873
Community development and housing	1,961
Education and manpower	6,825
Health	11,696
Income security	37,399
Veterans benefits and services	7,640
Interest	15,791
General government	2,866
Undistributed intragovernmental transactions:	
Employer share, employee retirement	−2,018
Interest received by trust funds	−3,099
Total	184,556

* Source: *The Budget of the United States Government, Fiscal Year 1971.*

amounted to about $800 million. Even a conservative apportionment of these costs and the costs of other programs that are advertised as necessary to national security, such as the oil-import program, would bring the total cost of defense to well over $100 billion. By this reckoning defense spending took at least 54 percent of all federal outlays. (See Table 1.)

However, let us take a closer look at the narrower meaning of defense spending, the expenditures of the Department of Defense, since it is these sums which support the more important segment of the defense industry and which stimulate related outlays, keeping in mind the fact that the related outlays have a profound impact on the nation.

The $78 billion spent by the Pentagon in 1969 accounted for about 42 percent of all federal spending and represented a per capita outlay of about $400. When we try to break down this budget into its constituent parts, we again run into difficulty. It can be done in several ways.

2. The Appropriations Budget and the Importance of Advanced Weapons

One way is to divide it up the way Congress does, by appropriation. The budget request submitted by the President to the legislative branch contains line items with sums of money alongside each one. When Congress finally appropriates for defense, it in effect fills in its own figures beside the line items, although for many years the tendency was merely to rubber-stamp the Presidential requests. Table 2 shows the appropriation budget for 1969.

It will be noted that the largest single item was $23.3 billion for procurement. Another large item—research, development, test and evaluation—amounting to $7.7 billion, is closely related. These two items represent the amount of money spent for the purchasing of weapons systems and other hardware. I will come back to them.

After procurement the next-largest items are military personnel, $21.9 billion, and operation and maintenance, $20.6 billion. Military-personnel outlays include pay and allowances, subsistence, and other costs such as the expenses of apprehending deserters and escaped military prisoners. (The budget document does not state whether the last expense has been rising in recent years, but one

TABLE 2.* **National Defense**

(IN MILLIONS OF DOLLARS)

Program or agency	Outlays 1969 actual
Department of Defense—military	
Military personnel	21,374
Retired military personnel	2,444
Operation and maintenance	22,227
Procurement	23,988
Research, development, test, and evaluation	7,457
Military construction	1,389
Family housing	572
Civil defense	87
Revolving and management funds and other	−1,534
Military trust funds	10
Deductions for offsetting receipts	−135
Subtotal, military	77,877
Military assistance:	
Grants and credit sales	685
Trust fund	103
Subtotal, military and military assistance	78,666
Atomic energy	2,450
Defense-related activities:	
Stockpiling of strategic and critical materials	18
Expansion of defense production	166
Selective Service System	65
Emergency preparedness activities	11
Deductions for offsetting receipts:	
Proprietary receipts from the public	−138
Total	81,240

* Source: *The Budget of the United States Government, Fiscal Year 1971.*

suspects it has.) Operation and maintenance expenditures pay for day-to-day costs of operating aircraft, naval and missile forces, troops in combat, forces providing airlift and sealift capability, logistics support, training, medical care, communications and intelligence activities.

Military construction totaled $1.6 billion and paid for the acquisition of land and construction of facilities such as those required to deploy the Safeguard antiballistic missile system (ABM), as well as medical facilities, service schools, troop housing and bachelor-officer quarters.

It should be seen from the discussion of the defense budget so far that the linchpin in the modern war machine is the expensive advanced weapons systems. It used to be that the principal cost of war was that of supporting masses of men who would wield their axes or fire their small arms in combat. We still support masses of men, in fact, larger numbers on a permanent basis than ever before. But the dominant expense is the cost of researching, developing, purchasing and maintaining the sophisticated weapons systems— the jet aircraft, the guided missiles and the nuclear-powered warships. The masses of men have become, for the most part, servants to machines.

For example, of the 3.5 million men in uniform in 1969, a little more than a million were in the Navy and slightly less than a million were in the Air Force. Obviously most of these men were not trained to go on fixed-bayonet charges or to board enemy ships for hand-to-hand combat. (The Marines are a notable exception.) Their mission was mostly to operate multimillion-dollar ships, planes and missiles and, when they were not in operation, to baby-sit for them. Further, a large if not predominant percentage of Army personnel had a similar assignment, for the Army has a substantial number of planes and missiles of its own. The ABM is an Army program.

Similarly a significant proportion of the operation and maintenance expense goes toward the upkeep of major weapons systems. The ten-year operation-and-maintenance costs, for instance, of a modern airplane equal and sometimes exceed its procurement cost. That is, if a jet fighter cost $10 million to buy, it will cost another $10 million to operate and maintain for the ten years following its purchase. Military construction, as has been pointed out, is in part devoted to the physical housing and support of weapons systems, in part for the housing of manpower attached to weapons systems. Even civil defense, an Army program, is related to electronic weapons systems, especially missiles, to the extent that it is supposed to defend against the all-out war that could be produced by the arms race in which we are a full participant.

The point here is that the largest part of the defense budget is directly related to or a by-product of the sophisticated weapons system. In this sense the production and acquisition of weapons is the moving force underlying defense expenditures.

3. The Program Budget:
Strategic and General-Purpose Forces

A second way of looking at the defense budget is by program, a method advocated by former Secretary of Defense Robert S. McNamara, who was instrumental in shifting the emphasis of our defense strategy from nuclear "massive retaliation" under Eisenhower and John Foster Dulles to the concept of "balanced defense" and "flexible response" under John F. Kennedy and Lyndon Johnson. To achieve a balanced program the Kennedy and Johnson administrations built up the conventional-warfare capabilities or general-purpose forces and reduced to some extent the investment in nuclear-warfare capabilities.[10] This strategy was intended to give the United States a "proper mix" of warfare capabilities so that when a crisis came, we would not be limited to an all-or-nothing choice of nuclear war or inaction. We would be enabled to engage in "brushfire wars" and major ground actions as well, with a balanced defense. It is interesting to note that this concept was specifically rejected by Eisenhower for the reason that it "required massive defense units of such size and capacity that no matter how universal and threatening the danger or how many the local 'disturbances' we could quickly defeat them by conventional means."[11] It was in rejection of this strategy that Eisenhower said, "I refused to turn the United States into an armed camp."

Under the program budget the dollars spent are related to missions, the key ones being nuclear war (strategic forces) and conventional war (general-purpose forces). (See Table 3.) In 1969 $8.6 billion was spent for strategic forces, $30.7 billion for general purpose forces. These figures are increased when other items in the program budget are properly charged to either strategic or general-purpose forces. For example, "airlift and sealift" is a general-purpose-force expense. It is sometimes maintained that the amount spent for conventional-warfare capabilities as compared with nu-

---

[10] See William W. Kaufmann, *The McNamara Strategy* (New York: Harper & Row, 1964), for an early exposition of the shift in emphasis.

[11] Eisenhower, *op. cit.*, pp. 453–54.

clear-warfare capabilities shows that the costs of ICBMs and nuclear bombers are exaggerated out of proper proportion and that it is the cost of ground and naval forces and their deployment around the world that accounts for the bulk of defense expenditures.

TABLE 3.* Summary of the Department of Defense Budget Program

(IN BILLIONS OF DOLLARS)

Major military programs	Total Obligational Authority 1969 actual
Strategic forces	8.6
General-purpose forces	30.7
Intelligence and communications	5.8
Airlift and sealift	1.6
Guard and Reserve forces	2.1
Research and development	4.7
Central supply and maintenance	9.4
Training, medical, and other general personnel activities	12.4
Administration and associated activities	1.3
Support of other nations	2.2
Total obligational authority	78.7
Of which:	
New budget authority	77.0
Prior-year funds and other financial adjustments	−1.7

* Source: *The Budget of the United States Government, Fiscal Year 1971.*

What this argument misses, however, is the fact that the large weapons systems dominate both missions. The important role of missiles, bombers and nuclear Polaris submarines in the strategic forces is self-evident. But the role of equally sophisticated and often more costly weapons in the general-purpose forces should also be clear. All tactical aircraft, such as the F-111 fighter and FB-111 fighter-bomber, the F-4, A-7, and the newly proposed F-14 and F-15, are general-purpose-forces weapons. Antisubmarine aircraft, helicopters, cargo planes such as the C-5 and C-141, tanks, aircraft carriers, attack submarines and fleet-escort ships are in the general-purpose-forces inventory. It is the major weapons systems around which the galaxy of other defense expenditures orbit.

4. The Cost of Weapons

It is important to note the enormous rise in costs that has taken place in the weapons-systems market in the past few decades and even in the past few years. Some examples:

World War II B-17 bombers cost $218,000, the B-29 cost $680,000, Korean War B-47s cost $2 million—while the FB-111s now cost $16 million each.

Korean War B-36s cost $3.7 million, the B-52s cost $7.9 million, and the RS-71s cost $24.6 million. The newly proposed B-1 (formerly called AMSA) has been estimated as high as $80 million each.

The World War II C-47 transport cost $94,000, the C-46 cost $262,000, the Korean War C-119 cost $663,000, but the C-141 costs $6.3 million, and the C-5 is costing an estimated $53 million each.

The World War II F-51 fighter cost $54,000, the F-47 cost $89,000, the Korean War F-84 cost $466,000, the F-101 cost $1.8 million, but the F-4 costs $2.1 million, and the F-111 costs $13 million each.

Attack submarines cost $4.7 million during World War II, $22 million during the Korean War—and from $77 million to $100 million presently.

Attack carriers, conventionally powered, cost $55 million in World War II; the last conventionally powered one cost $277 million. Nuclear carriers now cost from $500 million to $600 million each.

The M-1 rifle cost $31 in 1946; the M-16 costs $150. A 4.3-inch mortar that cost $834 in 1946 now costs $5,700. A machine gun cost $74 in 1946, but it costs $579 today.

Certainly inflation since 1945 accounts for part of the increased cost of weapons. Some weapons are much larger and more complex than those which have been replaced, and this would account for additional cost increases. But the Wholesale Price Index increased by only 90 percent from 1945 to 1968 and by only nine percent since 1959. Do inflation and modernization account for the 700 percent rise in the cost of machine guns? In the past two to ten years, according to Admiral H. G. Rickover, military equipment prices have doubled. As an example, nuclear-propulsion turbines and gears purchased for the aircraft carrier *Nimitz* were up nearly 100 percent over practically the identical equipment purchased eight years earlier for the carrier *Enterprise*—$10 million compared to $5.5 million.

More important is the fact that as the cost of weapons, and presumably their effectiveness, increases, their number tends to remain the same. The higher prices are supposed to pay for higher-quality weapons, yet they never seem to decline in quantity. The outstanding case is the aircraft carrier. We have had roughly 15 attack carriers since World War II. Now they are being replaced by nuclear carriers at an enormous cost, because, according to the Navy, the increased effectiveness is worth the price; yet the Navy still wants 15, and it would like more than that number. The same can be shown with planes, tanks and missiles. The effect is to create pressures on the budget to expand it.

5. Pentagon Property Holdings

A summary of the property holdings of the Defense Department will round out the financial picture. After almost two centuries of procurement the military has built a worldwide and practically incalculable empire of real estate, weapons and equipment, and foreign and domestic bases. For example, the Pentagon has estimated the value of its real and personal property at $210.1 billion in 1969. But the 29.5 million acres of real estate under its control, more than the land area of Ohio and roughly equivalent to that of the state of New York, was valued at $39.6 billion, a sum arrived at by simply toting up the *acquisition* costs of each purchase. Yet some of the real estate was acquired more than a century ago, some of it was donated, some withdrawn from the public domain. Much of it is located in cities and metropolitan areas, and its actual market value must be many times the acquisition cost. In addition, the Pentagon does not include in its totals property under the control of the Army Civil Works Division. In 1969 this Division controlled 9.7 million acres valued at $9 billion, plus additional property valued at $4.7 billion. Of the total land, 2.3 million acres were in foreign countries. There were in 1969 approximately 430 major foreign bases and about 3,000 other installations overseas. Weapons holdings were valued at $100.7 billion, supplies at $47.4 billion and plant equipment at $11.9 billion.

But the more important fact about the defense budget is that in the procurement process the military establishment has become wedded to many of the largest industrial corporations in America and has taken up various kinds of relationships with others as well as with educational institutions, including the so-called think tanks. It was to this conception of the defense establishment, the military organization embraced in the arms industry, that Eisenhower issued his farewell warning:

> In the councils of government, we must guard against the acquisition of unwarranted influence, whether sought or unsought, by the military-industrial complex. The potential for the disastrous rise of misplaced power exists and will persist.

Each year the Defense Department enters into about 22,000 defense contracts with private contractors, and more than 100,000 subcontractors are engaged in defense production. In 1969 about four million persons were employed in the defense-oriented industries. The contracts awarded by the Pentagon, including research and development contracts and production contracts, totaled $42 billion. (Since many contracts extend for periods of several years, the figures for contract awards and defense outlays for procurement are not the same.)

A PROFILE OF THE DEFENSE INDUSTRY

1. The Beneficiaries

Although a large number of contractors and subcontractors do some military business, the lion's share of procurement money is concentrated among a relative handful of giant contractors. In 1969, the 100 largest defense suppliers swallowed up $25.2 billion in contract awards, 68.2 percent of the money spent through contracts of $10,000 or more, a percentage that has been steadily growing. Firms defined by the Small Business Administration as "small businesses"—generally, independently owned with no more than a specified number of employees, usually not more than 500 or 1,000, depending upon the type of business—received less than 20 percent of contract awards compared to 57 percent a decade earlier. Table 4 lists the largest 100 military contractors and their subsidiaries according to net value of military prime-contract awards in fiscal year 1969.

TABLE 4.   100 Companies and Their Subsidiaries Listed According to Net Value of Military Prime-Contract Awards

FISCAL YEAR 1969
(1 JULY 1968–30 JUNE 1969)

Rank	Companies	Thousands of Dollars
U.S.	Total	$36,888,601
	Total, 100 companies and their subsidiaries	25,175,240
1.	Lockheed Aircraft Corp.	2,004,423
	Lockheed Shipbuilding Construction	35,752
	Ventura Mfg. Co.	61
	Total	2,040,236
2.	General Electric Co.	1,619,095
	General Electric Supply Co.	1,680
	Total	1,620,775
3.	General Dynamics Corp.	1,228,903
	Dynatronics, Inc.	448
	Stromberg Carlson Corp.	10,680
	Stromberg Datagraphics, Inc.	2,879
	United Electric Coal Co.	145
	Total	1,243,055
4.	McDonnell Douglas Corp.	1,031,752
	Advanced Communications, Inc.	524
	Conductron Corp.	32,021
	Hycon Mfg. Co.	4,862
	Tridea Electronics, Inc.	584
	Total	1,069,743
5.	United Aircraft Corp.	997,380
6.	American Telephone and Telegraph Co.	152,349
	Chesapeake and Potomac Telephone Co.	13,939
	Illinois Bell Tel. Co.	217
	Mountain States Tel. and Tel. Co.	1,688
	New England Tel. and Tel. Co.	564
	New Jersey Bell Telephone Co.	578
	New York Telephone Co.	52
	Northwestern Bell Telephone Co.	236
	Ohio Bell Telephone Co.	270
	Pacific Northwest Bell Telephone	145

Rank	Companies	*Thousands of Dollars*
	Pacific Telephone and Telegraph Co.	172
	Southern Bell Telephone and Telegraph	2,325
	Southwestern Bell Telephone	1,729
	Teletype Corp.	16,926
	Western Electric Co., Inc.	723,389
	Total	914,579
7.	Ling Temco Vought, Inc.	26,554
	Altec Service Co.	32
	Braniff Airways, Inc.	43,327
	Computer Technology, Inc.	54
	Continental Electronics Mfg. Co.	3,895
	Jefferson Wire and Cable Corp.	138
	Jones and Laughlin Steel Corp.	2,803
	Kentron Hawaii, Ltd.	15,448
	LTV Electrosystems	182,160
	LTV Aerospace Corp.	617,706
	LTV Ling Altec, Inc.	770
	Okonite Co., The	997
	Service Technology Corp.	10,645
	Staco, Inc.	11
	Tamar Electronics Industries, Inc.	125
	Wilson and Co., Inc.	9,154
	Wilson Sporting Goods Co.	295
	Total	914,114
8.	North American Rockwell Corp.	673,840
	Morse Controls, Inc.	201
	Remmert-Werner, Inc.	134
	Total	674,175
9.	Boeing Co.	653,638
10.	General Motors Corp.	584,407
	Frigidaire Sales Corp.	32
	Total	584,439
11.	Raytheon Co.	542,817
	Edex Corp.	15
	Heath, D. C., and Co.	25
	Machlett Laboratories, Inc.	3,470
	Micro State Electronics Corp.	102
	Raytheon Education Co.	73
	Seismograph Service Corp.	270
	Total	546,772

Rank	Companies	Thousands of Dollars
12. Sperry Rand Corp.		467,861
13. Avco Corp.		456,054
14. Hughes Aircraft Co.		438,756
Meva Corp.		260
	Total	439,016
15. Westinghouse Electric Corp.		424,175
Electro Insulation, Inc.		15
K-W Battery Co.		197
Sanford Marine Services, Inc.		67
Thermo King Corp.		294
Thermo King Sales and Service		12
Urban Systems Dev. Corp.		2,911
Westinghouse Electric Intl., S.A.		278
Westinghouse Electric Supply Co.		886
Westinghouse Learning Corp.		723
	Total	429,558
16. Textron, Inc.		13,776
Accessory Products Co.		29
Aetna Bearing Co., Inc.		34
Bell Aerospace Corp.		412,700
Camcar Screw and Mfg. Co.		140
Fafnir Bearing Co.		542
Textron Electronics, Inc.		606
Townsend Co.		435
Walker-Parkersburg		17
Waterbury Farrel		11
	Total	428,290
17. Grumman Aircraft Engineering Corp.		417,052
18. Honeywell, Inc.		405,575
19. Ford Motor Co.		67,202
Philco Ford Corp.		329,131
	Total	396,333
20. Olin Mathieson Chemical Corp.		354,359
21. Litton Industries, Inc.		14,586
Aero Service Corp.		200
Allis (Louis) Co.		220
American Book Co.		24

Rank	Companies	Thousands of Dollars
	Bionetics Research Laboratories	213
	Clifton Precision Products Co.	11
	Ingalls Shipbuilding Corp.	1,052
	Kimball Systems, Inc.	27
	Litton Precision Products, Inc.	8,524
	Litton Systems, Inc.	291,890
	Monroe International, Inc.	127
	New Britain Machine Co.	208
	Streater Industries, Inc.	20
	Total	317,102
22.	Teledyne, Inc.	62,559
	Adcon, Inc.	277
	Amelco, Inc.	3,816
	Brown Engineering Co., Inc.	3,256
	Columbia Steel and Shafting Co.	39
	Columbia-Summerill Corp.	27
	Continental Aviation and Engr. Corp.	38,116
	Continental Device Corp.	56
	Continental Motors Corp.	64,897
	Electro Development Co.	33
	Geotechnical Corp.	93
	Getz, William, Corp.	105
	Gill Electric Mfg. Corp.	755
	Gurley, W. & L. E.	308
	H and H Engineering Co.	20
	Hydra Power Corp.	289
	Isotopes, Inc.	1,103
	Kinetics Corp.	122
	King Metal Products, Ltd.	24
	McKay Co.	63
	Micronetics, Inc.	70
	Milliken, D. B., Co., Inc.	217
	Monarch Rubber Co.	74
	Ordance Specialties, Inc.	135
	Packard Bell Electronics Corp.	5,906
	Pines Engineering Co., Inc.	14
	Republic Mfg. Co.	119
	Ryan Aeronautical Corp.	121,233
	Techdata, Ltd.	37
	Thermatics Inc.	13
	Wah Chang Corp.	55
	Wisconsin Motor Corp.	4,698
	Total	308,455

Rank	Companies	Thousands of Dollars
23. R.C.A. Corp.		298,868
	National Broadcasting Co., Inc.	13
	RCA Defense Electronics Corp.	91
	RCA Institutes, Inc.	20
	Total	298,992
24. Standard Oil Co. (New Jersey)		
	American Cryogenics, Inc.	85
	Enjay Chemical Co.	216
	ESSO A G	1,302
	ESSO International Corp.	151,098
	ESSO Petrol Co., Ltd.	66
	ESSO Research and Engineering Co.	885
	ESSO Standard Eastern Inc.	224
	ESSO Standard Italiana	2,463
	ESSO Standard Oil Co., S. A.	5,001
	ESSO Standard Thailand, Ltd.	78
	Humble Oil and Refining Co.	129,635
	Total	291,053
25. Martin Marietta Corp.		264,279
26. General Tire and Rubber Co.		8,307
	Aerojet Delft Corp.	272
	Aerojet–General Corp.	212,924
	Batesville Mfg. Co.	41,154
	Frontier Airlines, Inc.	45
	General Tire International Co.	799
	Total	263,501
27. Intl. Business Machines Corp.		256,304
	Science Research Associates, Inc.	177
	Service Bureau Corp.	142
	Total	256,623
28. Raymond Morrison Knudsen (JV)		254,000
29. International Telephone and Tel. Corp.		120,206
	Barton Instrument Corp.	27
	Bobbs-Merrill Co., Inc.	11
	ITT Continental Baking Co.	1,746
	E T C, Inc.	79
	Federal Electric Corp.	66,088
	ITT Electro Physics Laboratories	3,044
	ITT Gilfillan Inc.	38,643

Rank	Companies	*Thousands of Dollars*
	ITT Hammel Dahl	11
	ITT Technical Services, Inc.	8,392
	Jennings Radio Mfg. Corp.	20
	Total	238,267
30.	Tenneco, Inc.	
	Davis Mfg., Inc.	203
	Gas Equipment Engrs, Inc.	15
	Newport News Shipbld. and Dry Dock Co.	236,024
	Tenneco Chemicals, Inc.	467
	Total	236,679
31.	DuPont, E.I., de Nemours and Co.	41,582
	Remington Arms Co.	170,383
	Total	211,965
32.	F M C Corp.	189,639
	Gunderson Bros. Engineering Corp.	3,807
	Kilby Steel Co., Inc.	2,179
	Total	195,625
33.	Norris Industries	187,553
34.	Bendix Corp.	177,806
	Bendix Field Engineering Corp.	5,923
	Bendix Westinghouse Automotive	129
	Fram Corp.	433
	Marine Advisers, Inc.	31
	P and D Mfg Co., Inc.	78
	Scott Testers, Inc.	37
	Total	184,437
35.	Hercules, Inc.	179,364
	Haveg Industries, Inc.	258
	Total	179,622
36.	Northrop Corp.	106,992
	Hallicrafters Co.	32,468
	Northrop Carolina, Inc.	4,874
	Page Communications Engineers, Inc.	34,311
	Warnecke Electron Tubes, Inc.	262
	Total	178,907

Rank	Companies	*Thousands of Dollars*
37.	Uniroyal, Inc.	174,061
	Uniroyal International Corp.	27
	Total	174,088
38.	T R W Inc.	169,487
	Crescent Insul. Wire and Cable Co., Inc.	73
	Globe Industries, Inc.	316
	Gregory Industries, Inc.	12
	International Controls Corp.	380
	Ramsey Corp.	33
	T R W Semiconductors, Inc.	29
	United-Carr, Inc.	49
	Total	170,379
39.	Pan American World Airways, Inc.	167,437
40.	Asiatic Petroleum Corp.	155,583
41.	Mobil Oil Corp.	151,479
	Mobil Chemical Co.	12
	Mobil Oil New Zealand, Ltd.	24
	Total	151,515
42.	Standard Oil Co. of Calif.	73,406
	Caltex Asia, Ltd. *c/*	2,866
	Caltex Australia *c/*	13
	Caltex Oil Products Co. *c/*	61,280
	Caltex Oil Thailand, Ltd. *c/*	2,058
	Caltex Overseas, Ltd. *c/*	311
	Caltex Philippines, Inc. *c/*	70
	Chevron Asphalt Co.	33
	Chevron Chemical Co.	552
	Chevron Oil Co.	3,323
	Chevron Oil Trading Co.	273
	Chevron Shipping Co.	192
	Standard Oil Co., Kentucky	4,396
	Total	148,773
43.	Fairchild Hiller Corp.	148,549
	Burns Aero Seat Co., Inc.	37
	Total	148,586
44.	Collins Radio Co.	145,751
45.	Kaiser Industries Corp.	495
	Hydromar Corp.	173

Rank	Companies	Thousands of Dollars
	Kaiser Aerospace and Electronics Co.	2,936
	Kaiser Jeep Corp.	118,517
	Kaiser Steel Corp.	11,095
	National Steel and Shipbuilding Co.	9,182
	Total	142,398
46.	General Telephone and Electn. Corp.	25
	Automatic Electric Co.	9,029
	Automatic Electric Sales Corp.	200
	Fleetwood Corp.	15
	General Telephone and Electronic Lab.	268
	General Telephone Co., Southeast	52
	General Telephone Directory Co.	58
	Hawaiian Telephone Co.	8,026
	Lenkurt Electric Co., Inc.	9,556
	Sylvania Electric Products, Inc.	113,247
	Total	140,476
47.	Day and Zimmerman, Inc.	137,793
48.	Texas Instruments, Inc.	132,483
49.	Federal Cartridge Corp.	131,901
50.	Magnavox Co.	126,245
	General Atronics Corp.	4,003
	Selmer, H. and A., Inc.	12
	Sentinel, Inc.	22
	Total	130,282
51.	Thiokol Chemical Corp.	127,901
	Delta Corp.	65
	Uniplex, Inc.	104
	Total	128,070
52.	Texaco, Inc.	22,966
	Caltex Asia, Ltd.	2,866
	Caltex Australia	12
	Caltex Oil Products Co.	61,279
	Caltex Oil Thailand, Ltd.	2,057
	Caltex Overseas, Ltd.	310
	Caltex Philippines, Inc.	70
	Jefferson Chemical Co., Inc.	695
	Texaco Export, Inc.	30,305
	Texaco Puerto Rico, Inc.	2,855

Rank	Companies	Thousands of Dollars
	Texaco Trinidad, Inc.	17
	White Fuel Co., Inc.	541
	Total	123,973
53.	Chrysler Corp.	117,688
	Chrysler Outboard Corp.	4,128
	Total	121,816
54.	Pacific Architects and Engineers, Inc.	120,959
55.	Sanders Associates, Inc.	117,707
	Mithras, Inc.	775
	Total	118,482
56.	United States Steel Corp.	109,720
	Reactive Metals, Inc.	291
	U.S. Steel International, Inc.	7,787
	Total	117,798
57.	Goodyear Tire and Rubber Co.	57,878
	Goodyear Aerospace Corp.	56,484
	Motor Wheel Corp.	2,098
	Total	116,460
58.	Singer Co.	1,301
	Controls Co. of America	439
	EMC Instrumentation, Inc.	73
	Friden, Inc.	1,906
	General Precision Equipment Corp.	40
	Graflex, Inc.	1,060
	HRB-Singer, Inc.	7,749
	National Theatre Supply Co.	29
	Singer General Precision, Inc.	91,822
	Singer Sewing Machine Co.	112
	Strong Electric Corp.	644
	Tele-Signal Corp.	9,099
	Vapor Corp.	1,968
	Total	116,242
59.	Chamberlain Mfg. Corp.	115,925
60.	Lear Siegler, Inc.	83,650
	American Avitron	443
	Astek Instrument Corp.	11
	L S I Service Corp.	31,247

Rank	Companies	Thousands of Dollars
	Lighting Products, Inc.	33
	National Broach and Machine Co.	11
	Transport Dynamics, Inc.	358
	Total	115,753
61.	American Machine and Foundry Co.	115,025
	AMF Beaird, Inc.	27
	AMF Tuboscope, Inc.	82
	Cuno Engineering Corp.	91
	Harley-Davidson Motor Co.	41
	Total	115,266
62.	Colt Industries, Inc.	7,866
	Chandler Evans, Inc.	9,273
	Colts, Inc.	84,792
	Crucible Steel Corp.	158
	Elox Corp.	89
	Fairbanks Morse, Inc.	5,596
	Holley Carburetor Co.	4,244
	Pratt and Whitney, Inc.	2,407
	Total	114,425
63.	Eastman Kodak Co.	108,998
	Eastman Chemical Products Corp.	48
	Eastman Kodak Stores, Inc.	764
	Kodak Export, Ltd.	38
	Total	109,848
64.	City Investing Co.	
	American Electric Co.	43,818
	Hayes Holding Co.	50,431
	Moe, A. E., and Co., Inc.	15
	Rheem Mfg. Co.	247
	Wells Marine, Inc.	14,613
	Wilson Shipyard, Inc.	75
	Total	109,199
65.	Whittaker Corp.	60,195
	Aircraft Hydro-Forming, Inc.	345
	American Finishing Co.	159
	Berwick Forge and Fabricating Corp.	174
	Columbus Milpar and Mfg. Co.	27,224
	Detroit Bolt and Nut Co.	35
	General Aerospace Materials Corp.	412

Rank	Companies	Thousands of Dollars
	Hol-Gar Mfg. Corp.	3,438
	Jenks Metals Co.	880
	May Aluminum, Inc.	402
	Nautec Corp.	66
	Precision Forge Co.	980
	Space Sciences, Inc.	266
	Straightline Mfg. Co.	13,112
	Total	107,688
66.	American Mfg. Co. of Texas	106,745
67.	Massachusetts Institute of Technology	100,519
68.	Gulf Oil Corp.	86,443
	Gulf General Atomic, Inc.	5,883
	Gulf Oil Trading Co.	2,988
	Industrial Asphalt, Inc.	298
	Pittsburgh Midway Coal Mining Co.	330
	Total	95,942
69.	National Presto Industries, Inc.	94,908
70.	Kidde, Walter, and Co., Inc.	10,632
	American Desk Mfg. Co.	72
	Associated Testing Labs, Inc.	51
	Audio Equipment Co., Inc.	565
	Carpenter Mfg. Co.	56
	Chatos Glass Co.	55
	Columbian Bronze Corp.	246
	Craig Systems Corp.	2,111
	Crane Hoist Engr. Corp.	185
	Dura Corp.	116
	Fenwal, Inc.	840
	Grove Mfg. Co.	845
	Harrington and Richardson, Inc.	25,767
	United States Lines Co.	50,380
	Total	91,921
71.	Signal Companies Inc., The	29
	Allison Steel Mfg. Co.	85
	Dunham Bush, Inc.	501
	Garrett Corp.	72,698
	Mack Trucks, Inc.	11,404
	Signal Oil and Gas Co.	5,606
	Southland Oil Corp.	942
	Total	91,265

Rank	Companies	Thousands of Dollars
72. Curtiss Wright Corp.		90,680
	Dorr-Oliver Corp.	28
	Marquette Metal Products Co.	213
	Metal Improvement Co.	90
	Zarkin Machine Co.	160
	Total	91,171
73. Harvey Aluminum, Inc.		21,606
	Harvey Aluminum Sales	68,852
	Total	90,458
74. States Marine Lines, Inc.		87,059
75. Reynolds, R. J., Industries, Inc.		18,474
	Equipment, Inc.	3,346
	Gulf Puerto Rico Lines, Inc.	384
	Reynolds, R. J., Foods, Inc.	456
	Sea-Land Service, Inc.	62,269
	Total	84,929
76. Aerospace Corp.		76,245
77. Motorola, Inc.		73,061
	Motorola Overseas Corp.	103
	Total	73,164
78. Automation Industries, Inc.		1,617
	Consolidated American Services, Inc.	550
	Facilities Mgmt. Corp.	4,986
	Spartan Aviation, Inc.	3,157
	Vitro Corp. of America	62,802
	Total	73,112
79. Talley Industries, Inc.		21,273
	Braincon Corp.	32
	General Time Corp.	50,665
	Lakeville Precision Molding, Inc.	38
	Waterbury Button Co.	77
	Waterbury Companies, Inc.	385
	Total	72,470
80. Harris-Intertype Corp.		1,159
	Gates Radio Co.	371
	PRD Electronics, Inc.	39,393

Rank	Companies	Thousands of Dollars
	R F Communications, Inc.	3,516
	Radiation, Inc.	27,167
	Total	71,606
81.	Firestone Tire and Rubber Co.	66,640
	Hamill Mfg. Co.	16
	Total	66,656
82.	Seatrain Lines, Inc.	41,906
	Commodity Chartering Corp.	3,169
	Hudson Waterways Corp.	15,822
	Transeastern Shipping Corp.	3,675
	Total	64,572
83.	Aluminum Company of America	64,331
	REA Magnet Wire Co., Inc.	109
	Wear-Ever Aluminum, Inc.	18
	Total	64,458
84.	Hughes Tool Co.	63,693
85.	National Gypsum Co.	63,214
86.	Hazeltine Corporation	60,472
	Wheeler Laboratories, Inc.	81
	Total	60,553
87.	Western Union Telegraph Co.	57,686
88.	Control Data Corp.	50,757
	Associated Aero Science Labs, Inc.	1,352
	C E I R, Inc.	541
	Electronic Accounting Card Corp.	894
	Pacific Technical Analysts, Inc.	3,293
	T R G, Inc.	76
	Total	56,913
89.	White Motor Corp.	25,056
	Hercules Engines, Inc.	30,751
	Minneapolis Moline, Inc.	465
	Oliver Corp.	12
	Total	56,284
90.	Continental Air Lines, Inc.	55,242
91.	World Airways, Inc.	54,930

Rank	Companies	*Thousands of Dollars*
92. Atlantic Richfield Co.		31,347
	Sinclair Koppers Co.	13
	Sinclair Oil Corp.	8,387
	Sinclair Refining Co.	14,590
	Total	54,337
93. Tumpane Co., Inc.		53,963
94. Cessna Aircraft Co.		52,685
	Aircraft Radio Corp.	732
	Total	53,417
95. Smith Investment Co.		
	Smith, A. O., Corp.	51,567
	Smith, A. O., of Texas	134
	Total	51,701
96. Sverdrup and Parcel and Assocs., Inc.		430
	Aro Inc.	49,817
	Total	50,247
97. Dynalectron Corp.		50,049
98. LeTourneau, R. G., Inc.		49,903
99. Flying Tiger Line, Inc.		48,261
100. Southern Airways Inc.		48,260

(Most of the criticism of the defense industry in this and succeeding chapters is directed against the large contractors. Small businesses doing defense work have many legitimate gripes against the government, the most important being that they are discriminated against. For example, in any pinch they are the first to get squeezed. Whenever contract awards are reduced, small business shrinks the most. In the past two years contract awards have gone down somewhat, but on each occasion small business has been affected disproportionately. Thus in 1967 the small-business share of defense contracts was 20.3 percent, in 1968 it went down to 18.4 percent, and in 1969 it went down further, to 17.5 percent. Most small defense contractors know this; however, they are afraid to speak out

about it or to criticize the special treatment given the large contractors, because of fear of reprisals. Meanwhile, the dinosaurs are
eating all the fodder.)

Similarly contracts awarded by the Atomic Energy Commission
and the National Aeronautics and Space Administration, both of
which deal largely with the same contractors as does the Pentagon,
tend to be concentrated in an élite group of corporations. Of approximately $1.6 billion awarded by the AEC in 1968 to prime
industrial contractors, all but $104 million went to 36 contractors.
The ten largest AEC contractors accounted for $1.2 billion. NASA
spends much more of its total budget for procurement than any
other federal agency. More than 90 percent of its funds are awarded
in contracts to industry and educational institutions. Of its $4.1
billion worth of procurement in 1968, 92 percent of the awards to
business went to NASA's largest 100 contractors.

Some firms do almost all their business with the government. Into
this category fall a number of the aerospace concerns—those which
specialize in advanced weapons and space vehicles—including such
giants as General Dynamics, Lockheed Aircraft and United Aircraft. For the more or less totally dependent government contractors
the benefits of a large and stabilized defense budget are easily
demonstrable. In 1949 none of the three firms mentioned had total
annual sales of so much as $250 million per year, and one, General
Dynamics, had only $45.2 million. By 1967 each was doing well in
excess of $2 billion in annual sales. By any other measure they and
others like them had grown like fabulous beanstalks after a steady
diet of defense-contract nourishment.

For other important defense contractors, such as General Electric,
AT&T and General Motors, government sales amount to only a
small percentage of total business. But the tendency for such powerful companies is to enlarge their dollar value of defense work,
if not their share, over the years. And whether defense contracts
represent five percent or fifty percent or more of a corporation's
annual sales, they become a solid part of the business, an advantage
to maintain or improve upon. A company may even work harder
to increase its military sales than it does to build commercial sales,
because military work is more profitable in many ways, less competitive and more susceptible to control through lobbying in Washington. Industrial corporations of the first order, those with assets
of $1 billion or more, have faithfully made their pilgrimages to the

TABLE 3. Largest National Security Contractors*

Pentagon	AEC	NASA	Largest Industrial Corporations**	
1. Lockheed	1. Union Carbide	1. North American Rockwell	1. General Motors	(10)
2. General Electric	2. Sandia Corp.	2. Grumman Aerospace	2. Standard Oil (N.J.)	(24)
3. General Dynamics	3. Reynolds Electrical	3. Boeing	3. Ford	(19)
4. McDonnell Douglas	4. du Pont	4. McDonnell Douglas	4. General Electric	(2)
5. United Aircraft	5. General Electric	5. General Electric	5. Chrysler	(53)
6. AT&T	6. Bendix	6. Bendix	6. IBM	(27)
7. Ling Temco Vought	7. Holmes and Narver	7. IMB	7. Mobil Oil	(41)
8. North American Rockwell	8. Westinghouse	8. Aerojet–General	8. Texaco	(52)
9. Boeing	9. Idaho Nuclear	9. Martin Marietta	9. Gulf Oil	(68)
10. General Motors	10. Douglas United Nuclear	10. RCA	10. U.S. Steel	(56)
11. Raytheon	11. Dow Chemical	11. TRW	11. ITT	(29)
12. Sperry Rand	12. E. G. and G., Inc.	12. Chrysler	12. AT&T	(6)
13. AVCO	13. Goodyear Atomic	13. Lockheed	13. Standard Oil of Cal.	(42)
14. Hughes Aircraft	14. Atlantic Richfield	14. TransWorld Airlines	14. McDonnell Douglas	(4)
15. Westinghouse	15. Monsanto	15. Sperry Rand	15. du Pont	(31)
16. Textron	16. Rust Engineering	16. General Dynamics	16. Shell Oil	
17. Grumman	17. Aerojet–General	17. General Motors	17. Westinghouse Elec.	(15)
18. Honeywell	18. Swinerton and Walberg	18. Federal Electric (ITT)	18. Boeing	(9)
19. Ford	19. Mason and Hanger	19. United Aircraft	19. Standard Oil (Ind.)	
20. Olin Mathieson	20. North American Rockwell	20. Service Technology	20. RCA	(23)
21. Litton	21. Kerr-McGee	21. Philco-Ford	21. General Tel. and Elect.	(46)
22. Teledyne	22. National Lead Co.	22. Catalytic-Dow (Joint Venture)	22. Goodyear Tire and Rubber	(57)
23. RCA	23. United Nuclear Corp.	23. LTV	23. Bethlehem Steel	
24. Standard Oil (N.J.)	24. United Nuclear Hanestake	24. Brown/Northrop (Joint Venture)	24. Swift	
25. Martin Marietta	25. Gulf General Atomic	25. Northrop	25. LTV	(7)

* 100 Companies and Their Subsidiary Corporations Listed According to Net Value of Military Prime Contract Awards, Fiscal Year 1969, Department of Defense; 1969 Financial Report, United States Atomic Energy Commission; Annual Procurement Report, Fiscal Year 1969, National Aeronautics and Space Administration.

** *Fortune*, May 15, 1969.

Pentagon, the Mecca of the world of contractors, with no less enthusiasm than their smaller associates.

Table 5 lists the 25 largest contractors of the Pentagon, the Atomic Energy Commission and the National Aeronautics and Space Administration, and the 25 largest firms listed in *Fortune* magazine's directory of the largest industrial corporations. The figures in parentheses beside the largest industrial corporations indicate their rank among the largest Pentagon contractors. Note that only four of the 25 biggest industrial corporations are not among the largest Pentagon contractors. Note also the high coincidence of firms on the Pentagon, AEC and NASA lists. The table suggests that defense contracting is extremely attractive to big business.

The enormous attraction of military and military-related contracts for the upper tiers of industry has deepened since 1965 along with the sharp increase in military procurement. For example, GE's defense contract awards went up from $783 million in 1958 to $1.5 billion in 1968; General Motors went from $281 million in 1958 to $630 million in 1968. While much of this increase can be traced to the Vietnam war boom—and many contractors would suffer a loss of business if the war ended or defense spending were cut back significantly for any other reason—there was steady growth in the defense industry during the 1950s and early 1960s (in 1964 and 1965, before the Vietnam buildup, there was a decline in contract awards). In the five years from 1958 to 1963—five years of peace—the value of GE's defense contracts increased by $217 million and General Motors' rose by $163 million. The same trend can be shown for many of the large corporations in the aerospace and other industries. The large sums of working capital (money), use of government-owned property, research and development financing, and freedom from competition and from other rigors of the marketplace offered as defense contract fringe benefits are just too much for many corporations to turn down.

It is not difficult to identify the corporate beneficiaries of military largesse. What also seems to be clear is that defense production is gradually spreading throughout industry, although the great bulk of defense contract money is still spent among a relatively few companies that receive their largesse on more liberal terms than the others. Still, as the defense budget has increased over the long term, the procurement dollars have gone further afield.

2. Geographical Distribution

The geographical concentration of defense production in the industrialized, high income states also suggests that military contracts have come less and less to be restricted to an isolated sector of the economy specializing in guns and ammunition or even warships. In 1969 the two regions receiving the highest percentage of contract awards were the Pacific and Middle Atlantic. California placed in the top five states in 18 of the 25 procurement programs, New York in the top five in 12 programs, and Ohio among the top five in nine programs. The New England region received the highest proportion of awards for weapons contracts, and the Middle Atlantic, for ships. The East North Central region received the highest number of tank and automotive awards, and the Middle Atlantic region received the most electronic- and communications-equipment contracts. California received over one-third of all military research and development awards. The South Central excelled in aircraft awards, largely because Texas is located in that region. Military business has become solidly impacted in industrial America.

3. Concentration and Entrenchment

Indeed, concentration and entrenchment are characteristic of the defense industry. A study by Dr. Murray Weidenbaum, now Assistant Secretary of the Treasury for Economic Affairs, showed the degree of concentration of sellers in the major military product categories. Weidenbaum applied concentration ratios to Air Force procurement during 1966. The concentration ratio shows how dominant small groups of sellers are in any given field. According to the Weidenbaum study, four firms received 86 percent of the aircraft engine contracts; eight firms took 92 percent. Four firms took 56 percent of airframe and spare-parts contracts, and eight firms accounted for 79 percent. Eight firms obtained 56 percent of total missile and space systems contracts. Finer breakdowns within product categories show further concentration. For example, two firms, United Aircraft and General Electric, received 65 percent of the aircraft engine contracts. Two firms, General Electric and Westinghouse, dominate nuclear turbine production. One firm, Newport News Shipbuilding and Drydock Company, has a monopoly on attack-aircraft-carrier production. Defense production at its upper reaches is characterized by oligopoly and monopoly.

4. Industrial Inefficiency

Orthodox economists like Weidenbaum associate oligopoly and monopoly with the absence of effective competition and therefore expect to find a high degree of inefficiency. This is precisely what has been found by Weidenbaum and others who have seriously studied the way the defense industry works. Industrial inefficiency has been demonstrated in two ways.

First, it has been shown by on-site investigations and first hand observations at defense plants. Albert Shapero, a defense consultant and professor of management at the University of Texas, concludes that aerospace contractors habitually overstaff, overanalyze and over-manage. In a study comparing engineering in a number of countries, he found that firms in the United States and, interestingly, in the Soviet Union tend to employ unnecessarily large numbers of scientists and engineers on government projects.[12] While a United States firm might use several hundred engineers on a single component of an aircraft project, the typical French or German project team varies from three to fifty engineers on an aircraft and from three to ten on an electronic project. The lead times necessary to get an aircraft into production are also much shorter. A major reason seems to be the expectation that the project leader in the European firm will stay within his budget and schedules. Says Shapero: "Funding increases, which remain the prerogative of top management, are much rarer than in U.S. practice, and are certainly not taken for granted."

In addition, administrative professionals in United States firms far outnumber their counterparts in Europe. In United States aerospace engineering offices, administrative personnel outnumber technical personnel by about twenty to one. The European ratio is the reverse.

The superabundance of money in the United States is having the

---

12 *Space/Aeronautics*, March 1969, pp. 58–65. Deputy Secretary of Defense David Packard came to a similar conclusion in a 1970 speech in which he said that both the military and the contractors tended to "over-organize, over-man, over-spend and under-accomplish." *Congressional Record*, August 21, 1970, pp. S 13917–13918.

effect of increasing the costs of aerospace development far above what it would cost with reasonable efficiency. It takes the French fewer than 150,000 man hours to develop a jet fighter, while it takes the U. S. about a million hours to develop a comparable plane. As for quality, many experts doubt whether any American fighter can outperform the French Mirage, the Swedish Viggens or the Russian MIG 21.

Colonel A. W. Buesking, who until his retirement from the Air Force in 1968 was Director of Management Systems Control, Office of the Assistant Secretary of Defense, in testimony before the Joint Economic Subcommittee on Economy in Government, headed by Senator William Proxmire, summarized a study he had conducted by saying that control systems essential to prevent excessive waste in defense production simply did not exist. Contractors, he observed, were inefficient, performed poorly and charged the government with excessive costs.[13]

A. E. Fitzgerald, former Deputy for Management Systems, Office of the Assistant Secretary of the Air Force, also in testimony before the Proxmire Committee, described poor work habits and poor discipline, attributable in part to "the emphasis in periods past, particularly during the so-called missile gap days, in which we were driving ahead full speed to field new weapons with primary emphasis on schedule and secondary emphasis on technical capability of weapons, and with a readiness to pay whatever the costs happened to be." Fitzgerald went on to say that inefficient conduct is contagious:

It has been my personal observation that companies, contractors, and Government organizations for that matter, having poor discipline in one area, cost control, for example, typically have poor discipline in other areas. Almost every situation in which we have found gross failings in cost control techniques through our examination of the systems for compliance to our criteria, have been also situations in which we have severe quality and workmanship problems.[14]

In one rare case where the Defense Department hired a management-consultant firm to find out why production costs of the en-

---

[13] Ninetieth Congress, second session, Joint Economic Committee, Subcommittee on Economy in Government, "Hearings on the Economics of Military Procurement" (1968), Part 1, pp. 156–66.

[14] *Ibid.*, pp. 229–230.

gines for the F-111 (the TFX) were running several times higher than initial estimates, an on-site investigation revealed inefficiency of about 50 percent, that is, costs were 50 percent higher than they should have been, assuming reasonable efficiency of operation. As a result of this study the government reopened price negotiations with the contractor, Pratt and Whitney (a subsidiary of United Aircraft), and reduced the contract price by more than $100 million. However, that useful exercise—on-site inspection by independent experts to determine what a given program "should cost"—has been carefully not made into a general policy.[15]

The other two major components of the F-111, the airframe, manufactured by General Dynamics, and the avionics, made by North American, also entailed substantial cost overruns. Had there been better management of these programs by the Defense Department and better efficiency by the contractors, great sums of money and a number of lives would probably have been saved. The cost of the aircraft was originally estimated at $4 million each. Current estimated costs are about $13.7 million each. Original plans called for purchasing 2,000 aircraft. By 1970 the number had been reduced to 547, yet the cost of the total program had risen steeply and the performance characteristics of the plane had been significantly degraded.

Three of the first eight F-111s sent to Vietnam were lost a few weeks after their arrival, and the plane was then grounded. In December 1969 all F-111s were temporarily grounded following yet another crash and they remained grounded throughout most of 1970. It was the fifth time this unusual action had to be taken toward the F-111. The Navy was so dissatisfied with the performance of its version that it was canceled altogether, and the British Royal Air Force canceled its order, too. As of the start of 1970, a total of 15 F-111s had crashed and 13 pilots had been lost—seven known dead and six missing. The 223 planes completed as of that time plus the 250 under construction were in the process of being overhauled because of a defect discovered in the wing carry-through box, the structure holding the movable wings. The cost of the "fix" was estimated at $80 million.

15 The Proxmire Committee, in its report on "The Economics of Military Procurement," urged the General Accounting Office to study the feasibility of incorporating the should-cost method into its audits of contractor performance. The GAO found the should-cost method to be feasible and useful. In 1970 the Army gingerly authorized a should-cost study of its Hawk missile program and learned that the contractor, Raytheon, was 30 percent inefficient.

A second way that gross inefficiency in defense production has been demonstrated has been by studies of weapons systems and components to determine their overall performance. Two highly significant studies of this nature were reported in 1969. One was a classified study done by an analyst in the Pentagon's Office of Systems Analysis.[16] It showed that the assumed superiority of costly aircraft avionics (electrical and electronics systems such as radar and guidance controls) is a myth. For example, according to the report modern avionics are less effective than World War II iron bombsights and in general range from 20 percent to 300 percent worse. Airborne track-and-scan systems are unreliable and perform worse than human operators. Offshore radar early-warning aircraft do not successfully warn pilots of imminent attack. This last finding may have been demonstrated in October 1969, when a Cuban defector successfully penetrated United States defenses by flying a Russian MIG 17 from Cuba to Florida, although the official Pentagon explanation was that our own early-warning flights had been curtailed for "economic" reasons. Antiradiation missiles are considered unreliable. The report further concludes that cost estimates of avionics are as poor as performance. Ten-year operating costs of these systems run from four to twenty times the cost of their initial purchase.

The second study was done by Richard A. Stubbing, a defense-budget analyst at the Bureau of the Budget. Stubbing's study, entitled "Improving the Acquisition Process for High Risk Electronics Systems," originated as a paper for a graduate course at Princeton University in 1967–1968, which he was attending on leave of absence from the Bureau of the Budget. Following his return to the government, however, the paper went through several drafts, including one in classified form, and was circulated within the Pentagon for comment. It stirred up great interest among defense analysts, many of whom had come to similar conclusions. After being referred to at least once before a congressional committee, it was leaked to the press and reported on in the *Washington Post* by Bernard Nossiter. Then more great interest was stirred up and there was a clamor for copies of the paper itself. Finally the Bureau of the Budget reprinted it for distribution on January 30, 1969, but with a number of disclaimers. It was inserted into the *Congressional Record* by Senator Fulbright on February 7.

A reading of the study makes it plain why so much consternation within government and industrial circles was provoked by it. (One

[16] Summarized in *Aerospace Daily*, August 7, 1969.

Pentagon official accused Stubbing of being a part of a conspiracy dedicated to unspecified but devious ends.) It begins with the assertion: "A growing and prosperous nation can afford many luxuries, but the low overall performance of electronics in major weapons systems developed and produced in the last decade should give pause to even the most outspoken advocates of military hardware programs." He then supports his statement by showing that of a sample of 13 major aircraft and missile programs with sophisticated electronics systems initiated since 1955 at a total cost of $40 billion, two programs were canceled because they did not work (cost, $2 billion), two programs were phased out after three years because of low reliability (cost, $10 billion), five programs were less than 75 percent reliable and gave poor performance (cost, $13 billion). Altogether, $25 billion was wasted.

Drawing on the work of other researchers, Stubbing showed that in the 1950s complex weapons systems, in addition to being poor in quality, increased in cost from initial estimates by an average of 240 percent, in some cases by more than 600 percent; that delays in scheduled deliveries to the government averaged two years, and that such poor contractor performance did not improve in the 1960s. In a number of case studies of current programs, unfortunately not identified by name of weapons system or contractor, similar problems were encountered—doubling and tripling costs, late deliveries, and poor performance, including failure under combat conditions.

Perhaps the most disquieting feature of the study concerns the question of defense profits. Stubbing found an inverse, or perverse, relationship between performance and profits. The contractors who earned the highest profits gave the worst performance.

Others have shown that between 1944 and 1965 a total of $4.2 billion was spent on the development of missile systems that were canceled before they were ever deployed.[17]

THE INFORMAL POLITY

To see the real defense establishment in action one must look beneath the surface of formal relationships, constitutional divisions of power, organization charts, laws, regulations, contracts, budget documents, profit-and-loss statements, and pious pronouncements about national security, the public interest and free enterprise. The

---

17 See tables placed in *Congressional Record*, March 7, 1969, p. S 2464, by Senator Stuart Symington.

fact is that vested interests lobby or bargain informally to get all they can of the benefits distributed through the political and economic system.[18] The economic pie is not divided according to an intelligent arrangement of priorities in light of the legitimate needs of all groups within society and the best use of national resources, but according to who sits at the various bargaining tables and with what strength. The only difference about the military table is that so much of the pie has been brought there under the shibboleth of "national security." Around that table sit an informal polity of military and civilian officials and private defense contractors. All meetings are held in secret, and nobody brings his organization chart or his rule book. This is not to say that military planning has no bearing on our defense posture or that many dedicated people, especially at the lower levels, are not trying to make the cockeyed procurement system work. The question is one of degree. Who decides how weapons are purchased? How much influence do the weapons salesmen exercise? How much public money is being squandered to satisfy private appetites?

1. Howard Hughes' Helicopters

Take the case of the Light Observation Helicopter (LOH). In 1966 the Pentagon submitted a supplemental request to Congress for $15 billion to meet its miscalculated military needs in Vietnam. Included in the request was a sum that the Army wanted for the purchase of 121 LOHs. Some quick arithmetic done by Representative Otis Pike, a member of the House Armed Services Committee, showed that the price of the helicopters had apparently increased by 250 percent within the past year. The committee approved the request but decided to investigate the helicopter situation. Shortly, the Army told the committee it had decided not to buy the helicopters after all and that the funds would be "reprogrammed" for other purposes, thank you. The committee decided to investigate anyway.[19]

[18] For a discussion of formal and informal political relationships see H. L. Nieburg, *Political Violence* (New York: St. Martin's Press, 1969) pp. 49–73. The classic study is Harold D. Lasswell, *Politics, Who Gets What, When, How* (New York: McGraw-Hill Book Company, Inc., 1936).

[19] The Hearings and Report on the investigation are in Ninetieth Congress, First Session, Subcommittee for Special Investigations of the Committee on Armed Services, U.S. House of Representatives, "Review of Army Procurement of Light Observation Helicopters" (1967).

The facts were that the Army several years earlier had decided it would need lots of little helicopters for observation, reconnaissance and support of ground troops. A design competition for the airframe (without the engine) was conducted with several potential manufacturers, and the list was soon narrowed down to three rivals: Hiller Aircraft Corporation, Bell Helicopter, and Hughes Tool Company. Under an interservice agreement the Navy was handling the procurement for the Army. The Navy originally intended to award design contracts to two firms. It then decided that only one design was acceptable, Hiller's, and it recommended that the contract be awarded to it. The Army thought that two contracts ought to be given, however, and it was then agreed to select Bell as well as Hiller.

The Army's deliberations were being conducted by a seven-man board, one of whose members, General Clifton F. von Kann, dissented from the decision to leave Hughes out. Von Kann, it happened, had been attending briefings during the board's deliberations, arranged by a close friend, Albert W. Bayer, vice-president for marketing of the Hughes Tool Company. Von Kann later said that Bayer was very effective in telling him of the superiority of the Hughes model and, out of the trust that is built only on friendship, he believed Bayer and became a proponent of the Hughes design. General von Kann filed a minority report recommending that Hiller be dropped instead of Hughes. Hiller's designs, he had concluded, were "extravagant and unproductive."

Von Kann had only begun to fight. Within a few days he persuaded his immediate superior, General Barksdale Hamlett, Deputy Chief of Staff for Military Operations, to write to the Army Chief of Research and Development, General Arthur G. Trudeau, stating that he, too, thought it was a travesty to leave Hughes out. General Trudeau, like a good soldier, agreed, although neither he nor Hamlett was a member of the selection board that had considered the designs. Trudeau told the story to General Clyde D. Eddelman, Acting Chief of Staff, who also agreed that an injustice was about to be done. Eddelman ordered the chairman of the selection board, General Gordon B. Rogers, to reconvene the board. The board was reconvened and in about ten minutes it unanimously overruled itself and added Hughes to the list of entries.

Von Kann had one more thing to do to close out this particular incident. When the board was making its earlier decision, one member, General Richard D. Meyer, actively opposed von Kann's efforts to give Hughes a piece of the action. The Navy had also opposed the Hughes design, and von Kann went to the Acting Chief of Staff, General Eddelman, to inform him of Meyer's transgression (siding with the Navy). Within three weeks General Meyer was transferred to a new command, given another assignment, removed from flight status (which reduced his income by $100 per month) and told that he was to have nothing further to do with Army aviation. When he asked for a short extension of time before leaving for his new assignment because of his daughter's wedding, his request was rejected.

The three contractors were given about $18 million to deliver five prototype models of each of their designs by November 1963. They were all late and none of them met the performance requirements specified by the Army. The contract had provided for certification of airworthiness by the Federal Aviation Administration. Because of the delays, the Army dropped the certification requirement and accepted delivery of the planes although they could not be certified for their intended use.

The Army then had to decide which of the defective prototypes was to be chosen for final production. The big money, of course, was in the production of large quantities. The Hughes Tool Company, owned by the Greta Garbo of the business world, Howard Hughes, was determined to get into the helicopter field even though it had never made a helicopter before this. Its previous most notable effort in aircraft production was the "Spruce Goose," a $20 million flying boat made during World War II that neither flew nor sailed. (Hughes' World War II contracts were investigated by the Senate Special Investigating Committee in 1947. The committee concluded that Hughes' firm had received $40 million in aircraft contracts but that no flyable planes had been delivered during the war and that Hughes had lavishly entertained government procurement officials with whom he was doing business. The committee also found that the evidence indicated that the awards of the contracts to Hughes had been influenced by political pressure.[20]) But Hughes had several invaluable assets—von Kann and his friends.

Since two other firms were bidding for the contract, there was one obvious way to win—submit the lowest bid. Hughes' strategy was to learn in advance what the Army board decision would be as to number of helicopters required, time allowed for production and

[20] See Eightieth Congress, second session, "Senate Report No. 440," Part 3.

other details in order to prepare the most attractive and lowest-priced bid. To be sure, it would also be necessary to find out what the other bidders were proposing. Hughes set out to learn all of these matters and, by all the evidence, succeeded. The Armed Services Committee concluded that the board's recommendations were disclosed to Hughes before they were publicly announced, a conclusion based in part on the fact that Bayer and von Kann had held meetings shortly after the board reached its decision and in part on the fact that Bayer, after the meetings with von Kann, tried to sell the same information to the Hiller Corporation. Bayer also told the Hiller Corporation that the Hughes Company had been given the details of Hiller's bid. The president of the Hiller Company had in his possession and turned over to the Army documented evidence of Hughes' intelligence (spy) system, including memoranda showing how Hughes was kept apprised of Army decisions by "informed sources" almost as they were made. The documents were received from Hiller by the Army before the decision was reached on the production contract, yet it did nothing to follow up the disclosure until more than a week after the contract was finally awarded. The winner was Hughes.

The committee also learned during its investigations that one of the "informed sources" who gave information about the rival bids to Hughes was William Leatherwood, Acting Chief of the Army Aviation Matériel Command, Evaluation Branch, who had access to the cost data submitted by the contractors. He also had a close friend with Hughes, one R. P. Pettengill. Their wives were friends, they attended the same church and they lunched together at the same Playboy Club on Pettengill's money.

General von Kann, after retiring from the Army, became a vice-president of the Air Transportation Association of America. General Eddelman retired to work first for the Hughes Aircraft Company, then to become vice-president of Universal Match Corporation, an important Army contractor.

What we see in the collaboration of General von Kann and Bayer, their determination to get a weapons contract for Hughes and the brutal humiliation of General Meyer, who tried to do his duty as he saw it rather than as one of the contractors saw it, is a not unusual example of the way the informal polity operates in the defense establishment. But it is not only a matter of friendship and favoritism. In the bargaining process something is exchanged for something. It is also a matter of jobs and contracts. Military officers want high-paying jobs after retirement. Contractors want contracts. Civilians want stepping-stones for career advancement in both the Pentagon and the defense industry. What better way to attain these goals than for contracting officials to "cooperate," bend the law, play favorites and sometimes connive with contractors? To believe that such practices do not take place or that they occur only as rare and insignificant exceptions to the general rule is to be blind to the evidence. It is not only common for generals, admirals and lesser military luminaries to take jobs with defense contractors; retired officers often go to work for the same contractors with whom they have been dealing in specific procurements.

2. Going Native

A *Look* magazine story quotes a senior Pentagon official as saying:

> It happens all the time. Almost all the officers who have anything to do with procurement go into the business. Naturally, they go to the companies they've had the most contact with. If you check the history of any missile or weapon program you'll find the same story.[21]

In the spring of 1969 the Proxmire Committee checked one missile program, the largest one we have—Minuteman.[22]

The Minuteman program, America's first line of land-based ICBM power (the Polaris submarines also carry ICBMs), was begun in the late 1950s and is still in progress. Actually the program has proceeded in three stages. Minuteman II was announced as a new-generation missile in the early 1960s, although some experts claim that the Kennedy administration, hoist on its own nose cone after it learned that the missile gap didn't exist, merely labeled some relatively minor improvements in Minuteman I as a brand-new weapon. Having installed most of the planned Minuteman Is and IIs, the Pentagon is now planning to replace them with Minuteman III, a larger missile with about 15 warheads on each one, called "multiple independently targeted reentry vehicles" (MIRV). The same consortium of contractors, except for one or two additions, has done all

---

[21] Berkeley Rice, "Generals for Hire," *Look*, August 26, 1969, p. 31.

[22] Ninety-first Congress, first session, Joint Economic Committee, Subcommittee on Economy in Government, "Hearings on the Military Budget and National Economic Priorities" (1969), Part 2, pp. 495–519, 547, 610, 751–67.

the work so far: North American Rockwell, Boeing, Thiokol, Hercules, Aerojet–General, Sylvania, General Electric and Avco. The total cost of Minuteman I and II has escalated from $3.6 billion to about $7 billion.

The committee looked into one aspect of Minuteman II, the guidance-and-control-system contract with the Autonetics Division of North American, and found the usual history of cost overruns, schedule slippages and performance failures. For example, the orignal contract grew from $170 million in 1963 to $320 million in 1964. The problem, according to Merton Tyrrell, executive vice-president of the private consultant firm that looked into this problem in behalf of the Air Force, was that "there has been little intent and little action taken to control costs," on the part of either the contractor or the Air Force personnel responsible for the program.[23] And one major reason for the cost-careless military attitude was "the switchover of personnel between Government and Industry."

One general, three colonels and one major, all of whom had direct responsibilities for the Minuteman guidance-and-control system being manufactured by Autonetics, subsequently retired from the Air Force and went to work for North American, two of them at the Autonetics Division. General W. Austin Davis was the head of the Air Force's Ballistics Systems Division, which had charge of the contract. General Davis became a vice-president of North American. Two colonels were the Air Force plant representatives at the Autonetics Division. Their job was to monitor the program for the Air Force. They retired and both went to work for North American, one at the Autonetics Division. The guidance-and-control project officer retired and became an assistant program manager at Autonetics. General Davis' head of missile procurement also went to work for North American.

It is no wonder that the chances of a military plant representative "going native," that is, becoming in all respects indistinguishable from the contractor, are said to be excellent. Those who make the switchover on the higher levels, general or admiral, are referred to within the defense community as "rainmakers."

The pattern repeats itself. Captain Patrick Keegan signed the contract with Pratt and Whitney for the F-111 engines; Keegan later went to work for Pratt and Whitney as a special assistant to the executive vice-president. General Nelson M. Lynde headed the Army Weapons Command, which set up the procurement of the M-16 rifle from the original sole-source contractor, Colt Industries, Inc. He personally approved the prices negotiated. A congressional investigation of the contracts with Colt found that excessive profits were taken and the rifles delivered were defective. Upon retiring General Lynde went to work for Colt as a consultant. While employed by Colt, Lynde wrote to the Army requesting copies of four classified documents relating to the M-16. The investigating committee, headed by Representative Richard H. Ichord, concluded "that it was at least unethical for Major General Lynde to accept employment with the producer of the M-16 rifle upon his retirement from the Army." [24]

But apparently the value of a rainmaker exceeds the cost of such occasional admonitions. General Harry Evans left the Air Force's Manned Orbiting Laboratory program in 1967 to become vice-president and general manager of Raytheon's Space and Information Systems Division. General Hamilton Howze, former Chief of Army Aviation, went to work in 1966 for Bell Aerospace Corporation.

Similar paths are even more well-trod by civilians who use their Pentagon experience as credentials for higher-paying positions in the defense industry or for lucrative relationships with defense firms, such as legal counsel. Willis Hawkins was a corporate officer at Lockheed before becoming an Assistant Secretary of the Army for research and development in 1963. He sold his Lockheed stock before going with the Army, but following his appointment, until 1965 he continued to receive deferred compensation from his old employer, Lockheed. While he was an Army official, his office made the decision to award the Cheyenne Helicopter contract to Lockheed, despite the fact that Lockheed had never produced a military or civilian helicopter before and although the designs of rival contractors were rated superior by an Army evaluation board. The costs of the Cheyenne subsequently increased from $1 million to $3 million each. The helicopter performed so badly in tests that production was terminated in 1969. After leaving the Pentagon, Hawkins went back to Lockheed. Hawkins' assistant chief of staff, General William W. Dick, Jr., went with him.

---

[24] Ninetieth Congress, first session, "Report of the Special Subcommittee on the M-16 Rifle Program of the House Committee on Armed Services," p. 5371.

Roger Lewis was an Air Force Assistant Secretary under President Eisenhower, later became a vice-president of Pan American World Airways, then president of General Dynamics. Roswell Gilpatrick has also had a profitable relationship with the Pentagon and General Dynamics. He served as Undersecretary of the Air Force in 1951–1953 and Deputy Secretary of Defense in 1961–1964. After each tour of duty he returned to his Wall Street law firm, Cravath, Swain and Moore. Before leaving the Pentagon the second time, however, he was interrogated intensely by Senator McClellan's Permanent Investigating Subcommittee concerning the award of the F-111 contract to General Dynamics. It turned out that Gilpatrick's law firm had represented General Dynamics before he was sworn in as Deputy Secretary and that he personally had helped settle a dispute between the Air Force and General Dynamics, facts he failed to disclose at his confirmation hearings. While Deputy Secretary, Gilpatrick took an active role in the competition for the F-111 contract and recommended that it be given to General Dynamics. One month after General Dynamics got the contract, one of Gilpatrick's law partners, Moore, was made a member of its board of directors. One of the lesser-known tragedies of John F. Kennedy's assassination is that it occurred a few days after these matters were disclosed by the McClellan Committee and after the hearings had been temporarily recessed.[25]

Men like Hawkins, Lewis and Gilpatrick are regularly recruited from the defense industry to help make and carry out defense policy. It is not only that the Pentagon civilian hierarchy constitutes, for the most part, a business élite that is very disturbing. What is most disturbing are the unlimited and unchecked possibilities for conflicts of interest.

There is a conflict-of-interests law, but it is toothless and nearly worthless because it is vague, narrow and practically never enforced. It applies only to retired military officers, not to civilians who may have handled military procurement, and provides that a military retiree may not "sell" to the Department of Defense for three years or to his service branch during his lifetime. The word "sell" is the catch. Military retirees do not "sell"; they become technical consultants or special assistants or are given other innocuous titles.

25 See I. F. Stone, "Gilpatrick and General Dynamics: Some Unanswered Questions," *The New York Review of Books,* January 2, 1969, pp. 10–12. The McClellan Committee hearings were resumed in 1970.

What's in a name? All that is necessary is for the rainmaker to make rain. He can beat his drum for his employer in a hundred ways, by calling old friends in the Pentagon, arranging meetings, bending an ear, leaning on a former subordinate, etc.

Jack Raymond, who covered the Pentagon for *The New York Times,* recounted the story of Admiral William M. Fechteler in a *Harvard Business Review* article. The admiral retired as Chief of Naval Operations and went to work as a consultant to the Atomic Products Division of General Electric. In testimony before a congressional committee, Admiral Fechteler explained how he arranged appointments in the Pentagon for a GE vice-president:

> I took him in to see Mr. Gates. I took him to see Admiral Burke. He had not met Admiral Burke before. And then I made appointments for him with the Chief of the Bureau of Ships. But I did not accompany him there, because those are matériel bureaus which make contracts, and I studiously avoid even being in the room when anybody talks about contracts.[26]

Thomas L. Gates was then Secretary of the Navy and later became Secretary of Defense. As of this writing the Pentagon has moved on the conflict-of-interests law in only one case since 1962.

The danger, of course, is that procurement officials, military and civilian, will influence policies and decisions concerning the purchase of weapons while in the Pentagon, then benefit from their actions or those of their former associates when they join the defense industry. At the same time, the defense budget gets bloated by a hodgepodge of unnecessary weapons. In early 1969 Senator Proxmire compiled data showing the number of retired military officers of the rank of colonel or Navy captain or above holding jobs with the 100 largest defense contractors.[27] Approximately 2,100 retired regular officers were employed by the 100 firms. Ten of the larger contractors employed almost 1,100. These figures represent a tripling of comparable data gathered ten years ago by Senator Paul H. Douglas. Senator Proxmire concluded that the community of interests between the military and the large contractors is growing and militates against the public interest.

An investigation by a Navy team in 1969 revealed that of approxi-

[26] "Growing Threat of Our Military-Industrial Complex," *Harvard Business Review,* May–June 1968, p. 60.

[27] The data, broken down by each of the 100 largest contractors, may be found in the *Congressional Record,* March 24, 1969, pp. S 3072–81.

mately 300 officials employed by the Navy to administer its ship-building contracts with the Electric Boat Company, a division of General Dynamics, more than a third formerly worked for the Electric Boat Company. "The situation," according to the Navy report, "is not conducive to proper and objective relationships between the Government and the shipyard." After studying the procurement and cost control practices at the shipyard, 98 per cent of whose work was under Navy contracts, the report concluded that there was inadequate control over the costs charged to the government and that unwarranted charges were being made, that government surveillance of contractor operations was inadequate, and that the shipyard was wasting millions of dollars.[28]

3. The Board of Directors

Representatives of the defense industry do a great deal of lobbying, individually through their own Washington offices and collectively through various industry associations, such as the Aerospace Industry Association. With their military counterparts—the Air Force Association, the Navy League, and the Association of the U.S. Army—they make up an effective pressure group in Congress. Perhaps the most heavily financed and sustained lobby program is carried on directly by the services—Army, Navy and Air Force—which maintain direct contact with Congress through offices of congressional liaison with branches located in the House and Senate office buildings.

The informal polity works best through the semi-institutionalized organization called the "business advisory group."[29] As of December 31, 1969, there were ninety-nine of these groups that meet regularly with Pentagon officials to discuss problems of mutual interest—everything from foreign policy to proposed changes in the rules governing weapons procurement. They are the defense industry's early-warning defense system and ministers plenipotentiary. Inside the Pentagon, members of the more powerful groups, such as the Coun-

[28] The report is reprinted in Ninety-first Congress, first session, Subcommittee on Government Operations of the Committee on Government Operations, U.S. House of Representatives, "The Efficiency and Effectiveness of Renegotiation Board Operations," Part 1, pp. 44–60 (1969).

[29] They were first authorized by an Executive Order of President Kennedy in 1962.

cil of Defense and Space Industry Associations (CODSIA), are known as "our Board of Directors." Their function clearly is to influence defense policy. They keep abreast of new developments at the Pentagon, do their best to veto unwelcome changes and exert pressure to get the government to do things industry's way. They are obsessed with two problems: profits and criticism of the defense establishment.

An important advisory group is the Industry Advisory Council (IAC), which used to call itself the Defense Industry Council (DIAC).[30] In 1969 some of its members were:

> Ruben E. Mettler, Assistant President and Executive Vice-President, TRW
> William M. Allen, Chairman, Boeing
> George R. Brown, Chairman, Brown and Root
> Eugene G. Fubini, former Vice-President, IBM
> Daniel J. Haughton, Chairman, Lockheed
> Donald J. Holden, Chairman, Newport News Shipbuilding
> Thomas J. Jones, Chairman, Northrop
> James R. Kerr, President, Avco
> Roger Lewis, Chairman, General Dynamics
> Thomas S. Nichols, Chairman, Olin Mathieson

Of those, three formerly held high positions in the Pentagon. Eugene Fubini was Assistant Secretary of Defense and Deputy Director of Defense Research and Engineering (1961–1965). Roger Lewis was an Assistant Secretary of the Air Force (1953–1955). Ruben Mettler was aide to the Assistant Secretary of Defense for Research and Engineering (1954–1955). Also members of IAC were the Deputy Secretary of Defense, David Packard, and the Assistant Secretary of Defense for Procurement, Barry J. Shillito. Both were with the defense industry before coming to the Pentagon.

A typical IAC meeting was held in October 1968. The meeting was attended by the usual crowd of giant-contractor representatives and about thirty of the highest-ranking officials of the Defense Department, military and civilian. One of the first orders of business was the presentation by the then Assistant Secretary of Defense for

---

30 See Ninetieth Congress, second session, Subcommittee on Economy in Government, "Economics of Military Procurement," Part 1, pp. 127–34; Donald May, "Washington Pressures/Industry Advisory Council," *National Journal* (March, 1970), pp. 682–84.

procurement, Thomas Morris (later a vice-president of Litton), and Ruben Mettler, of TRW, of what they called a "blueprint" for the 1969 activities of the council. It was agreed that this blueprint would be circulated among members of the council so that it might be approved as the next year's agenda for action.

Following the meeting this blueprint was distributed to the members and throughout the Pentagon on the assistant-secretary level, attached to a memorandum from Morris. It was entitled, "Fundamental Problem Areas: key areas worthy of joint exploration by DOD and industry in calendar year 1969." It is an intriguing document for the insight it offers into the defense establishment. From all the pressing issues before the highest, mightiest chieftains at their annual powwow, what had they selected as "fundamental key areas"? The impact of defense spending on the national economy? The relative strength of the United States and the Soviet Union? The need for better coordination of force levels among the service branches? Ways to eliminate cost overruns? One could think of a score of topics this group could usefully occupy themselves with. Instead, the blueprint combines an outline of their fears and anxieties with a Dale Carnegie list of how to win public funds and influence politicians.

The number one major problem area was labeled "Achieving Higher Public and Congressional Confidence in Integrity and Effectiveness of the Defense Procurement Process." Listed beneath this key issue were a number of "Detailed Problems." Some of these were:

Government Property Management Hearings
Excess Profits Hearings
Renegotiation Act Expansion
Truth-in-Negotiations
Lack of Competition Hearings
Specific Program Investigation (e.g., TFX, M-14, LOH, etc.)
Economy in Government Procurement
Property Management Report, Statutory Profit Limitations

All of these "problems" describe congressional hearings, reports and efforts either critical of defense contracting or aimed at trying to regulate it. In other words, what worried this business advisory group was the possibility that Congress might try to tighten up contracting and gain better control over the defense establishment.

Chapter Three

THE ORIGIN OF WEAPONS: RESEARCH AND DEVELOPMENT

Research and development plays a critical role in the acquisition of major weapons, with long-range effects on total defense spending that far exceed the $8 billion or so spent in this area per year.

In the first place, the future makeup of our arsenal of weapons depends to a large extent on present decisions to fund research programs. All weapons begin as a research project and evolve into the development of a prototype. At some point the program is given a green light and production of the new weapon is ordered. While most of the costs of weapons are incurred in the production phase, the research and development must come first. Obviously the research, though only a fraction of the total cost of a program, determines how huge amounts of money will be later spent. The research, therefore, is considered the thin edge of the budget wedge. A few million dollars spent on a research program in one year may lead to billions of dollars spent in the future.

To the Pentagon, research and development means "science" and is automatically sacrosanct, in line with the conviction that military and space research and accomplishment are of preeminent importance to American, if not global, life. Government expenditures for research and development go mostly to private contractors, where much of it is used inefficiently and much not used at all on government programs, but diverted to the contractors' own commercial purposes. Despite this, the belief is that America's safety depends upon the development of new technology, upon winning the "technology race," especially military and space technology.

The irrational extension of reason, the elevation of science to sacred heights, has been anticipated for many years. In 1927 C. E. Ayres wrote: "If we would only reflect upon it, our very faith would show us that science is the object of our devout belief. It is the great constant, superstition in another guise."[1] Long before, during the Civil War, Henry Adams had foreseen the danger inherent in the utter devotion to science, namely, that with science, the epitome of reason, as his excuse man would do something insane. Adams warned:

> Man has mounted science, and is now run away with. I firmly believe that before many centuries more, science will be the master of man. The engines he will have invented will be beyond his strength to control. Some day science may have the existence of mankind in its power, and the human race commit suicide by blowing up the world.[2]

Science has made the military planner a convert to new technology, although for centuries the Army and the Navy were famous for their hidebound resistance to even the slightest changes in the techniques of war. James B. Conant, who worked on the Manhattan atomic bomb project, recorded the sudden transformation that came over the military during World War II. He became deeply concerned over "the almost fanatic enthusiasm for research and development" that had seized the men in uniform. "It is," he said, "a phenomenon not unlike that of an old-fashioned religious conversion. The Defense Department, in regard to research, is not unlike the man who sprang onto his horse and rode madly off in all directions."[3]

[1] *Science: The False Messiah* (Indianapolis: Bobbs-Merrill, 1927), p. 19.

[2] Quoted in Robert V. Bruce, *Lincoln and the Tools of War* (Indianapolis: Bobbs-Merrill, 1956), p. 60.

[3] *Modern Science and Modern Man* (New York: Columbia University Press, 1952), pp. 116–17.

SPIN-OFFS, FALLOUT AND
INCIDENTAL BENEFITS

For a long time and still to a certain extent advocates of defense, space and atomic-energy research tried to justify the enormous drain on public resources on the grounds that the "spin-offs" from the technology of war and space conquest contributed to social and economic progress. NASA, especially hard-put to demonstrate the relevance of its activities to earthly problems, regularly disseminates long lists of technical achievements supposedly adaptable or already in medical or industrial use. It used to refer to these incidental benefits as "astronomical fallout" and to assert that they would spur economic development to new heights, a claim that so far has no basis. Throughout the late 1960s, the economy was spurred only to the dangerous heights of inflation, largely as a result of the impact of military and space extravagance.

One social scientist, Amitai Etzioni, investigated some of the space agency's claims and found certain discrepancies.[4] For instance, NASA took credit for a new kitchenware ceramics, but the Corning Glass Works showed that it first developed the glass-ceramics material for pots and pans, and it was then used in nose cones. NASA claimed that an electronic device developed by space research was being used to restore hearing in deaf people. The fact was the device had been used on only one person and was then discontinued. NASA reported that its telemetry system had been adapted by a Detroit hospital to monitor patients by remote control. A spokesman for the hospital insisted that it was the other way around, that the hospital had been experimenting with the system since 1948 and NASA took it from them.

The military have also claimed great contributions to the civilian economy, and no doubt some small fraction of military and space research has trickled down to civilian technology. But the $14.4 billion in research money that went to the three big defense and defense-related spenders, or more specifically to their contractors, cannot be justified on the basis of fallout, spillovers or incidental benefits.[5] As Dr. Wolfgang Panofsky once said to the Joint Com-

---

[4] *The Moon Doggle* (New York: Doubleday & Co., 1964), Chapter 4.

[5] Of the $16.8 billion in total federal outlays for research and development in 1968, DOD, NASA and AEC spent 85 percent. Twenty-eight other government agencies shared the remaining 15 percent.

mittee on Atomic Energy, "If you want the by-product, you should develop the by-product." In other words, it would make much more sense to invest public funds directly into civilian technology, and it would be less costly, than to expect civilian benefits to justify military research. The overwhelming proportion of technology produced by military, space and atomic-energy science has no earthly civilian application, and the little that does is not worth the cost.

Possibly because this fact is becoming clearer all the time, some space proponents have now adopted the essentially metaphysical position that space science creates *spiritual* value and is therefore worthwhile. In the days following the first successful moon landing the spirituality of space conquest was unfurled like the flag on the moon. For example, NASA's space-flight director, Dr. George C. Mueller, in a prepared public statement on splashdown day, demanded to know whether Americans would be so shortsighted as to "substitute temporary material welfare for spiritual welfare and long-term accomplishment." In other words, would citizens forego the divine achievements of space travel by denying to NASA the public funds it wanted, in order to satisfy its mean pedestrian needs? Then, calling for a "great leap" to Mars, Dr. Mueller suggested that we "dedicate ourselves to the unfinished work so nobly begun by three of us to resolve that this nation, under God, will join with all men in the pursuit of the destiny of mankind, will lead the way to the planets." Mueller resigned from NASA in December 1969 to become a vice-president of General Dynamics. Prior to joining NASA in 1963, he worked for Space Technology Laboratories, an Air Force contractor. He was succeeded as NASA's administrator for space flight by Dale D. Meyers, a vice-president of North American Rockwell, also an important Air Force contractor.

President Richard Nixon's declaration upon greeting the three new wise men soon after their return, that the moonshot events comprised the greatest week in history since the Creation, underlined the point. Flushed with success, space proponents immediately began softening up the public for more ambitious and expensive projects—magical mystery tours of the planets and eventually intergalactic trips. On the other hand, a strange exodus was begun of the leading scientists in the program, including Dr. Wilmot N. Hess, the science director of the Manned Spacecraft Center, who complained that NASA is not really interested in scientific discoveries, but only in the engineering and technical feats associated with space travel.

Other scientists, including Nobel prizewinner Harold Urey, have criticized NASA for restricting the free flow of scientific information. Some have accused NASA of maintaining a blacklist of scientists who have objected to agency policies but have remained anonymous because of fear of reprisals.

The ascension of the space agency, of course, follows the successful staircase to heaven built by the Defense Department. Military spending for research and development has long been justified on the emotional appeal of "the technology race" and the need to be faithful to the almighty purpose of advancing "the state of the art," a phrase dear to the military, for it appears often in their testimony for funds. The true believers are working in the new vineyards of the Lord, the military laboratories of the great corporate and educational contractors, expanding man's universe by pushing against the frontiers of knowledge. This compulsion to advance the state of the art is not subject to rational analysis, least of all the overall effects any given project may have on national security, but is produced, as Richard J. Barnet has written, by a mystical power for which reason is a poor match.[6] Contrary to the opinions of the existential philosophers, God is not dead, He is alive and well in the military-industrial complex helping NASA pursue the destiny of mankind in space, helping the Pentagon pursue the state of the art of warfare and helping contractors pursue private profits.

It can be seen how important research and development decisions are to the arms race. The initiation of research on a new missile or bomber may be interpreted by the Soviet Union as a potential threat to its security and cause it to embark on a countermeasure, and vice versa. The action-reaction phenomenon leads to arms escalation on both sides. It is for this reason that intelligence estimates of what the other side is doing become of crucial importance, as the Pentagon's decision to go ahead with a new project is generally based on a not always correct interpretation of what the Soviet Union or any other potential enemy has or may have in the near future.

For example, the missile gap that Lyndon Johnson and John F. Kennedy thought they saw was based on intelligence estimates of a Soviet missile buildup. Billions of dollars were then spent on research and development of new missiles, primarily in the Minuteman program, to counter the assumed threat. Fortunately the intel-

6 *The Economy of Death* (New York: Atheneum, 1969), p. 53.

ligence estimates turned out to be wrong, as the official intelligence estimators later conceded. Senator Symington said in 1968 to the Pentagon's chief of research and development programs, Dr. John S. Foster:

In the late 1950s we were told about the tremendous number of missiles they had. Between December 1959 and August of 1961 the CIA reduced the number of Soviet missiles estimated on launching pads ninety-seven and one-half percent, in four separate reductions. As a result of that type and character of false information, I have become a convert to the theory of overkill.[7]

Unfortunately, we had already spent great sums on the program and forged so far ahead of the Soviets in intercontinental missiles that they accelerated their own missile program in order to catch up with us. The Safeguard antiballistic missile system (ABM) has been partly justified on the basis of that Soviet effort, which will probably be followed by a new Soviet response, and so on.

THE BOMBER AND THE SUPERSONIC TRANSPORT

Through research and development awards, the military are able to maintain some programs on a relatively meager diet until the time is ripe to make the big move for major funding. Requests for research are the most difficult of all military programs for the President and Congress to resist. Who would be so stingy and shortsighted as to prevent the defense establishment from investing in America's continued military superiority, on which weapons innovation is dependent? Who would be so irreverent and unpatriotic as to deny the defense establishment the opportunity to advance the state of the art? Through the miracle of science, programs that many have thought dead, live again.

The decline and resurgence of the manned bomber is a case in point. Ever since the advent of missiles after World War II the bomber has been threatened with extinction. The B-52, built by

[7] Ninetieth Congress, second session, Senate Appropriations Committee, "Hearings on Department of Defense Appropriations, Fiscal Year 1969" (1968), Part 4, p. 2109.

Boeing after the Korean War, went into service in 1956. According to the logic of military weaponry it should have been superseded by a "new generation" of long-range bombers within a few years (the B-47 and its follow-on, the B-58, were medium bombers). The supersonic B-70 was duly chosen as its replacement. Later versions were called the RB-70 and RS-70. By the end of the Eisenhower administration more than $790 million had been spent on the new bomber, although additional funds for it had been drastically reduced by the President in 1959.

The bomber question became a major controversy of John F. Kennedy's administration as he first cut the Pentagon's requests for the program in half, then backed Defense Secretary Robert S. McNamara's refusal to spend the full amount appropriated by Congress for production and deployment. The basic objection was that it simply made more sense to develop a long-range nuclear-offensive capability through the intercontinental missile than through the manned bomber. The missile is more difficult to defend against and is less vulnerable in a hardened underground silo or in a nuclear-powered submarine than an airplane. Bombers are also more expensive than missiles. In 1962 the Air Force estimated the cost of 150 of the RS-70 versions at more than $10 billion, not including annual operating costs.

Despite these objections, the bomber concept was able to survive the lean years of the early and mid-1960s. One technique was to feed it small amounts of research and development money—small by military standards. By the time the program was canceled following the crash of one of the prototypes built, $1.5 billion had been wasted.

Another indirect way the manned-bomber idea was pursued by the Air Force and its constituency was through the promotion of the supersonic transport, the SST. Frustrated by the failure to get a large, long-range supersonic plane into full production, both the bomber users and the bomber builders got behind the notion of a government-subsidized commercial plane, which coincidentally would have many of the characteristics of the B-70. This was a reversal of the usual process, the historical experience having been for the government to purchase large military aircraft and for private industry to spin off commercial versions. Most large commercial transports originated in military procurements. When the bomber lobby began pushing for the SST, it was saying, in effect, let the government subsidize this new plane as it has subsidized new planes in the past. Except, this time we will go directly for a subsidized commercial aircraft and spin off a military plane.

Contrary to his efforts to retire the manned bomber, President Kennedy promoted the SST, perhaps to appease the bomber builders, perhaps in the belief that commercial-aviation activity, like space activity, was relatively benign. Whether he knew that the Air Force supported the SST because it expected to benefit from the military fallout is not clear. Among his reasons were that it would "maintain the historic United States leadership in aircraft development" and that it would "enable this country to demonstrate the technological accomplishments which can be achieved under a democratic, free enterprise system."[8] It is difficult to fathom how Kennedy could believe that a plane built with federal money by private contractors would demonstrate the accomplishments of free enterprise.

The SST program began in 1961 with a modest appropriation of $11 million for research to be conducted jointly by the Federal Aviation Administration (FAA), NASA and the Defense Department. A year later the amount was doubled. Although the SST program is under the control of a civilian agency, the FAA, the Air Force has been able to exercise great influence over it, particularly from the time that President Johnson appointed retired General William F. McKee, former Vice Chief of Staff to General Curtis LeMay, as head of the FAA. In 1966 McKee chose another retired Air Force general, Jewell C. Maxwell, to be director of the Office of Supersonic Transport Development.[9]

Still a third route taken by the bomber protagonists was through the conversion of the TFX fighter plane into a bomber. For a time, in the mid-1960s, things were going well for the bomber lobby on all fronts. Both the B-70 and the SST were being heavily financed, and plans were being laid for the TFX bomber. Then, with the crash of one of the B-70 prototypes, came a temporary hitch. McNamara was able to scrap the B-70 program, and a little later Johnson "stretched out" the SST program, that is, he extended the target

8 Message to Congress, June 1963.

9 In 1966 the FAA was made a part of the newly created Department of Transportation. In 1970 William M. Magruder, of the Lockheed Aircraft Company, was named SST program director. For a typical defense of the SST from the military point of view see "The SST Is Vital to the National Interest," *Air Force/Space Digest* (Feb. 1970), pp. 51–53.

date for making the final decision to begin production. Many thought the day of the long-range bomber was over.

But a little-known research program had been started up in 1964 that would change everything. In that year McNamara decided to support a $5 million request for funds "for initial study and development of a manned bomber," called the Advanced Manned Strategic Aircraft (AMSA). On the other hand, he opposed General LeMay's request that an additional $50 million be spent on the AMSA program. The Chairman of the Joint Chiefs of Staff, General Maxwell Taylor of the Army, sided with McNamara, as did the Air Force Secretary, Eugene Zuckert, and LeMay's request was turned down.

General LeMay must have been shaken. Ever since World War II there had always been new bombers and widespread support for even newer bombers. Testifying in the 1964 House Appropriations Hearings he said:

This is something new for us. We have always replaced our airplanes before we wore them out in the past. As a matter of fact, the B-29s, B50s, B-36s were all phased out of the inventory at around the 2,000 or 3,000 hour mark.

No doubt it was hard for him to understand the opposition to manned bombers by three Presidents—Eisenhower, Kennedy and Johnson. McNamara remained adamantly opposed to the end of his term. In February 1968 he told the Senate Armed Services Committee: "There is no reason in my opinion to move to accept the Air Force proposal, because the national intelligence estimate threat, as presently projected, does not appear to require the AMSA."

In 1964 General Taylor termed the question of whether or not to accept the Air Force recommendation for a follow-on bomber as an "emotionally charged decision." Taking sides were a potent combination of vested interests in the bomber concept versus civilian experts who claimed the bomber had become obsolete. On one side were arrayed pilots and commanders of bomber squadrons led by LeMay; bomber manufacturers led by Boeing, Lockheed, North American, General Dynamics, General Electric, and Pratt and Whitney; and members of Congress who represented districts and states where bombers were built and where the decision would have a heavy economic impact. On the other side were McNamara and the Whiz Kids, and the White House.

The issue was never really confronted. The B-70 program had been kept alive for years with funds for "research and development." The same technique was used with the SST. By the end of 1970 over $700 million had been spent on the SST. The same technique was used on AMSA, which, as Air Force Secretary Harold Brown admitted to the Senate Committee on Defense Appropriations, is very much like the TFX bomber. In fact, AMSA is a giant TFX, including the variable (swing) wing. In 1969 the opposition evaporated and Congress approved the first large amount, $100 million, for further research and development, and the Air Force began getting ready to award some contracts. Out of the rubble of the B-70 rose the phoenix, AMSA.

As a bonus and without much notice given to the fact, the TFX bomber, officially the FB-111, will also be used as a long-range strategic bomber, despite contrary assertions by General LeMay when he was struggling to get research money for AMSA. LeMay told the Senate Armed Services Committee in 1965 that the TFX bomber "is going to do the job fine in a tactical role but in the strategic role it is just not big enough to do it."

In the running for the AMSA program were the same five contractors who had won the contracts on the pre-AMSA programs, plus a sixth, Lockheed. North American built the airframes for the B-70 prototypes, General Electric built the engines, General Dynamics is the airframe contractor for the TFX, Pratt and Whitney builds the engines. Boeing and General Electric make up the SST team. They were all on the list of the top ten defense contractors for 1969, accounting for $7.2 billion in contract awards during that year. In 1970 the prime contracts were awarded to North American and General Electric.

AMSA (now called the B-1A) could be the most expensive aircraft program in history. Senator Proxmire has reported estimated costs as high as $80 million each. The official Air Force estimates range from $25 million to $50 million. If 300 planes were built at $50 million each, the acquisition cost would be $15 billion. This would not include the expensive air-to-ground missiles they are expected to carry or operation and maintenance costs.

The SST also moved closer to success. In September 1969 President Nixon gave his blessing to the program, although his own SST Ad Hoc Review Committee did not give its blessing to him. The committee, made up of his subcabinet government appointees, including Henry Houthakker of the Council of Economic Advisors, and Lee A. Dubridge, Nixon's National Science Advisor, reported that there was little or no justification for further federal support of the SST. It found that there would be insubstantial technological fallout and that economically there were too many uncertainties to warrant continued subsidization. Dubridge himself opposed further federal subsidies and recommended that remaining development and all production be turned over to private enterprise. Fortified in his belief, however, that America's prestige as world leader of aviation technology was at stake and convinced that the program would be successful, although his hand-picked advisors were not, Nixon approved a request for just under $100 million of federal funds for fiscal year 1970 and $290 million for fiscal year 1971. The program is expected to cost the government in excess of $1 billion if research and development is continued.

THE ANTI-BALLISTIC MISSILE: THE ARMY AND WESTERN ELECTRIC

The evolution of the antiballistic missile system (ABM) represents an even greater tribute to the efficiency of research and development, but not because it contributes to a sane defense program. The ABM is supposed to be able to intercept an incoming ballistic missile and destroy it before it destroys us. An operational ABM still does not exist, and even if the system is ever made to work, it will probably reduce national security rather than increase it, because of the response it would provoke from the Soviet Union. On the other hand, ABM has been formally approved and funded, with a promise of billions to come in the future. That makes the Army and its contractors very happy and, to them, it spells success.

ABM is the Army's missile program, one that it believes is a natural follow-on to the antiaircraft mission it has always had. It therefore fought fiercely against Air Force efforts to grab the antimissile mission. The Air Force program was called Wizard; the Army called its program Nike-Zeus and by 1959 was trying to get funds for production and deployment.

Actually the Army was given the antiballistic missile mission as a consolation prize for having lost the Thor-Jupiter contest for the intermediate-range ballistic missile (IRBM). The rivalry for the

IRBM assignment had raged in the mid-1950s with the Army field-
ing its Jupiter missile and the Air Force pushing Thor. Fighting
desperately for a major role in nuclear missilery, the services sabo-
taged one another, pirated manpower and withheld technical information. Secret data were leaked by the military to members of
Congress in an effort to influence the decision, and an Army officer
was court-martialed for revealing Air Force and contractor irregularities. Unsurprisingly there were lengthy schedule delays, cost
overruns and performance failures in both missile programs.

One of the important matters that this contest helped determine,
more important in many ways than the outcome of the Army–Air
Force missile race, was the question of whether in-house government laboratories like the Army's Huntsville, Alabama, facility
would continue to play a major role in military weapons research
and development. The Air Force and its contractors had already
worked out an alternative system of contracting out whereby public
funds would be funneled to private laboratories, and the Army's
stubborn adherence to in-house capabilities was a major threat to
the Aircraft Industries Association, which was envisioning the demise of the manned bomber and the fighter aircraft and which was
determined to capture the missile market.

In the end the Air Force's missile won and the Huntsville team
of scientists and engineers was transferred from the Army Ballistic
Missile Agency to the National Aeronautics and Space Administration. The missiles, by the time they were finally produced, turned
out to be obsolete before they were deployed, and most of our
European allies refused to have them, which made this $2.2 billion
program embarrassing as well as wasteful.

President Eisenhower did not fully support Nike-Zeus, although
it successfully knocked Wizard out of the rivalry, and he would
allow funds only for research and development. Eisenhower's former science advisor, Dr. George Kistiakowsky, testified to the Senate
Foreign Relations Committee in March 1969 that had the full Nike-
Zeus been authorized in 1960, we would have spent "what was then
estimated as $20 billion and could have been, judging by analogy
with other weapons systems, twice as much," and that it would now
be obsolete.

As with the manned bomber, Kennedy and McNamara opposed
moving Nike-Zeus into production. In 1964 it was abandoned in
favor of a modified program called Nike-X. That year McNamara

estimated it would cost at least $16 billion, not including annual operation and maintenance, and he suggested that it would have to be expanded if it were to meet the threat of Soviet attack and that additional costs would be imposed upon related programs such as civil defense, fallout shelters and bomber defenses. McNamara's opposition to the program was typical of the resistance it had met since its inception. Nevertheless, it managed to carry on for a decade with a little help from its friends and a lot of research and development money.

The prime contractor for Nike-Zeus and Nike-X was Western Electric, a subsidiary of AT&T, the sixth largest defense contractor in 1969. The Army–Western Electric relationship is a very special one, dating back at least to 1945, when the Army selected it as the prime contractor and program manager for its latest anti-aircraft program, the Nike. (Nike was the Greek goddess of victory in war.) Western Electric was also the prime contractor for the Sentinel, successor to the Nike-X, and is now the prime contractor for the current version of the ABM, Safeguard.

In the early 1960s the Senate Permanent Subcommittee on Investigations, headed by Senator John L. McClellan, investigated the "Pyramiding of Profits and Costs in the Missile Procurement Program" and made a devastating analysis of the dealings between the Army and Western Electric throughout the Nike programs. It showed, among other things, how Western Electric managed to make millions of dollars in excess profits by obtaining fees from the government for jobs on which it did absolutely no work. Western Electric's principal subcontractor, Douglas Aircraft (now merged into McDonnell Douglas, also one of the top ten contractors), did the same thing with its subcontractors.

For example, on one contract for launcher loaders, the platforms from which the Nike missiles are fired, Western Electric sent invoices to the Army totaling $16.4 million, including its profit of just under $1 million. What had Western Electric done for its fee? The bulk of the $16.4 million was the price paid by Western Electric to its subcontractor, Douglas. Western Electric's direct costs incurred on that contract were only $14,293, "for checking over the equipment at Army bases." Thus Western Electric was able to parlay a $14,293 expenditure into a $1 million fee, a profit of 6,684 percent. The manufacture of the launcher loaders was done by a third firm, the Consolidated Western Steel company, which subcontracted for the job with Douglas. Consolidated's costs of production were $13.5 million, on top of which Douglas added a profit of $1.2 million, while spending the grand sum of $3,316.21 of its own money. The Douglas profit totaled over 36,000 percent of its costs. The Army ended up paying $16.4 million for $13.5 million worth of effort, assuming the integrity of Consolidated Western's costs. Almost $3 million went for brokerage.

On another contract Western Electric was again two steps removed from production, yet was allowed to add a $3.2 million profit for itself to the government's bill. Once more the pyramid steps led from Western Electric down through Douglas to the worker firm on the bottom. In this case the Fruehauf Trailer Company produced rocket trailers for $53.8 million, including its 9.2 percent profit. Douglas took Fruehauf's invoices, added the sum of $3.7 million for its own services, which were in the nature of a toll gate, and passed them along to Western Electric. Western Electric added $3.3 million for itself and turned the final bill of $60.8 million in to the Army. According to the McClellan Committee report, Western Electric and Douglas "did absolutely no work" to earn their fees. The Army paid without asking questions.

Although major contractors have been able to hide their profits from defense contractors in a multitude of ways and it is difficult to separate defense from nondefense business, an analysis of Western Electric's financial reports for the ten-year period 1951 through 1960 shows an extraordinary jump in its profits with the increase in Nike sales. In 1951, a year when Nike sales were relatively low, Western Electric's government sales totaled 12.8 percent of its business, and its profits on net investment for government business were only 12.1 percent. By the next year there was a dramatic increase of Nike sales by Western Electric and an equally sharp upturn in the firm's profits. For 1952 Western Electric's government sales rose to 24.2 percent of total business, and profits on investment increased to 27.7 percent. For the ten-year period government sales averaged 26.6 percent of Western Electric's business; return on investment averaged 28.3 percent on its government work. The McClellan Committee concluded that Western Electric had taken large unearned profits out of the Nike programs.

But the real issue concerns the part played by the Army. Was this an isolated case of contractor abuse, of furtive actions committed by Western Electric and the others against which the Army took corrective and punitive steps as soon as it learned the facts, or did the Army condone the practices? The McClellan Committee reprimanded the Army for its inept administration of the program. It used inadequate numbers of personnel and none in the higher grades to manage billions of dollars of contracts. Since its own personnel was not competent, it constantly relied on Western Electric for technical and engineering advice. It had allowed its own in-house capability to deteriorate and was doing nothing to build it back up. When it was stated during the hearings that because the Nike-Zeus ABM could cost as much as $10 billion it was imperative for the Army to reconstruct its in-house capability, one of the Army chiefs of procurement, Colonel Henry Wishart, could only reply: "I think we have to consider the dangerous threat to this country to provide the kind of defense that we need to get on with the job."

The committee observed that it had learned to its distress, through General John H. Hinrichs, Chief of Army Ordnance, that the Army intended to continue the Nike-Zeus in the same manner as the earlier Nike programs, through Western Electric as prime contractor. It also observed that the Army had awarded $146 million for research and development on the Nike-Zeus since the completion of its public hearings and that two years afterward the same military official was still the Army's contracting officer with Western Electric. The committee concluded:

> The Army must be severely criticized for its past actions and for its contemplated future actions. . . . A showing of deficiencies in the past should bring steps to correct them. Apparently this has not been so.

Further, the committee found something in the Army–Western Electric relationship beyond ineptness. For one thing, the Army knew about the profiteering and did nothing about it. When a government auditor found evidence of the excess profits and showed it to the Army's contracting officer, Colonel John Graham, he simply ignored it. When Senator McClellan pointed this out to Colonel Graham during the hearings, the colonel replied that it was not the government auditor's function to comment about excess profits. In other words, it was nobody's business but the Army's what profits it paid its contractors. As the committee's report stated,

> Apparently the Government should be pleased that Western Electric Co. asked for and received a profit of only $995,000 on its $14,000 of work.

Had it asked for over $2 million profit, Colonel Graham apparently would have found authority to pay that amount.

For another thing, the Army's dependence on Western Electric as a consequence of its own technical and engineering ignorance placed the contractor in a monopoly position. It then demanded certain concessions from the government, and the Army capitulated. For example, Western Electric threatened to relinquish responsibility for the integrity of the systems until the Army agreed to buy all Nike parts through it, that is, to make the contractor the super-broker. The Army, unable to manage its own program, agreed. However, Western Electric generously permitted the Army to buy standard items such as screwdrivers, pliers, antifreeze and paper cups from other contractors. The Army, perhaps to reciprocate for the paper cup dispensation, permitted Western Electric to retain technical drawings prepared under Army contracts, so that it was impossible for it to purchase components of the program from other contractors or to open the program to competitive bidding.

From such facts the committee reached an important conclusion about the nature of defense contracting and the relationship of the government to the defense industry:

> The advanced technology of the space age, requiring huge expenditures of Federal funds, has created between Government and contractors new relationships to accomplish research and development and carry out production. The contract has, in effect, become a quasi-governmental service agency, usually operating without competition in supplying major weapons systems. The rule of the marketplace quite evidently no longer applies to the procurement of modern weapons. The contracts which provide them can no longer be considered commercial transactions between buyer and seller and there is need for spelling out a new legal, economic relationship.[10]

The McClellan Committee also criticized Boeing for taking excess profits in the Air Force's Bomarc missile program (part of the SAGE bomber defense system) and General Dynamics for doing the same in the Titan missile program (predecessor of Minuteman). Boeing beefed up its profits in two ways, by playing the profit-pyramiding game and by intentionally overestimating its costs during contract negotiations so as to increase its profits under the incentive-contract provisions.

---

[10] Eighty-eighth Congress, second session, Senate Report No. 970, "Pyramiding of Profits and Costs in the Missile Procurement Program," p. 149.

THE AIR FORCE GOES INTO ORBIT

The Air Force space program further demonstrates the salvation of weapons programs when they are zealously anointed with research and development funds.

The Air Force fought bitterly throughout the 1950s, first to gain control of the entire space effort, then, after NASA was created, to acquire the military franchise. By 1958 it had put down its service sisters and cornered the market on military space systems. Its tactics toward NASA, a potential rival for both the Air Force's industrial and political constituency, have been to infiltrate that civilian agency with as many Air Force people as possible, to conduct joint space ventures with it and to exercise maximum influence over it. NASA has always been well-stocked at the policy-making level with military and civilian Air Force officials, and the traffic of people between the two has been great. Air Force contractors, such as Thompson-Ramo-Wooldridge, have also played an important part in the space agency's affairs.

The Air Force's space program, though overshadowed by NASA's, has been substantial. It includes an extensive number of orbiting satellites for espionage and other military purposes, most of which have been shrouded in secrecy. In addition, there has been one overriding goal of the Air Force—to gain military dominion over space. The reasoning, first articulated by Air Force former Chief of Staff General Thomas D. White, is that just as military control of the land, followed by control of the sea, and then of the air, once meant control of the world, now control of outer space will give to its masters control of earth. Therefore it is necessary for the United States to investigate the military uses of space and to prevent any other nation from dominating it. Officials of NASA and the Air Force have always considered all space exploration to be at least in part imbued with a military purpose. James E. Webb, NASA's former administrator, once stated that the policy is "to develop the space program as a civilian peaceful effort . . . but always pressing with the kind of technology that would permit us to move rapidly in the military field if we were required to do so." And Air Force General Bernard Schriever spoke of "the artificial division between space for peaceful purposes and space for military purposes."[11]

11 The Webb and Schriever quotes may be found in H. L. Nieburg, *In the Name of Science* (Chicago: Quadrangle Books, 1966), pp. 15, 52.

The effects of such statements have been to assure an Air Force role in space despite the clear mandate given to NASA.

Characteristically the Air Force turned to the concept of manned flight in its military space program. Its first major effort was aptly called Dynasoar, for, as it turned out, behind it there was more political brawn than brains. Urged upon the Congress by General LeMay, among others, its purpose was to propel one man into space in a vehicle that could be maneuvered during reentry from orbit and "to explore man's military usefulness in space."[12] But by 1963 the cost overruns during the research and development stage had risen higher than Dynasoar ever would, and it was canceled. At the time of its cancellation over $400 million had been spent on it, and it would have cost at least $1 billion to complete. McNamara conceded in 1964 that "we will have spent close to $400 million and we will not be able to salvage any of the $400 million." His only regret was that he did not cancel it sooner.

But the manned-military-space idea was far from abandoned. While McNamara was announcing the demise of Dynasoar, a new manned-military-space putsch was being organized; in 1965 the birth of the Manned Orbiting Laboratory (MOL) was heralded by President Johnson as a research and development program. As with Dynasoar, its purposes were described in vague generalities ("conceived to enhance national security by providing support for our military forces"), and assurances were given that it would not duplicate NASA's program. The major distinction from Dynasoar seems to have been that Dynasoar would have carried one man while MOL was supposed to carry two. Like the earlier program, MOL would "enable us to ascertain the full extent of man's utility in space for defense purposes."[13]

Despite the Air Force's assurances, it grew increasingly difficult to distinguish the MOL program of manned space flight from NASA's program of manned space flight, especially as MOL's failures became conspicuous. The program called for providing several two-man 30-day earth-orbit trips at an estimated cost of $1.5 billion. The launching was supposed to be in 1968. But by the end of 1968 almost all of the $1.5 billion had been spent and the 30-day orbit had been

12 Harold Brown, then the Pentagon's Director of Research and Engineering, before the Senate Armed Services Committee, 1964.

13 John S. Foster, Jr., the Pentagon's Director of Research and Engineering, before the Senate Committee on Appropriations, 1968.

postponed to 1972. When faced with their own dismal performance, Air Force officials used the old stab-in-the-back excuse, namely, that Congress had not given them enough funds.

On May 6, 1969, John S. Foster, Jr., the Pentagon's research director, told the Senate Space Committee:

> We have conducted a comprehensive review of this project, its objectives, present development status, numerous detailed analyses of prior years, and its relationship to NASA manned space-flight undertakings and other DOD space activities. The results of our review can be summarized briefly as follows: The anticipated benefits of the Defense Department to be derived from the MOL justify the continuance of this program.

One month later, on June 10, 1969, the Pentagon announced its cancellation. The grounds given for the cancellation were the need to reduce federal spending and the advances made in the development of unmanned satellites. At the time of its cancellation about $1.5 billion had been spent and another $1.5 billion would have been needed to complete the program.

But within a few days plans were being made known to enlarge the Air Force's spy-satellite program and, more importantly, to embark on a new joint venture with NASA, incorporating manned space flight: a space shuttle. According to *Electronic News*, June 16, 1969:

> The Air Force plans to use the shuttle for short one-to-two-day orbital missions, to carry into orbit piggyback spy satellites and retrieve and service previously orbited spy craft. The shuttle would also inspect and destroy enemy satellites.

The space shuttle was being promised as a vehicle that could perform all the missions planned for MOL at a fraction of the cost. However, soon after the contracts were awarded to a team of contractors headed by McDonnell Douglas, North American Rockwell, Aerojet–General, and Pratt and Whitney it became apparent that the project, which might properly be labeled Dynasoar III, would cost more, not less, than MOL. Ralph Lapp estimated in congressional testimony that the shuttle would cost $6.8 billion and that the space station to receive it would cost $5.1 billion, not including cost overruns.

RESEARCH WITHOUT RISK

Military research and development awards often lock the government into long-term relationships with private contractors. The firm that obtains the research money for a complex weapons system almost always walks off with the even more lucrative production contract. Lockheed did the research on the Polaris program, then built the Polaris missile. Subsequently Lockheed did the research on Poseidon, successor to Polaris, and is now the prime contractor for the Poseidon program. The original research and development estimate for Poseidon was $900 million. This portion alone has grown to more than $2 billion, and the total cost of the program, including production of the missiles, will be more than $7 billion and will take several years to complete. Through the research laboratory contractors often gain a monopoly position for a particular weapon. This is an important factor in the concentration of defense, space and atomic energy business among a relatively few large contractors.

The fact that research money flows so freely from the government has had the important effect of shifting the risk of developing new weapons from the contractors to the public. It used to be that a corporation's laboratory had to justify every dollar it spent by proving it was benefiting the firm with new or improved products that would sell, because prior to the advent of federal spending in this area the contractor had to use his own money for research. Now the laboratory justifies itself simply as a source of military money. If a research project turns into something that the military wants to invest further in, so much the better, and if a production contract follows, jackpot. Either way, the contractor benefits, as the public pays the costs of his research laboratory.

In addition, research and development is a most difficult product to measure from the government's standpoint. There is no easy way to tell whether the government is getting its money's worth out of a contractor's laboratory, whether the charges for which reimbursement payments are made are reasonable, whether a contractor might be padding the government's bill with the costs of his own commercial research, or whether he is efficient. In typical fashion the military meets these difficulties in the "What? Me worry?" manner of Alfred E. Neuman. Having downgraded the government laboratory, which at one time provided the government with a way to compare the costs and quality of private work, the Pentagon refuses to concern itself about such matters, trusting as always in the ability of almost unlimited sums of money to get the job done.

The trend toward the decline of the government in-house military laboratory supports H. L. Nieburg's claims that they are being systematically destroyed and that an important yardstick is being intentionally thrown away. At the same time, the out-house contract system permits the payment of high salaries and extravagant rewards to corporate scientists and managers. This has had a harmful effect on an important natural resource, scientific and technical manpower. In 1964 the House Select Committee on Research and Development reported that contractors were stockpiling scientists and engineers by keeping more of them on their payrolls than current work required, to be in a more advantageous position to bid on and undertake new projects. As such labor costs can be part of a research and development contract or charged indirectly to the government as overhead expense, in some instances the government is subsidizing contractor laboratories not to get the benefit of its scientific output, but to enable the contractor to bid on future contracts. Also a serious domestic "brain drain" is created as scientists and engineers drift out of government, university and nonmilitary industrial employment into defense-subsidized laboratories.

The absence of adequate controls over the uses of government research and development funds has been documented by a series of recent investigations by the General Accounting Office. In 1967 it reported on an aspect of research and development that comes under the heading of "bidding and related technical efforts." The preparation of bids is considered closely related to the contractor's *independent* research and development. Independent research is not authorized by specific contracts, but is reimbursable under a variety of informal agreements between the Pentagon or NASA and its contractors. It is supposed to provide an incentive for contractors to do innovative research that will open up new avenues of weapons technology and, naturally, extend the frontiers of knowledge. The investigation looked into the propriety of reimbursing contractors for certain bidding costs connected with their independent research. The cases studied all involved the Lockheed Aircraft Corporation, but the report noted that similar problems have been revealed by audits of numerous other contractors.

In one case Lockheed analyzed a proposal for Eurospace, a European space organization. The arrangements for the work were made between Lockheed and Eurospace and had nothing to do with NASA. Yet Lockheed submitted the costs of the study as part of its bidding expense and requested reimbursement. NASA made reimbursement. In another case Lockheed incurred bidding on three projects after NASA informed it that it was not interested in receiving proposals for the work the contractor was doing. Nevertheless, Lockheed requested and received reimbursement for its bidding costs on the three projects. On one of the projects, a study of a space shuttle bus, Lockheed had been advised by NASA that a contract was being awarded to another firm. Still Lockheed ran up its costs of preparing a bid for eight months, then submitted its bill to NASA and was reimbursed. NASA ended up paying almost the same amount to Lockheed for that particular bid as it did to the other contractor for actually doing the study.

The problem in this area, according to the General Accounting Office, is the absence of good controls in the Defense Department as well as in NASA. Because the government's regulations are inconsistent and vague, "the interpretations made by contractors most often prevail." One instructive aspect of the investigation was the Pentagon's reaction to the report. Prior to its issuance the Pentagon was in the process of amending the regulations dealing with independent research. Upon receiving a copy of the critical report for comment, however, the Defense Department informed the General Accounting Office that it had discontinued its efforts to tighten up the rules and, no, it would not be feasible to issue even interim guidelines as the GAO had suggested. NASA made a similar reply. Both responses were similar in tone to the Army's reaction to the McClellan investigation where, it will be recalled, the Army told the McClellan Committee in effect to mind its own business and the Army would take care of the profits it allowed its contractors.

The almost frivolous way some research and development funds are handled is illustrated by one 1968 report by the General Accounting Office dealing with Herman Kahn's defense-supported "think tank," the Hudson Institute. The Institute received three research contracts totaling $600,000 from the Army's Office of Civil Defense. The General Accounting Office found that of the 11 study reports submitted by the Hudson Institute, seven had been judged by the government to be less useful than had been expected or to require major revision. One of the studies "added no new thoughts and failed to provide any information not previously known." Another was considered "a rehash of old, if not tired, ideas." Three others were criticized as not having sufficient depth to justify general distribution or the loading of bookshelves. One might reasonably ask why the government pays for such poor performance.

Chapter Four

PROCUREMENT AND PROFITS

The Pentagon has replaced competition with negotiation as the principal method of doing business with the defense industry. Almost always it negotiates on industry's terms, especially with regard to the giant contractor. As a result defense purchasing is a card house of false promises, "overoptimism," lock-ins, buy-ins, cost overruns, get-well devices, late deliveries and poor performance. Pull out one part for close examination, and any advanced weapon is likely to fall on its face as a program failure. What allows the system to continue to operate despite itself is money, tons of public funds spooned out to the large contractors in sums so great it requires the mentality of an astronomer to comprehend them. Problems are not solved, they are dissolved in rich applications of government capital.

THE DECLINE OF COMPETITION

To minimize the opportunities for fraud and favoritism in military procurement a general rule evolved long ago that government purchases should be made through competition, that is, by the invitation of written bids and the award of contracts to the lowest bidder. In theory, competition provides objectivity in government purchasing and efficiency in defense production. Generally speaking, government officials required to accept the lowest-priced offers are less likely to give government business to their friends. At the same time, private suppliers, knowing that their competitors have an equal opportunity to obtain government contracts, are encouraged to lower their prices and control their costs. Former Secretary McNamara estimated that items procured through competition cost the government 25 percent less than similar items procured through negotiation. Others have estimated the savings to be as much as 50 percent. Competition also increases the probability of small-business participation in defense work, as small firms are not included in the select group of large contractors with whom the Pentagon negotiates.

During war the practice has been to relax or suspend competitive buying in order to mobilize more swiftly. The price of haste and waste, the argument goes, is cheaper than the price of defeat. But in peacetime, so long as government purchasing was substantially competitive, the worst procurement abuses were held at bay and the rise of a military-industrial juggernaut was at least retarded. Until World War II competitive bidding was reinstituted after each of our wars.

The change began in 1947, when Congress enacted the Armed Services Procurement Act,[1] restating the general rule of competition but setting out seventeen exceptions—circumstances under which negotiation would be authorized instead of competition. The exceptions are very broad and vague and permit subjective determinations as to whether an item is critical or complex, whether delivery is urgent, whether competition is "impractical," whether emergency conditions exist, whether security considerations preclude advertising, or whether industry experience is lacking and costs cannot be accurately estimated. Under any of these and other exceptions the Pentagon is authorized to negotiate for what it wants from whomever it wants. In contrast, the requirements for formal advertising for competitive bids are quite specific. For instance, specifications must be made available to all potential bidders and not restricted because

[1] This act replaced the Civil Sundry Appropriations Act of 1861. Other procurement legislation was passed in 1795, 1809 and 1870.

of security. (The procurement official who lacks the imagination to determine that one of the conditions for negotiation exists would be wise to change careers.)

When President Truman signed the Armed Services Procurement Act into law, he saw the possibilities for abuse and wrote to the heads of the armed services and the National Advisory Committee for Aeronautics:

This bill grants unprecedented freedom from specific procurement restrictions during peacetime. . . . There is danger that the natural desire for flexibility and speed in procurement will lead to excessive placement of contracts by negotiation and undue reliance upon large concerns, and this must not occur.

As early as 1960 the House Armed Services Committee, under Representative Carl Vinson, concluded that Truman's admonition had proven to be something of a prophecy, that the Defense Department had become "an emergency negotiated-purchasing organization" and that there had been a failure to achieve reasonable costs and profits. The committee also found that "there has been a concentration of production facilities in the hands of a relatively small production base in which the Government is heavily interested. This segment of industry is the beneficiary of public necessity."[2]

Despite numerous recommendations for many years by members and committees of Congress that the Defense Department take steps to arrest the long-term trend away from competitive awards, the trend has continued. From 1951 through 1967 formal advertised procurement represented 13.9 percent of total contract awards. In 1968 the figure was 11.5 percent, and in 1969 it declined further to 11 percent. Thus about 90 percent of the Pentagon's contract awards are negotiated under the "exceptions."

The Pentagon argues that it is unrealistic to expect competition for weapons systems when only a few large firms have the competence to manufacture such items as airframes, jet engines and turbines for nuclear reactors. But this argument ignores the fact that it is possible to "break out" subsystems and components of weapons into relatively small units for which competition could be obtained and

[2] Eighty-sixth Congress, second session, House Report No. 1959, "Report Pursuant to Section 4, Public Law 86-89," pp. 11, 14, 15, 37.

that the Pentagon could, if it wanted to, encourage rather than dis-
courage competition. For one example, small firms can produce
many of the spare parts needed for large weapons. The practice,
however, is for the government to allow the large contractor to
monopolize production of spare parts as well as major systems. For
another example, the government has been purchasing an increasing
amount of computers and computer services. Many smaller manufacturers produce parts of complete computer systems called "periph-
erals," which can be plugged into the larger systems and which
when bought in this manner substantially reduce the cost of the
entire system. Yet at least until recently the government has failed
to take advantage of the potential savings. One member of Congress, Representative Martha Griffiths, accused the Pentagon in 1967
of permitting IBM to draw up the government specifications for
computer purchases, and the Proxmire Committee concluded in a
1968 report that there was evidence that government procurement
practices have tended to favor the larger computer manufacturers
and that competition from smaller companies was being stifled.[3]

The Pentagon also argues that it utilizes a less stringent form of
competition, in addition to formal advertising, called "competitive
negotiation." Under this procedure a number of potential suppliers
of an item are identified by the Pentagon and asked to submit bids
for the contract. The bidding is thus not open to anyone but is
restricted to a few. Many persons were persuaded that this was a
sensible compromise between the goal of competition and the demands of modern defense, until it was learned in the latter part of
1967 that the Pentagon was misclassifying purchases as competitive
when they were not. It would consider competition to be present
when two bids were solicited and only one received. After being
criticized for this practice, the Pentagon now requires that at least
two bids be received before classifying purchases as competitive.

Even where two or three bids are received "competitive negotiation" can hardly be considered as real competition. The most obvious distinction is that the military gets to select the élite group of
firms that are given the opportunity of bidding. Secondly, the lowest
bidder does not necessarily get the contract. The Pentagon claims
that the proposed price of an item is an important—but not the

3 Ninetieth Congress, second session, Report of the Subcommittee on Economy
in Government of the Joint Economic Committee, "Economy in Government
Procurement and Property Management," p. 6.

only important—factor. Technical performance, time of delivery and other considerations may be more crucial in a given case. Though this may be so, the history of procurement does not demonstrate the Penetagon's ability to obtain quality from its contractors, much less timely or economical performance.

The fact is that contracts awarded on any basis other than price must be based on subjective determinations, as whether in the opinion of the procurement official the product of company X will be of better workmanship or delivered earlier than the product of company Y. One of the principal advantages of competition—objectivity—is thus lost.

Economists have labeled this kind of bidding as "rivalry" rather than competition, to distinguish it from cases where price is the controlling factor. Businessmen other than the privileged few who are tapped as rivals—and the public—might call it "government-engineered oligopoly."

Sometimes even the oligopolists get upset with this procedure. In the "competitive negotiation" for the second round of the M-16 rifle contract awards General Motors was selected as one of the two winners over the Maremont Corporation, even though Maremont's bid was considerably lower than GM's. The Army explained that it had more faith in GM's ability to do the job and price was not the important factor. Since Maremont had a 20-year history of manufacturing small arms behind it and GM did not, Maremont remained unhappy with the decision.

In 1968 Representative Richard H. Ichord, a member of the House Armed Services Committee, condemned the awards of the M-16 contracts as "the climax of a long history of incompetence and bungling that has characterized the entire program from 1964 to the present." As a result of what Ichord called "the sloppy contracting procedures used in these awards, the callous disregard of Government funds, and the subversion of competitive prices in defense procurement," at least $40 million had already been squandered on the M-16, and the eventual waste in the program could amount to $100 million.[4] Later that year a Special Senate M-16 Rifle Subcommittee headed by Senator Howard W. Cannon issued a formal report substantiating Ichord's charges. The report showed that General Motors did not have test-range facilities and would have to build new ones at considerable expense while Maremont had test-range facilities, criticized the Army for removing price as a factor in the award, and concluded that the procurement was "a most inept performance."[5] As it turned out, GM was not able to deliver the rifles on time, and the other firm selected to supply M-16's, the Harrington-Richardson company, provided a defective product.

What this illustrates is that the Pentagon has largely abandoned objective criteria for measuring the fairness of contract awards and that the marketplace no longer acts as a control over the costs, quality and time of performance.

NEGOTIATION: LOCK-INS AND COST OVERRUNS

Negotiation is the Pentagon's way of saying that it reserves the right to refuse service (contracts) to anyone. It is also the Pentagon's way of playing ball with the large contractors. The tendency of the research and development contractors to obtain production contracts, as well as the tendency for the Pentagon to purchase spare parts and even off-the-shelf items from the prime contractor, is what is generally meant by the phrase "locked-in." That is, the government becomes "locked-in" with a contractor. Because the contractor knows good times are ahead when he gets a research and development contract, he has an incentive to stretch a few facts during the negotiations, such as how inexpensive the program will be and how well it will perform. The winner of a research and development contract gains know-how, including patent rights, the use of government-owned equipment and other advantages over his rivals, if there are any rivals, for the more enduring and profitable part of the program—the production.

In most cases the contractor is aware that costs will probably increase as the program proceeds and that technical performance might not be quite so spectacular as he has claimed. The Pentagon probably knows as much, from its historical experience with cost overruns, schedule slippages and performance failures, if nothing else.

---

[5] Ninetieth Congress, second session, Special M-16 Rifle Subcommittee, Senate Armed Services Committee, "Report on Additional Procurement of M-16 Rifles" (1968).

A cost overrun is commonly understood as the amount by which the final cost of a weapons system exceeds the amount originally planned. Technically, until 1969 an overrun occurred whenever costs exceeded the contract target price. In a negotiated contract there are usually two prices, the target price and the ceiling price. Typically the contract provides that if the final costs meet the target price, the contractor will be paid some portion of the difference between the target and the ceiling price in addition to his normal profit. For example, a contract for airplane engines with a target price of $1 million and a ceiling price of $1.2 million might provide that the contractor receives as a bonus (incentive) profit 30 percent of the difference between target and ceiling, or about $60,000. If he goes above target, he is still entitled to a share of the amount that actual costs fall below the ceiling. If he goes through the ceiling, he gets no bonus. The serious overrun cases involve costs that have gone far above the ceiling. In a non-negotiated, competitive contract the overrun problem is one for the contractor to worry about, since he must absorb any cost increases above the amount of the contract price. On negotiated contracts the contractor must pay for costs that go above ceiling, in theory only. As a matter of practice the contractor is reimbursed for most overruns, no matter what the contract says, as will be shown later.

Cost overruns in weapons procurement are an old problem, dating from the earliest usage of the contract system. Eli Whitney, for example, exceeded his rifle-contract price with the government by a wide margin in the early part of the nineteenth century. It was a little-noticed problem, however, probably because of the general neglect of military procurement until the recent past and also because prior to World War II weapons contracting required large amounts of public funds only during periods of war. It is the magnitude of the sums involved in cost overruns during the past two decades that is startling and indicative of the huge amount of public resources being diverted into the defense industry. During the 1950s and 1960s cost overruns regularly consumed two or three times the amounts originally planned for the major weapons systems, but this fact was mostly concealed from the public. In 1968 and 1969 the phrase became a household word for the first time, due primarily to the $2 billion cost overrun revealed in the C-5A cargo plane program. Yet the percentage of the overrun in that program was less than for many other weapons.

One of the most extreme instances of an overrun to come to light was in the Deep Submergence Rescue Vehicle (DSRV), built by Lockheed and the Massachusetts Institute of Technology. The DSRV is a small submersible vehicle designed to rescue men trapped in disabled submarines. In 1964 the Navy estimated that 12 rescue vehicles could be developed in four years at a cost of $36.5 million, including the costs of one year of operation. In addition the Navy claimed $37 million would be saved by phasing out an existing rescue system after the DSRVs were built. By 1969 the cost estimates had jumped to $463 million for six DSRVs, to be developed in ten years. In other words, the unit price had grown from $3 million each to $80 million each, a rise of over 2,500 percent, and the delivery schedule had slipped by six years. Further, the decision to phase out the existing rescue system had been reversed.

To make matters worse, an investigation indicated that the entire program may have been unwarranted to begin with or, at best, that no more than two of the vehicles should have been planned.[6] Submarine disasters where rescue is possible are rare, only one having occurred in peacetime operations from 1928 to 1970. Today, with nuclear-powered submarines cruising at depths where any mishap would cause the external hull and the internal bulkheads to collapse, rescue is possible in only a small percentage of the ocean area. The *Thresher*, for example, had descended far below her collapse depth in the 1963 disaster, and rescue of survivors could not have been accomplished with the DSRV. The Navy admits that it is unrealistic to contemplate submarine rescue during wartime conditions.

Pressed by the cost overrun disclosures made in Congress, principally by the Proxmire Committee in 1968 and 1969, the Pentagon belatedly released data on a number of weapons systems showing costs over varying periods of time. A comparison of the estimated costs of an individual program at the planning stage with the current estimated cost through completion provided a rough measure of the overrun using the figures supplied by the Pentagon. The data, contained in an information system called System Acquisition Reports (SAR), showed that the problem was much more serious than

6 GAO report B-167325, "Evaluation Needed of Cost-Effectiveness of Four More Deep Submergence Rescue Vehicles Before Purchase by Navy," February 20, 1970. The program is discussed in Ninety-first Congress, first session, Subcommittee on Economy in Government of the Joint Economic Committee, "The Weapons Acquisition Process," part 1 (1969).

most people had realized. At the request of Congress the General Accounting Office reviewed the SAR, and the results of the review intensified concern over the problem.[7]

Fifty-seven weapons programs were selected by GAO for study. On only 38 of those programs was sufficient detail provided in the Pentagon's information system to allow a comparison of cost estimates at different points in time. For some programs no figures were supplied for critical time periods, such as planning estimates, so that comparisons were impossible. The cost overruns for the 38 programs totaled $21 billion, 50 percent of their combined original planning estimates. Overruns ranged from $304 million on the Gama Goat, a jeeplike vehicle with a trailer whose numerous wheels don't seem to go in the same direction, to $498 million on the A-7E aircraft, $663 million on the FB-111 (bomber version of the F-111), $3.9 billion on the Mark 48 torpedo, and $4.5 billion on the F-111 aircraft. The General Accounting Office pointed out in its report to Congress that the cost increases were continuing to occur and that the Pentagon's information system did not include a number of major systems which were too early in the acquisition process to forecast overruns, such as the AMSA bomber, the F-15 aircraft, the S-3A aircraft, and Minuteman III.

A further check into the status of the 57 weapons programs revealed that many of them were performing or were expected to perform significantly below the levels originally expected and that a majority would be delivered from six months to more than three years late. The reasons given by the Pentagon for the schedule slippages were found not to be helpful to an understanding of the basic causes, nor was any attempt made in the SAR to show the impact of delays on the costs of the programs or on other related programs. Studies of the performance of individual weapons disclosed failures not revealed in the Pentagon's report. The SAR itself contained no comparison of the technical performance of any given weapon with that required by the contract.

Other omissions in the SAR reflected how seriously deficient and misleading it was as an information system. On some programs major systems were delivered and accepted by the military without essential subsystems. Delays and problems of technical performance

[7] GAO report B-163058, "Status of the Acquisition of Selected Major Weapon Systems," February 6, 1970.

were not reported. Costs incurred and reimbursements paid on individual programs were not related to physical progress. Changes in quantities were not reported and a number of inconsistencies were detected in the way data was reported. For 20 percent of the systems, required program costs were left out of the SAR and no provision was made to indicate the amount of claims by contractors pending against the government on some of the programs.

One example of the exclusion by the military of major items of costs from the totals so as to minimize the overrun problem is the DE-1052 destroyer program. The Navy gave this program a clean bill of health, reporting only a miniscule $1 million increase for it. But the program had in fact grown by at least $300 million, as was revealed in the December 1969 hearings of the Proxmire Committee.[8] The Navy had simply transferred several major costs of the program into other accounts so that they would not show up as part of the DE-1052 program. Cost omissions were also discovered in the C-5A, Shillelagh missile, F-111, 1968 and 1969 attack aircraft carriers, SRAM missile, Poseidon, and Minuteman programs.

There is, in short, still no clear knowledge of the extent of the cost overrun problem. The Pentagon has consistently understated costs of ongoing programs in a misguided attempt to hide them under the rug. That what the Congress and the public do not know about weapons costs will not hurt them appears to have been the controlling attitude in the Department of Defense. But the sheer bulk of the overruns, the dollars involved, led to their exposure; if millions can be hidden in the labyrinth of Pentagon expenditures, billions cannot. A point was reached when what was under the rug exceeded the size of the rug.

We do not understand in sufficient detail why cost overruns occur, although government mismanagement and contractor inefficiency are prime suspects. How much is unnecessarily spent on the huge bureaucracies, military and civilian, that have grown like ancient incrustations around defense procurement? How much is wasted on duplication and fruitless efforts? How much is spent as a result of

---

[8] Ninety-first Congress, first session, Subcommittee on Economy in Government of the Joint Economic Committee, "The Weapons Acquisition Process," Part 1 (1969). In 1970 another major omission of the full costs of the DE-1052 was revealed: the DASH Helicopter program intended to be used on the ships had been canceled because of technical deficiencies. At the time of its cancellation at least $275 million had been spent for the production of 750 drone (unmanned) helicopters, 411 of which had crashed in tests.

the policy of keeping a contractor in business regardless of his real contribution to national defense? How much is carelessness, how much corruption?

On the contractors' part, we do not know or do not want to know how much public money winds up as profits, concealed or unconcealed. One way to break down the costs of any manufactured product is by labor, materials, and overhead. An understanding of what happens to those items of costs during the performance of a weapons contract should be seen as fundamental to the responsibility of government managers to account for the monies entrusted to them. The managers in the Pentagon exhibit neither the understanding nor the accountability. No system had been developed, at the time of this writing, to track the costs of labor, material, and overhead for the purpose of pinpointing and taking corrective action against problems in weapons procurement. No knowledge of these facts exists in Congress. We do not know, for example, whether the multibillion-dollar overruns in the F-111 and C-5A programs were caused by excesses of manpower or exorbitant prices paid for materials or costs of unrelated programs, including purely commercial programs, charged as overhead to the government contracts. Needless to say, the Pentagon has been extremely reluctant to analyze its weapons costs in this way.[9]

After costs of labor, materials, and overhead are paid by the manufacturer what remains from revenue generated by sales may be considered as profit. Supposing a contractor forecasts a profit on a weapons program of several million dollars. How much of that money is spent by raising the salaries of management, buying new office equipment, picking up the costs of commercial projects rather than declaring it as profit? Because of the absence of uniform accounting standards as well as the unwillingness to look very hard, the government is unable to discern if costs are being accurately charged or if profits are being passed on to the government as hidden costs. To what extent do contractors recover the cost of expenditures twice by charging them as indirect and direct costs? The fact that these practices are common has been amply documented.[10]

[9] For an attempt to inquire into this problem see Ninety-first Congress, second session, Subcommittee on Economy in Government of the Joint Economic Committee, "The Weapons Acquisition Process," Part 2 (1970).

[10] See for example GAO report B-39995, "Feasibility of Applying Uniform Cost Accounting Standards to Negotiated Defense Contracts," January 9, 1970.

Barry J. Shillito, Assistant Secretary of Defense, attributes colossal overruns like that of the DSRV to "just plain overoptimism." The Pentagon generally offers a four-pronged explanation for cost overruns and other program failures: inflation, program stretchouts, unanticipated technical difficulties, and changes made necessary because of technological advances or other reasons. When the facts of the case do not square with those arguments, the Pentagon retreats to its fallback position: The contractor and the government were "overoptimistic" about how much the program would cost, when it would be completed, etc. This kind of explanation puts the problem in the honest mistake category, which is at first glance hard to resist. After all, lots of things cost more than we thought they would—new houses, public buildings, highways. Should one conclude that all contracting is inherently risky and overoptimism endemic?

The process has other explanations. Gordon Rule, Director of Procurement Control and Clearance for the Navy, testifying before the Proxmire Committee in June 1969, said:

> I think that one of the things that we have got to stop doing in our con-tracting is playing games—the Government and the contractor. We play games. We know that if we tell the DOD across the river how much some-thing is really going to cost, they may scrub it. And they know that if they tell the Congress how much it is really going to cost the Congress may scrub it.

The former Navy captain added: "So you start in with both sides knowing that it is going to cost more. And that is not an overrun, because we know." [11]

Moreover, the contractor and the government know something else that enables them to do business in the essentially dishonest manner that Rule describes. The contractors know that no matter how high the costs go, the government will pay. Late delivery and less than promised performance will be accepted without penalty. The Pentagon knows that Congress will hardly blink at program failures. Requests for additional funds for military programs are generally approved without question.

In fairness it ought to be pointed out that the Pentagon did take steps to solve this problem and in late 1969 came up with an idea

[11] Ninety-first Congress, first session, Subcommittee on Economy in Government. Joint Economic Committee, "The Military Budget and National Economic Priorities," Part 2, p. 510 (1969)

that, while it may not reduce the costs of weapons programs, does do something about cost overruns. In a memorandum from David Packard, Deputy Secretary of Defense, dated November 26, 1969, the phrase "cost overrun" was ordered purged from the military lexicon, because it cast "confusion in the minds of the many." It is a comfort to know that the few who run the military establishment care enough about the many to want to make life simpler for them.

BUY IN NOW, GET WELL LATER

The contractors and the Pentagon engage in the charade known as "buy in now, get well later." The contractor buys in to a program by offering more than he can deliver. If the military sets a dollar ceiling on what it says it will pay for a program, the contractor agrees to meet it or beat it. If there is a rivalry for a major contract among three or four giants, one may bid extremely low in order to be assured the award. Promises about performance and delivery are made in the same way.

Technically the contractor can be penalized for his failure to fulfill promises made during the negotiations. There are clauses in the contract providing for financial penalties for exceeding the contract price or for failing to meet delivery schedules, and if the weapons system, or whatever the contractor is supposed to supply, does not perform in accordance with performance specifications, the government can refuse to accept delivery and declare the contractor in default. But the government rarely insists on full performance, and the contractor knows this. The contractor is confident that on practically any major weapons contract he can reasonably expect the government to extricate him from any difficulty. If he gets "sick," that is, runs out of the money alloted to him, the Pentagon will get him "well" by providing more money.

CHANGES, CLAIMS, AND LETTER CONTRACTS

The get-well stratagem operates in a number of ways. If costs run higher than anticipated, the Pentagon can simply agree to pay them. But the most commonly employed device is the change notice, referred to in defense circles as "contract nourishment." On a typical complex weapons-system contract, changes will number in the thousands. They usually relate to technical specifications that, because the contractor is "pushing at the frontier of man's knowledge," are in a state of flux. Some are justifiable, especially in the development of advanced new weapons systems such as supersonic aircraft, where new metals and electronic equipment are being used under extreme conditions. But many changes are unnecessary or nonexistent, mere bookkeeping entries intended to support claims for additional reimbursement.

The government is in a particularly disadvantageous position when the change is of an urgent nature. Some changes are negotiated. When either the government or the contractor requests the change, the increased costs are estimated and adjustments to the contract price are made. But frequently there is some urgency involved, as when the contractor telephones to the Pentagon and informs the government that unless it can obtain an immediate authorization to modify the specifications, work will have to be halted or later undone—and the costs of the change will be several times more than if the contractor were permitted to proceed. As Admiral Rickover has stated, once a large unpriced change has been made, the door is open to a future claim by the contractor for a lump-sum payment to reimburse him for a number of such changes.

There is no requirement that the contractor keep a record of the costs of changes on a change-by-change basis. "Thus," Rickover stated,

contractors can use change orders as a basis for repricing these contracts. They have almost unlimited freedom in pricing change orders because their accounting system will never show the cost of the work. The Government can never really evaluate the amounts claimed or check up to see if it paid too much.[12]

The opportunities for burying real or phony cost increases in change notices are obvious.

The sheer volume of the claims and the contractor's persistence in pressing them sometimes overwhelms the government's ability or

[12] Ninetieth Congress, second session, Subcommittee on Economy in Government of the Joint Economic Committee, "Economics of Military Procurement," Part 2, p. 41.

willingness to oppose full payment. Rickover reports one case where a contractor submitted a claim for $70 million on a $70 million fixed price contract. The Pentagon paid about 90 percent of the claim, thus agreeing to increase the cost of the contract to $133 million. In another case a contractor submitted a $2 million claim on a $1 million contract. After six years the claim was still pending.

A case involving a series of Navy contracts with the Westinghouse Electric Corporation illustrates how a tenacious contractor can use the maze of Pentagon procedures and bureaucracy to pursue a claim for excess profits despite the honest efforts of the few in government who regard concern for the public interest as the reason for their government employment. Beginning in 1956 several contracts were awarded to Westinghouse for the production of nuclear components for a number of submarines and for the aircraft carrier *Enterprise*. The prices negotiated seemed high to some persons and the Government Accounting Office decided to investigate.

The GAO found in 1962 that Westinghouse had made profits of from 40 to 65 percent on the contracts, instead of ten percent, and that the contractor was not entitled to the excess profits. (Westinghouse had submitted cost breakdowns to the Navy at the time the contracts were entered into indicating that it would earn a ten percent profit; but the cost breakdown included the estimated costs of purchasing items from a Westinghouse subsidiary for much more than the actual costs of those items.)

The Navy agreed with the GAO and withheld about $4 million in payments to the contractor.

The case was initially turned over to the Justice Department. According to John Finney of the *New York Times,* the Department reportedly agreed the profits were excessive but concluded it would be difficult to prove fraud and referred the case back to the Navy, recommending that administrative action be taken.

In 1964 the Navy auditor formally determined that the $4 million was not reimbursable. In 1965 Westinghouse appealed the decision. This appeal was turned over to the Defense Contract Audit Agency, created in 1965, and in 1966 the auditor handling the case approved the disallowance of the $4 million. In 1967 Westinghouse appealed that decision to the Defense Contract Audit Agency Headquarters. In 1967 Headquarters sustained the appeal of Westinghouse for more than $1 million of the amount witheld. Westinghouse then proceeded to press its claim for the remaining $3 million.

In 1968 Admiral Rickover stated in a congressional hearing that the Defense Contract Audit Agency had reversed its earlier findings and was in agreement with Westinghouse. Rickover said, "There is no question in my mind that the Government will ultimately have to pay the $4 million."

In March 1969, in response to an inquiry from Senator Proxmire, the director of the Defense Contract Audit Agency denied that it had reversed its position, asserting that the earlier views of one of its auditors did not constitute the position of the agency. At about that time the audit agency sent the case back to the Navy for another round of determinations, where, at the end of 1969, the case remained.

In the event that the Pentagon finally rules against Westinghouse the case could be taken to the courts, where another round of protracted hearings and appeals could last several more years. As a good part of Westinghouse's legal expenses for pursuing the claim can be recovered either as a tax deduction or as an overhead charge against other defense contracts, and as its legal department has already recaptured more than $1 million of the profits in question, there are excellent incentives for the contractor to continue its efforts.

No matter how the case is resolved, the public loses, for it ultimately will pay the excess profits that Westinghouse is claiming, or the costs of processing the appeal and the salaries of the numerous government employees who have worked on it, or both.

In late 1969 it became known that about $800 million in claims by shipbuilders were pending against the Navy, a figure that had risen phenomenally in just a few years.

Somewhat related to the change notice and claim devices is the letter contract. These are the most informal kinds of written authorizations for a contractor to proceed on government work, providing a minimum of protection against increased costs or other variables. The number and value of letter contracts issued each year is a good measure of the Pentagon's relaxed attitude toward contract costs, since it can exercise the least amount of cost control under a letter contract. Unsurprisingly both indicators have risen steeply in the last few years. In 1968 about 1,500 letter contracts valued at $7 billion were awarded, compared to 1,300 valued at

$6.7 billion in 1967. Yet in 1965 there were only 488 letter contracts valued at $1.2 billion.

Change notices have also increased sharply in number and value, insofar as the inadequate records kept by the Defense Department are able to show. There were 12,563 change notices valued at $2.6 billion in 1968, an increase of more than 50 percent in the value of changes authorized in 1967.

DEFAULTS AND CONVENIENCES

Another way for the government to get a sick operator well is to pay the full price for a weapon that performs poorly, say at only 50 percent or 75 percent of contract performance specifications, or to accept late delivery without imposing the contractual penalty.

If things really get rough and the military decides to curtail or cancel a program, there are still a number of options that can be exercised before doing anything as drastic as causing a contractor to lose money. The Pentagon can cancel a program for the "convenience" of the government rather than for default. A company whose contract is canceled for default, that is, because he failed to perform, stands to lose a great deal of money, while cancellation for convenience reduces or eliminates the loss; the government makes reimbursement for costs incurred plus a reasonable profit. Technically, a cancellation for convenience is made because the military decides it doesn't want the program any longer. Actually it may be used to bail out a contractor in deep difficulty.

An example of this occurred recently in connection with the F-111B, the Navy's fighter-bomber version of the TFX. In a Senate speech on the F-111B delivered in August of 1967,[13] Senator John McClellan pointed out that (1) the costs of the research and development had tripled since 1962 and the costs of the total program had doubled from $5.8 billion to $11.6 billion despite the fact that the number of planes had been reduced from 1,700 to 1,300; (2) the plane was performing poorly because of excessive drag; (3) it was more than eight tons overweight; and (4) twice during 1964 Navy technical experts had recommended suspending the program because of deficiencies.

---

[13] *Congressional Record,* August 22, 1967, pp. S 11981–82.

McClellan quoted a Navy report on the plane's defects:

The F-111B airplane remains unfit for service use as previously reported and was found to be incapable of carrier-based operations. . . . The large disparity between observed performance and the specification performance requirements of the airplane is a cause for concern.

In fact the program had been seriously criticized for several years, and in 1967 a team was set up by the Pentagon to make recommendations for termination of the contract held by General Dynamics. The head of the team was Assistant Secretary of the Air Force Robert Charles. The number two man was Gordon Rule. Rule took issue with the fact that Charles was ignoring the team and dealing directly with Roger Lewis, the chairman of General Dynamics and a former Assistant Secretary of the Air Force under President Eisenhower.

In November 1968 Rule wrote to Deputy Secretary of Defense Paul H. Nitze, objecting to Charles' suggestion that the program be terminated for convenience. Rule stated that the contractor was in default and should not be paid any more than he could receive under a default termination. Nevertheless the contract was terminated, in effect for convenience, since no penalties were invoked, and General Dynamics was reimbursed its costs. In addition, the contractor was given a kind of credit, amounting to $1 million, for research and development work done on the Air Force version, the F-111. The final negotiations were handled directly between Nitze and Lewis.

It is no wonder that Rule concluded in a later memo written to his superior that the reason for industry's failure to produce a quality product on time and at a reasonable cost is the Pentagon's permissive attitude. "No matter how poor the quality, how late the product and how high the cost, they know nothing will happen to them." The problem, Rule concluded, is brought about by "representatives of the government who today are condoning and acquiescing in the failure of industry to perform as they should."

In a similar vein Admiral Rickover has been critical of the propensity of government officials to be swayed by the views of industry:

Manufacturers and their advisory groups can be very persuasive. They have sold many Government agencies on the idea that the prerogatives of industry must be preserved. This explains why high-ranking Government officials often seem more interested in placating industry than they are in protecting the Government's rights. This is evident in the way new policies are implemented. The Department of Defense tends to trade away something for each new procurement policy it implements. Its preoccupation appears to be in making the policy palatable to industry.

Industry, according to Rickover, "would very much like to nationalize its losses but privatize its gains."[14]

A variation on the theme of "cancel a bad program but don't kick the contractor off the gravy train" was played out with the Cheyenne Helicopter, made by Lockheed. Again enormous cost overruns and poor performance alarmed some members of Congress, particularly Otis Pike, who tried to delete funds for it in 1968. After the crash of a test model killed a pilot in 1969, Secretary of Defense Melvin Laird announced the cancellation of the program with much fanfare. Within a few weeks, however, a new $10 million contract was quietly awarded to Lockheed for further research and development on the Cheyenne.

An even more novel get-well technique was revealed during the investigation of the C-5A, the giant cargo plane, also made by Lockheed. Here instead of relaxing the enforcement of the government's contractual rights the government built into the contract a get-well clause to be triggered automatically when the contractor's costs increased. This clause contained a repricing formula, now celebrated as "the golden handshake," amounting to a cost-escalation guaranty. (The case is discussed more fully in Chapter Five.)

It should be seen that the military-industrial "team," as they like to characterize themselves, has managed to invent a get-well scheme for all seasons and all contingencies. Contractual agreements are richly custom-tailored to the contractor's operations and his financial needs.

THE REVIVAL OF COST-PLUS PLUS

The cost-plus-a-percentage-of-costs contract was prohibited after World War I. The reason for this was that when the government

---

[14] Ninetieth Congress, second session, Joint Economic Committee, "Economics of Military Procurement," Part 2, pp. 69–71.

was obligated to pay the contractor's costs, plus a percentage of his costs as profit, all the contractor had to do to increase his profit was to increase his costs. No matter how high the costs went, the government paid, and the contractor's profit was increased accordingly.

A number of different contractual devices have since replaced cost-plus, most of them designed to prevent large cost overruns. The most commonly used contract type today is the so-called fixed-price contract. There are actually several kinds of fixed-price contracts and innumerable provisions intended in theory to protect the interests of the government and the contractor and to permit the contractor to earn a reasonable profit. But the outstanding feature of contracting today is the rubberiness of the commitments on price, delivery and performance, and the fact that in practice almost any agreement can be transformed into a cost-plus situation, even if it is called "fixed-price." This means contractors are paid in full no matter how large the cost overrun. The "fixed" price is simply stretched to fit the contract costs.

"Fixed" prices, in the sense of prices which remain the same from the time the contract is signed to its completion, are a myth. Cost-plus arrangements are the reality.

GOVERNMENT-OWNED PROPERTY AND PROGRESS PAYMENTS

In the negotiation of contracts the Defense Department can allow contractors to use government-owned property. It can also agree to make "progress payments" to the contractor up to 100 percent of the amounts spent in the performance of the contract. In other words, the Pentagon can provide the contractor with practically all of his working capital and most of his fixed capital.

The rationale of the policy whereby the government buys plant and equipment for the use of private contractors is that it is neither possible nor feasible for the contractor to invest large sums, given the uncertainty of defense production and the fact that he might not be able to recoup his investment during the life of the contract. In order to induce private industry to participate in the defense program it is supposed to be necessary to relieve the contractor of this burden, especially where specialized and expensive equipment is necessary. Also it is claimed that government-owned property reduces the costs of production, resulting in overall savings to the government.

The policy of permitting contractors to use government-owned property is very old, dating back perhaps to the beginnings of government contracting. However, it took on immense proportions, as did the concept of national defense, during World War II, when as a matter of course land was purchased and plants built and equipped so that contractors could produce for the war effort. After the war many of these plants were sold for far below their acquisition costs, but the practice continued of permitting some contractors to use the remaining government-owned plants free of charge, although in most cases rental payments were made to the government.

The government does not know how much government capital was used by private firms during World War II, how much was allowed to remain in private hands after the war or how much has been placed with contractors since the war. Nor is this ignorance an insignificant thing. One economist estimates that the government purchased $45 billion worth of plant and equipment for the use of private firms between 1940 and 1965.[15] In 1967 the Government Accounting Office at the request of the Proxmire Committee made a study of government-owned property. It found that the total value of such property was unknown, although available Defense Department data showed it to be about $15 billion.

As might be expected, government-owned property is mostly in the hands of the giant contractors. For example, one of the most important categories of government-owned property is called "industrial production equipment," used in the manufacturing process. In 1967, 15 companies—including nine of the largest defense contractors—held 84 percent of the $2.6 billion of government-owned industrial production equipment. Two companies, General Electric and North American, held more than $100 million each. Four companies, Avco, General Motors, General Dynamics and Lockheed, each held over $75 million. Medium-sized contractors hold very little, and small contractors use practically no government-owned property.

Many defense contracts are performed mostly with government-

15 Robert J. Gordon, "$45 Billion of U.S. Private Investment Has Been Mislaid," *The American Economic Review,* LIX: 3 (June 1969).

owned property in government-owned plants on government land with government machinery, tools, test equipment and even office furniture. Thus to a large extent the big contractors are able to operate on government fixed capital rather than risk their own. The current policy is to charge rent for use of government property, but where rentals are paid, they can be charged back to the government as part of the costs of the contract and the contractor is reimbursed for the amounts paid.

What is also disturbing is the slipshod manner in which the program of government-owned capital is administered. As indicated, the Pentagon does not have a good inventory of the public property it has loaned out to the defense industry, nor does it know how much of it is being used or whether it is lying idle. It collects inadequate rent, and it buys much new equipment for contractors who can afford to buy their own. The lack of government control over its own property has led to the most extreme abuses by contractors.

The investigation by the Government Accounting Office revealed that some contractors were using government equipment in their own commercial operations without the permission of the government. In one case, TRW, Inc., obtained from the government an 8,000-ton mechanical forge press costing $1.4 million after asserting that the older government-owned presses in the contractor's plant were inefficient and unable to handle all the government orders for jet-engine midspan blades. Yet over a three-year period, from 1962 through 1965, the company used the 8,000-ton press 78 percent of actual production time for commercial work, while the government contracts were being performed on the supposedly obsolete smaller presses. In addition, the same company had used ten machines, costing from $29,000 to $141,000 each, 100 percent of the time for commercial work during the first six months of 1966, without government approval.

In another case the Rohr Corporation used government equipment valued at $6.1 million on commercial work 58.5 percent of production time during the six months ending July 31, 1966, without approval of the government. One ammunition contractor used government equipment worth $4.2 million to fill his own commercial orders while producing military rockets only 24 percent of the time. For years an aircraft company manufactured engines for commercial customers with government equipment without paying rent to the government.

In these and other cases not only were contractors not requesting advance approval for private use of public property, but the Defense Department was not requiring them to do so.

In the 1967 hearings of the Proxmire Committee, Elmer Staats, head of the General Accounting Office, was asked whether there was any case where the Defense Department penalized a contractor for unauthorized use of government equipment. Staats replied, "I do not know of any."

In the same hearing Representative Martha Griffiths observed that the illegal use of billions of dollars of government equipment appears to be a matter of little importance to the Defense Department. Senator Proxmire stated that contractors were using the equipment "as a subsidy to compete unfairly with others who have to buy their own equipment, and to produce at a lower cost and to make excessive profits subsidized by the Federal Government."

So-called progress payments also comprise a multibillion-dollar subsidy to the defense industry. These are payments made on a pay-as-you-go basis to contractors, but they are not based on progress in the sense of work completed on any contract. Rather, they simply reimburse the contractor for up to 100 percent of his incurred costs, which often run far ahead of actual progress. For example, a contractor may be working on a project with a $10 million price tag, have completed only 50 percent of the work but received $8 million in progress payments.

In reality the payments are interest-free loans that permit the contractor to operate entirely on government money, insulate him against the risk of using his own liquid capital and save him the expense of making interest payments on money he might have to borrow in order to continue production.

In the C-5A program Lockheed received "progress" payments of $1.2 billion on $1.3 billion of incurred costs as of the end of December 1968. By February 1970 the government had paid $2.038 billion on incurred costs of $2.114 billion. At both dates the contractor was far behind the schedule of performance called for under the contract.

As with government property, discriminations are made between larger and smaller contractors. All large contractors get progress payments; most small contractors are expected to finance their own operations. The Pentagon puts representatives in all large contractors' plants, and part of their duties is to expedite progress-payments disbursements on a prompt and regular basis, usually at least twice a month. Smaller contractors who receive progress payments, and even those who have completed their work and are awaiting final payment, are in constant danger that their payments will be late. For them a delay of a week or two could be disastrous. More than one small contractor has been literally driven up against the wall and broken by a recalcitrant or spiteful procurement chief.

Several experts have claimed that no large prime contractor has ever lost money on a contract with the Defense Department, and in January 1969, when a congressional committee asked Assistant Secretary of the Air Force Robert Charles to name one, he could not. Subsequently he submitted the name of a contractor who allegedly had lost money on a military contract, but it was later revealed that the transaction was a subcontract with another contractor, not a prime contract.

The value of the progress-payments subsidy is seen in the fact that in mid 1970 progress payments outstanding totaled close to $10 billion. In other words, there was nearly $10 billion dollars in contractors' hands as partial payment on contracts not yet completed, a phenomenal increase over 1964, when there was just over $3 billion in outstanding payments. Using a conservative 6 percent interest rate, the value of interest payments alone that defense contractors did not have to pay amounted to $600 million annually.

Progress payments confer still another benefit on the contractor. A firm receiving substantial payments for costs incurred on a weekly basis is able to develop a flow of funds in excess of its real needs. This is because a company does not make outlays at the same time it incurs costs. A firm may not have to pay its own bills several days or even weeks after incurring an expense. Thus the contractor gets to hold on to his progress payments for a period of time before he has to apply them to his obligations. One way he can profit from this is by establishing an interest-paying bank account that he can maintain at a fixed level during the life of the contract. Since contracts may extend for several years, interest income from this source can be considerable.

Another way a contractor can profit from progress payments is by diverting them to commercial projects or using them to establish lines of credit in order to finance commercial projects. We have seen how contractors have used government fixed capital for this purpose. Unfortunately no serious investigation has ever been conducted to inquire into the uses of working capital advanced by the government.

But some of the possibilities for diverting working and fixed capital to private use were revealed in a court case involving the Boeing Corporation.[16] The federal government sued Boeing for return of excess profits taken during the Korean War, and in 1962 the United States Tax Court held that Boeing had in fact taken $13 million in excess profits. In the course of its opinion the court revealed that (1) $630,000 of advertising and entertainment expenses, including the purchase of meals and general entertainment of visitors and business associates, were improperly charged to the government and reimbursed through progress payments; (2) Boeing, in the production of the B-47 as well as in the production of the B-50, the Bomarc missile, the B-52, the C-97 and the KC-97, had operated in government-owned plants and facilities on government-owned land furnished free of charge to the contractor, and in the B-47 plant in Wichita, Kansas, Boeing's investment in plant and equipment amounted to only $2.4 million compared to $34.9 million worth of government-owned facilities; (3) in 1952 Boeing received reimbursement for costs incurred of more than $347 million; and (4) Boeing's profit for 1952, the year in question, was $56.7 million, equivalent to 98 percent of the company's net worth. Thus Boeing had been able to operate almost entirely on government capital and make almost a 100 percent profit on its total company investment.

The contractor was able to make a little something in addition to its book profits. In the same year that Boeing could afford to put only $2.4 million of its own investment into the B-47 in Wichita, the company was sinking $1.7 million into construction of a new prototype aircraft being built in a walled-off area of another government-owned plant in Renton, Washington. Previously it had tried unsuccessfully to extract a contract from the Air Force for construction of a jet-powered tanker. So it was proceeding in secret behind the walls of Renton without a military contract to build what it called on its books "model 367-80 prototype," the expenses of which were being charged to 1952 profits on its government work.

16 *Boeing Airplane Company v. The Renegotiation Board,* 37 T.C. 64 (January 10, 1962).

Model 367-80 later became known as the Boeing 707, and a military version, the KC-135, was eventually sold to the Air Force. But in 1952 it was a private venture. A full decade later the court ruled that Boeing was not entitled to deduct its costs from the 1952 profits and was not entitled to reimbursement for them from the government.

By the time of the court's ruling Boeing could well afford to pay the money back along with the rest of its excess profits. Prior to 1952 the company had tried desperately to break into the civilian-aircraft market. It had failed up to that time and lost millions on projects such as its Edsel-like airplane, the Stratocruiser. This, too, Boeing tried to charge against the government by claiming reimbursement for the costs of advertising it in newspapers.

For ten years it was able to sell the 707 commercially and, as a consequence, partly to wean itself away from the Pentagon. Boeing might well have thanked the court and the rest of the government for the use of public resources for so long. Even the reduction of its profits by the $13 million determined to be excess left it with a 75 percent return on its net investment.

The problem of government-owned property in the hands of contractors is further illustrated by the Olin Mathieson Chemical Corporation case. In the early 1960s the Air Force decided there was a critical need for fuel for the Titan II ICBM. At that time, Olin Mathieson was the only company producing this fuel. The Air Force, rather than encourage others to get into the business and offer some competition, negotiated with its "sole-source" contractor for increased production of the fuel, ten million pounds annually instead of three million pounds.

The contractor suggested that in addition to producing more at its plant in Lake Charles, Louisiana, a new plant to be built in Saltville, Virginia.

Coincidentally Olin Mathieson owned some land in Saltville. The Air Force and the company agreed it would be a good place to build a new anhydrous hydrazine propellant-fuel plant. The contractor even offered to construct the plant for the government at the government's cost, and the Air Force thought that was a good idea, too.

Olin Mathieson proceeded to build a government-owned plant in the middle of its land in Saltville. Although it was true that the government plant and machinery would be completely surrounded by the contractor's real estate and that this might create difficulties in the future, the contract for the construction of the plant solved this problem. It provided roads and utility easements to the government, enabling it to reach the plant, to be available as long as the government owned the plant. In the event the government wanted to sell the plant, the contract came to the rescue there, too. The government could sell it to anyone it wanted to. All the purchaser had to do was dismantle the facilities and take them off Olin Mathieson's land. Of course, Olin Mathieson had an option giving it the right to buy the plant at the price offered by any buyer foolish enough to bid on it.

To one proposition the Air Force would not agree. In addition to the profit included in the contract price, the contractor demanded a fee amounting to $720,000 for the "know-how" it was giving to the Air Force in building the plant. Here the Air Force drew the line. It would do no such thing, and the fee was not included in the construction contract. Instead, the Air Force entered into another contract with Olin Mathieson for the production of the urgently needed rocket fuel, and into this production contract it incorporated the $720,000 fee.

The production contract contained one other notable feature. All military contracts include a standard clause recognizing the right of the government to inspect and audit the contractor's books for a reasonable time after the contract has been performed, so that costs charged to the government can be verified. Since the government often has little basis on which to evaluate the proposed price during the negotiations, it is important that it be able later to satisfy itself that the charges were reasonable. In this case the contractor insisted that the inspection and audit clause be deleted, and it was. Later, when the Pentagon's audit agency attempted to check production costs at the Saltville plant, the contractor refused to let it. When the General Accounting Office investigated subsequently, it found that many of the costs were unreasonably high and that the Air Force should not have agreed to them. For example, the Air Force agreed to pay Olin's initial estimate for operating labor at the Saltville plant, amounting to $952,000. GAO found that the number of employees had been vastly overstated and that the contractor had incurred only $495,000 for labor, a little more than half the amount estimated.

The production contract was amended by supplemental agreements several times and ended up costing $28 million. Olin's profit amounted to nearly 60 percent of its costs. Its profit as a return on its investment was never discovered. In 1966 the Air Force concluded that the arrangement with Olin for construction of the plant at Saltville saved money for the government.

A new way to divert government funds from their intended use on military contracts was more recently disclosed. From 1964 to 1967 the Air Force entered into supplemental agreements to basic contracts with three of the largest defense contractors—Thiokol Chemical Corporation, Aerojet-General Corporation (a subsidiary of the General Tire and Rubber Company) and the Hercules Powder Company, Inc. The basic contracts were for the purchase of motors for the Minuteman program. According to the General Accounting Office $18.1 million of the sums paid out to the contractors under the supplemental agreements was used to finance "apparent research and development effort."

The GAO's criticism was that the funds had been earmarked for missile procurement by the congressional appropriation, as distinguished from research and development, and that none of the projects for which the funds were used had been approved by the Air Force for incorporation into Minuteman or any other weapons system. The GAO believes that money appropriated by Congress for procurement of Minuteman should not be used for research and development, an excellent although not the only important point about this case.

Equally significant was the revelation that the real purpose of the supplemental agreements was to make it possible for the contractors "to maintain a standby pool of engineers and scientists" who could help in the solution of possible production problems, and the research projects were to keep them busy until they were needed for that. The GAO report does not indicate how many employees were given busy-work with Air Force funds or exactly how the money was distributed by the contractors for salaries, pension funds, Christmas bonuses or whatever.

Fortunate is the business firm that the government subsidizes to enable it to maintain standby pools of workers, ready to solve the problems of those engaged in production when and if they should arise. Whether nondefense business firms and the general public agree that the government ought to be supporting cadres of troubleshooters for the defense industry who, among other things, might be tempted, if not directed, to make themselves busy in the interest of their employer's commercial profits, is something else.

The contractors would vigorously deny any wrongdoing in this case and would point out that the Air Force approved of the way the funds were used by entering into the supplemental agreements. Of course, that is the essence of the problem—that the Air Force knew and condoned the practice of using funds appropriated for procurement toward another purpose and most especially the practice of maintaining standby pools of employees. Defense contractors have learned how easy it is to siphon off the public treasury without actually violating the code of criminal conduct.

PROFITS: THE TRADITIONAL VIEW

Contemporary knowledge of defense profits as traditionally defined is not difficult to survey. The Defense Department makes a carefully controlled annual review of profit rates negotiated on certain types of contracts. Omitted are all the spongy so-called firm fixed-price contracts, comprising more than half of all negotiated contracts. The Pentagon kept the results of these reviews secret until a copy was obtained by Senator Proxmire and the contents made public by him in 1968. The findings of the review explain why the Defense Department preferred to keep them away from the prying eyes of outsiders. Two periods were compared: 1959–1963 and 1964–1967. According to the Pentagon's own figures profit rates increased by 22 percent in the two time spans. A similar study made by the General Accounting Office in 1967, also kept hidden until revealed in congressional hearings, found a 26 percent increase. The defense establishment insists that profits have been going down in spite of these studies. It points out that profit rates negotiated are only the "going-in" rates agreed to in the contract. The "coming-out" profits, those actually realized by the contractor after the job is done, are what count. The actual profits, it claims, are less than the going-in rates. In support of this assertion studies done by the Logistics Management Institute (LMI, a Defense Department think tank) are relied upon.

The LMI study that the Pentagon likes to refer to shows that actual profits are not high in the defense industry; they are low. Others have questioned the validity of LMI's findings. In addition to the fact that the Defense Department paid for the study, the information on which the study was based was gathered in the most relaxed fashion, raising questions about its validity. LMI sent questionnaires to contractors requesting data. Those who wanted to participate sent data. Those who did not sent none. All figures of individual contractors remain confidential. There was no attempt to verify the data by making actual examinations of contractors' books and records. There is no way for an outsider to know whether the profits reported are for the large contractors or the smaller ones.

A private study, done by Murray L. Weidenbaum, came to opposite conclusions. The study was done in 1968 while Weidenbaum was the chairman of the economics department at Washington University in St. Louis, Missouri. (He was formerly an economist with Boeing and has been a consultant to NASA.) Weidenbaum used a relatively small but extremely important sample of six giant contractors whose defense work accounted for at least 75 percent of the company's total sales and compared their profits with six companies of the same size doing civilian-oriented business. Each group reported total sales of $7.3 billion in 1965. The defense contractors were North American, Lockheed, General Dynamics, McDonnell, Grumman and Thiokol. The companies were chosen not only because they were representative of the larger firms, but also because they were not subsidiaries of other companies or conglomerates whose defense profits would be mixed in with their commercial profits and impossible to separate. A conglomerate such as Litton could not be studied in this way because the data it publishes combine the profits of nondefense subsidiaries with defense subsidiaries.

Weidenbaum looked at profits both as a percentage of sales and as a return on investment. The only signficant measurement, as mentioned earlier, is profits on investment, for this is what tells a stockholder how much the company has earned in proportion to its capital investment. Profits on sales or costs compare income to the volume of transactions; this can be a misleading guide to how much the company is actually taking in. This is especially true in the defense business, where larger contractors tend to use great amounts of government property and government funds; their investment in defense contracts is sometimes exceedingly low. Defense contractors thus like to measure profits on sales or costs rather than on investment. Both the Pentagon's profit review and the GAO's study measured profits on costs, not on investment.

Weidenbaum found that defense profits were low when measured as a percentage of sales, but high when measured as a percentage of investment—much higher than for the nondefense firms. In the 1962–1965 period the defense firms studied showed a 17.5 percent return on investment. For the same period nondefense firms showed only a 10.6 percent profit. Although the defense profits were slightly less than during the 1952–1955 Korean War period, the spread between defense and commercial profits had widened considerably.

Fortune magazine, in an otherwise competent article on defense profits, has attacked the Weidenbaum study and attempted to discredit it on the grounds that in two years excluded from the study, 1960 and 1961, the defense firms lost money.[17] It is a completely spurious charge. Weidenbaum first presented his study to the Senate Subcommittee on Antitrust and Monopoly, chaired by Senator Phillip A. Hart. When the same issue was raised there, Weidenbaum showed that in the two years in question the defense firms indeed lost money. But the losses were a result of the defense contractors' *commercial* flops. They had made high profits on their military business in both 1960 and 1961. Their unprofitable·commercial ventures had brought their averages down.

Most of the losses, as Weidenbaum showed a year prior to the *Fortune* article, were experienced by General Dynamics and Lockheed on the 880, 990 and Electra commercial airliners. The Lockheed Electra, it will be recalled, was the turbojet plane whose wings tended to fall off in flight. General Dynamics' 1960 annual report stated that "the unsatisfactory results for 1960 are attributable directly to our commercial transport program."[18] In January and February of 1962 *Fortune* carried an in-depth analysis of General Dynamics' civilian business failures in 1960 and 1961, described its financial plight as close to receivership and predicted that it would have to shut down unless it got the contract for the TFX.

Aside from this low bow toward its business clientele *Fortune* does make some useful observations about defense profits, among them the fact that the giants get preferential treatment from the Pentagon over the medium-size and small firms, and the fact that the contractual incentives relied upon by McNamara to induce

17 Allan T. Demaree, "Defense Profits: The Hidden Issues," *Fortune*, August 1, 1969.

18 Ninetieth Congress, second session, Subcommittee on Antitrust and Monopoly of the Committee on the Judiciary, U.S. Senate, "Competition in Defense Procurement," pp. 21–22, 94–95.

contractors to keep costs down have had the opposite effect. The incentive contracts, as mentioned earlier, work this way: If the final costs of the contract turn out to be less than the negotiated ceiling price, the contractor gets to retain a percentage of the difference (the underrun) as additional profit. This bonus is supposed to be the incentive for the contractor to control his costs. Instead, as Irving N. Fisher, a Rand economist, showed to the Proxmire Committee in 1968,[19] the real incentive is for the contractor to overstate his costs in the bargaining period. The higher he can push the price, the more profitable the contract.

[19] Ninetieth Congress, second session, Joint Economic Committee, "Hearings on Economics of Military Procurement," Part 1, pp. 166–98.

Chapter Five

INSTITUTIONAL ACCOMMODATIONS

On paper the organization of the government appears to make it difficult, if not impossible, for a defense contractor to make and keep excess profits or otherwise to overreach the public purse. There is an independent agency (the Renegotiation Board) that reviews defense contracts and recaptures whatever excess profits slip through the network of contractual safeguards. There are statutory requirements for "truth" in negotiations, making it necessary for contractors to certify that their cost estimates are accurate. There is Congress' investigative arm (the General Accounting Office) to audit contractors and uncover illegal and inequitable practices and to make recommendations for greater efficiency. There is the Office of Management and Budget (OMB), until mid-1970 called the Bureau of the Budget, to scrutinize defense requests for funds, and there is the Council of Economic Advisors to study government policies and expenditures, including defense, and evaluate their impact on the economy. And finally there is Congress, a co-equal branch of government, with Constitutional power over the purse strings, authorized to provide for the common defense and to exercise legislative oversight toward the Defense Department.

The problem is that the organizational chart for defense spending and defense contracting has as little bearing on reality as organizational charts have for most other activities. In fact there are only halfhearted attempts to recapture excess profits, stumbling enforcement of the law, toothless watchdogs, a crippled budget review, a one-eyed Council of Economic Advisors and a legislative branch that has spent much of the twentieth century learning that some co-equal branches of government are less co-equal than others.

The institutions established to control defense contracting and to restrain defense spending have instead accommodated themselves to flagrant contract abuses and extravagant defense expenditures. The adjustments that have been made take various forms. In some cases they have been made through debilitating statutes, in others through executive obfuscation. Either way, it amounts to an advanced case of bureaucratic sleeping sickness complicated by acute steatopygia.

HOW NOT TO RECAPTURE EXCESS PROFITS: THE RENEGOTIATION BOARD

On December 16, 1968, the United States Tax Court ruled that the LTV Aerospace Corporation had realized $4,250,000 in excessive profits on defense contracts over a two-year period. There was a time when such an event would have been newsworthy. LTV is one of the largest defense contractors in the country, a Texas-based conglomerate whose subsidiaries as of 1969 included Braniff Airways, Jones and Laughlin Steel Corporation, the National Car Rental System and Wilson Sporting Goods Company, all of which did defense work. Among its many programs is the problem-ridden A-7 attack aircraft, canceled by the Senate in 1969 because of huge cost overruns but brought back to life in the House by Representative Mendel Rivers.

The excess-profits ruling against LTV was barely reported in the press, hardly noticed in Congress and shrugged off by the Pentagon.

For the case stemmed from contracts awarded during the Korean War and questioned by the Renegotiation Board. The unwarranted profits were taken in 1952 and 1953. LTV, for its part, moved up from tenth largest contractor in 1967 to eighth largest in 1968 and in 1969 received a major share of a new multibillion-dollar program, the S-3 antisubmarine aircraft, an amazing record for a company that started out making popcorn machines in the postwar doldrums of the late 1940s.

Apparently it is difficult to get worked up over such an old indiscretion. Yet the length of time it took for this instance of what might once have been labeled "war profiteering" to surface and the inattention it received when it was made public illustrate how difficult it has become to examine the question of defense profits and how little control there is over the procurement process. Fifteen years is a long time to find out that something went wrong with a military procurement and that a contractor has been holding over $4 million of public money that he was not entitled to. For the Renegotiation Board, which started the case, the delay was quite normal.

The Renegotiation Board is practically all that is left of the efforts beginning in the post-World War I period to place direct limitations on defense profits. In 1934 the Vinson-Trammell Act was passed, limiting profits on naval ship and aircraft contracts to ten percent of the contract price, and in 1939 it was extended to Army aircraft. In 1940 an excess-profits tax was passed. Wartime profiteering spurred demands for additional controls, and in 1942 the Renegotiation Act became law, providing for a clause in defense contracts that would enable the government to renegotiate the price on any contract on which excessive profits were realized. An immediate outcry went up from the defense industry, and the act was soon amended so that renegotiation was conducted on an annual basis rather than contract by contract. The effect of this was to require the government to wait till the end of the fiscal year before examining the profits of contractors and to require that all the contracts be considered together instead of individually. Thus a contractor who made excessive profits on one contract could average them out by lumping together all his others. This was the first of a series of amendments that would continue to whittle away at the act until it was terminated in 1945. Nevertheless, during the war a total of $11 billion was recaptured in excess profits under the Renegotiation Act, not a bad record for an agency forced to operate in low gear.

A watered-down version of the act went into effect in 1948, and in 1951 a new act, patterned after the World War II law, was passed, setting up an independent civilian agency, the Renegotiation Board, to administer it. Again amendments soon began to blunt the edge of the act. A great variety of products purchased by the military was exempted from renegotiation as were all contractors who did less than $1 million in nonexempt defense work in a given year. Still over $750 million in excess profits was recaptured out of Korean War contract awards. In the late 1950s and most of the 1960s the act was further weakened by amendments increasing the exemptions and by reducing appropriations for the board. In 1953 the board had its highest number of personnel, 742. In 1969 it had about 200.

Since 1964 the board has returned about $20 million annually to the treasury in recaptured excess profits, a fact that surprised many people who thought the board was defunct until Representative Henry B. Gonzalez began fighting in 1966 to save and strengthen it. Were it not for Gonzalez' effort from 1966 to 1968, the board might have been demolished. Senator Proxmire has been the board's leading advocate in the Senate. His personal intervention in 1968 prevented a proposed personnel cut for the board. This agency's tenuous lease on life is seen in the fact that it is temporary and must be renewed periodically by an act of Congress. In 1969 it was extended for three years.

The board has had some notable victories in contested cases, notwithstanding its critics in industry and Congress who try periodically to water it down further or kill it altogether. The LTV case was one. The Boeing B-47 and 707 case discussed earlier was another. Both cases are among those known as the Airframe cases which arose during the Korean War. Another in this group was the North American Aviation (now North American Rockwell) case decided by the United States Tax Court in 1962.

North American, maker of numerous aircraft including the F-86 and F-100, made profits amounting to 612 percent and 802 percent, based on return on investment, in two successive years. The tax court upheld the findings of the Renegotiation Board and ordered the company to return $15.5 million in excess profits. Other cases arising out of the Korean War where the court ordered millions of dollars in excess profits paid back involved Martin Marietta ($17.9 million), Lockheed ($15.7 million), McDonnell Douglas ($18.5 million), Fairchild Hiller ($1.8 million) and Grumman Aircraft ($8.5 million).

Yet, as one writer put it, one develops a sense of eternity reading court cases as late as 1968 describing war-profiteering activities that occurred during the Korean War, in the early 1950s.[1] Reinforcing this impression is the fact that at least two of the airframe contestants, McDonnell Douglas and Grumman, were back in the tax court in 1969 protesting Renegotiation Board findings of excess profits totaling $15.5 million. For all we know, some of the others may also be in various stages of litigation. McDonnell settled one with the board outside of court in 1960, after the contractor agreed to pay back $2 million. At this rate it will be 1980 before the Indochina war court cases are completed, assuming the war ends soon.

This is so because the board's work is done in secrecy. Its only public utterances are in annual reports, where the totals of excess profits recovered are printed. It does not identify contractors or weapons programs by name, and in the board's opinion it is prohibited from doing so by the Renegotiation Act, although this narrow interpretation of the law is open to serious question. In 1970, under pressure from a taxpayer's lawsuit requesting a federal court to force disclosure of government information about profiteering, the board placed some of its records on public view. However, the most important information, the names of the contractors who took excess profits, was not revealed. It was learned that the board charges only 4 percent interest, far below market rates, for moneys held by contractors which they ought not to have held. The board does not even advise the Pentagon of the reasons that it has made a determination of excess profits against a contractor, nor does the Pentagon give weight to the board's findings in awarding new contracts.

The only time a real case is made public is when a contractor refuses to comply with a board determination and appeals to the tax court. If the case actually goes to trial, the court will publish its opinion and the facts will become known for the first time. Also, because the board reviews the profits of contractors on a fiscal year basis and because the board is severely restricted in manpower, there is a time lag between the award of a contract and the board's final

[1] Sanford Watzman in *The Nation,* January 27, 1969, p. 113.

action that can amount to several years. For example, a contract awarded in 1969 might not be performed until 1971 and the board might not complete its review of it until 1974. Then the contractor could appeal the board's action and assure the passage of several more years.

The time lag and the probability that an individual case may never be made public should be considered in light of the budgetary and personnel limitations and the restrictions of scope and jurisdiction imposed upon the board. Exempt from renegotiation are purchases of raw materials such as oil and gas, transportation and public utility services, and contracts with educational institutions. In addition, the large firms that come before the board have the advantage of averaging their profits. They can make excess profits on contracts where there is no competition and they have a lock-in, and make lesser profits on contracts where there is competition.

This has two effects. First, the entry of large contractors into new markets is subsidized at the expense of small contractors whose only opportunity for government contracts is through competition. The ability of the large contractor to average his profits allows him to underbid the smaller firms. Second, the trend toward mergers and greater concentration of corporate power is facilitated because it has become difficult, if not impossible, for the Renegotiation Board to focus on the different types of defense production. The board cannot review a conglomerate's subsidiaries one by one, even if one sells apples and the other sells aircraft carriers to the Pentagon. The contractor's entire business is reviewed together. As a result, the traditionally inefficient and high-profit industries such as shipbuilding escape the careful scrutiny they deserve. Since passage of the Renegotiation Act of 1951 virtually every remaining independent shipbuilding firm has been acquired by a conglomerate, including Newport News Shipbuilding and Dry Dock Company, which was taken over by Tenneco in 1968. Other shipbuilders have been absorbed by Litton, Lockheed and General Dynamics. This is not to say that the board was intended to promote conglomeration, but rather that statutory obstacles prevent it from functioning properly.

Even the courts have joined in the placing of constraints around the board's activities. In the 1962 Boeing decision the court invented a new rule for calculating a contractor's total investment that has gone far toward effecting the slow death of renegotiation. Previously the court followed the general rule of figuring profits as a percentage of net worth, defined as the company's total investment (such as land, buildings, equipment and inventory). Most of that kind of investment is usually made by the government in the form of government-owned property, so that profits as a return on the contractor's investment tend to be high. But the Boeing court discovered a company asset not previously included in the consideration of investment, called "know-how." According to the court, a contractor's engineering and manufacturing know-how is a valuable asset and should be included as part of its investment, and it proceeded arbitrarily to place a value on Boeing's know-how equal to the value of all its book assets combined. The court gave no explanation for this measure and showed no statistics or other facts to justify it. It simply said: "It is reasonable to conclude that this asset in petitioner's [Boeing's] case was at least the value of all its book assets combined." Boeing's profits were thus made to look like 37 percent on "adjusted net worth" rather than 77 percent on book net worth. Even so, the court found $13 million in excess profits, though it would have found much more had it not come up with its arbitrary new way of figuring investment. The recent cases have followed the Boeing rule, providing a windfall worth many millions of dollars for contractors.

Supporters of the board correctly point out that, despite its limitations, millions of dollars are returned to the treasury each year as a result of its activities, and, in addition, the board's very existence probably has a salutary deterrent effect. Measured by its annual appropriations, the board recaptures $18 in excess profits for every $1 it spends, a record few other agencies, other than the Internal Revenue Service, can come near matching. Doubtlessly industry considers this agency a nuisance and a government invasion of the rights of private enterprise. No one likes to have to file financial reports and face the possibility of being dunned by the government for money, even if the money came from the government in the first place. Contractors, their national associations and their spokesmen in Congress regularly call for abolition of the board.

On the other hand, the shrewder advocates of defense spending have recently begun to allay fears of profiteering by pointing to the board as the public's safeguard, so that excess profits are quickly detected and recovered by the government. They thus use the existence of the board to answer charges of contract excesses. This, of course, is a deception. Renegotiation today is a more sluggish version of what it once was, operating not only in low gear but with inadequate fuel and, in many respects, traveling down a bumpy side road, far outdistanced by the defense industry zooming down the superhighway.

If it had thought about it, the defense industry couldn't have invented a better way to divert attention from the need for effective regulation.[2] Renegotiation has the unintended effect of placing a government good-housekeeping seal of approval on the defense industry; the requirements of secrecy guarantee that all profiteering can be done in the strictest confidence, to be broken by the contractor alone in the event he wants to take his case to court. Implicit in this arrangement and in the fact that profiteers are never punished, only made to give back their excess gains when they are caught, is the recognition that defense contractors occupy a special status, somewhere between citizen and sovereign, and that profiteering is not a transgression but an indiscretion.

"TRUTH" IN NEGOTIATIONS

As a result of numerous revelations of unnecessary costs loaded onto defense contracts, Congress passed the Truth-in-Negotiations Act in 1962. This law was designed to keep contractors honest during negotiations by requiring them to submit to defense procurement officials certified, detailed pricing information to back up their estimates of what a contract will probably cost to perform. For example, the contractor is supposed to show the government what the cost of labor and materials has been on similar contracts so that the government will be on a more even footing with the contractor and the price agreed upon will be fair to both sides. Having committed itself into the hands of private industry years ago, to the point of phasing down government in-house capabilities of developing and manufacturing its own weapons, the Truth-in-Negotiations Act was a belated effort to prevent overpricing in the absence of competition.

---

2 For a critical analysis of the role of the board see the testimony of Admiral H. G. Rickover in Ninety-first Congress, first session, Subcommittee on Government Activities of the Committee on Government Operation, House of Representatives, "The Efficiency and Effectiveness of Renegotiation Board Operations," Part 1 (1969).

The effort has failed to prevent overpricing. Contractors still overcharge the government, thanks largely to the Pentagon's failure fully to implement the law. Noncompliance is widespread. In many cases neither the government nor the contractors pay any attention to the law, negotiating their deals over the telephone on occasion. At times a government request for pricing data may be denied by the contractor, whereupon the government may manfully ask again before granting a waiver.

A few recent examples of overcharges and hidden profits will partially illustrate the noncompliance. Aerojet–General Corporation received a series of contracts to produce BLU-3/B bombs from 1961 to 1963. On its 1963 contract for four million bombs it was paid $27.4 million including a $2.8 million overcharge. Aerojet was able to overprice the contract by submitting to the Army as backup data estimated costs for subcontracted parts and raw materials and estimated labor costs, instead of the actual costs that it had incurred under the preceding contract. Of course, the estimated costs, on which the price was based, were higher than the real costs that Aerojet had experienced on a similar contract.

In 1964 General Electric contracted to supply to the Navy propulsion equipment for a nuclear submarine. During the negotiations GE obtained price quotations for parts for the equipment from subcontractors. The prices quoted were substantially less than the cost estimates it later provided to the Navy for those same parts. In other words, the contractor knew the cost information it was giving the government was padded. GE later purchased the parts from a subcontractor at the lower costs. The contract, totaling $7.5 million, contained $564,000 in overcharges related to the parts.

Between 1965 and 1967 the Army awarded contracts to the National Union Electric Corporation for ammunition fuses in the amount of $23.3 million. Overcharges on materials and labor totaled $3.5 million, and an additional $1.6 million for the estimated costs of price increases, production losses and rework had no factual support.

Many other cases could be cited. In 1967 the General Accounting Office reported on a survey it had conducted on the enforcement of the truth-in-negotiations law. Of the 185 cases it selected for review where certified cost data were required, none had been supplied in 165 cases and the implication was that none had been requested. The following year an Armed Services Subcommittee headed by

Representative Porter Hardy investigated truth-in-negotiations and found very little of it. The Hardy Committee in its unanimous report concluded that despite the act, "the negotiation process, as conducted over the past several years, has permitted mistakes, misunderstandings, half-truths (and, in some cases, even various shades of fraud) to creep into the establishment of prices to the Government."[3] The subcommittee referred to 26 reports of specific contract examinations identifying faulty certifications of cost data and failures to disclose data to the government at the time of negotiations. (The contents of the reports and the names of the contractors were not made public.) The refusal of some contractors to allow government analysts to examine their books in order to verify cost information supplied by the contractor was deplored, and the absence of government enforcement of the law was criticized by the Hardy Committee.

Also in 1968 the Proxmire Committee unanimously concluded that the act was not being enforced: "The most glaring fact about the Truth-in-Negotiations Act is that it has still not been fully or even substantially implemented, although five years have elapsed since its passage."[4]

There are two techniques of nonenforcement of the law, in addition to the simple disregard for it by procurement officials and contractors alike. It will be recalled that about 90 percent of defense purchases are negotiated. However, the act does not necessarily apply to all negotiations. Like most laws intended to regulate business, this one has some exceptions or loopholes. The first is that the contracting officer can make a determination that competition is adequate, although the contract is being negotiated. That is, because two or three rivals have submitted bids for a negotiated contract, the official can conclude that there is sufficient competition and it is not necessary to require the winner to submit backup price information. Second, the government can simply grant a waiver to the contractor, whether or not there has been more than one bid.

Admiral Rickover, in testimony before the Proxmire Committee,

---

[3] Ninetieth Congress, second session, House Armed Services Committee, Report of Subcommittee for Special Investigations, "Review of Defense Procurement, Policies, Procedures and Practices," p. 1.

[4] Ninetieth Congress, second session, Joint Economic Committee, Subcommittee on Economy in Government, "Economy in Government Procurement and Property Management," p. 4.

explained how these techniques work. In one case the Navy solicited
bids early in 1968 for a multimillion-dollar contract.[5] The low bid
was substantially higher than the government estimate, based on experience with similar jobs. An examination of the low bidder's
proposal showed many areas where the costs were padded. The
rival's bid was much higher than the low bidder's. Yet the Navy
concluded that there was adequate competition and that it was not
necessary to review the low bidder's cost breakdown. Rickover objected, pointing out not only that the government was being over-
charged, but that the high price would establish a precedent and
the next job would cost even more. The Navy accused Rickover
of simply wanting to keep the contractor from realizing enough
profit. Ultimately, by going over the heads of his immediate superiors, Rickover succeeded in obtaining the low bidder's cost breakdown, and the contract price was reduced by $27 million as a result.
But there are very few Rickovers willing to make waves in the Pentagon, and the point is that the path of least resistance for the military bureaucrat is simply to award the contract without entering
into lengthy and difficult negotiations, and this is done in many
instances.

The government may assume this diffident attitude whether there
is an obvious overcharge or the opposite, a buy-in, depending upon
the contractor's stratagem. It will be recalled that in the Army's procurement of the Light Observation Helicopter there were three
rivals, Hiller Aircraft Company, Bell Helicopter Company, and
Hughes Tool Company. In the final bidding in 1965 Hughes bid
so far below cost and government estimates that the negotiators
knew it was a buy-in. It later became known that Hughes anticipated a large profit from the sales of the commercial version of the
helicopter it intended to sell to the Army and therefore decided it
could afford to lose as much as $10 million in the Army version in
order to gain entry into the market. Despite the unrealistic nature
of the bid, the Army awarded the contract to Hughes and determined the procurement was competitive so as not to invoke the
Truth-in-Negotiations Act. Hughes' failure to deliver the helicopters
on time when they were needed in Vietnam subsequently imposed
substantial costs on the program.

The waiver ploy (as distinguished from the determination that

5 Ninetieth Congress second session, Joint Economic Committee, "Hearings on
Economics of Military Procurement," Part 2, p. 33.

there is adequate competition) is the second technique. This is generally employed when a contractor or a group of contractors have been allowed to assume a monopolistic role as government supplier. For example, computer manufacturers simply refuse to provide the government with cost data on orders for new-design computers. If the government insists on truth-in-negotiations, the companies say they will not sell, and because the government has nowhere else to go for this equipment, it waives the act. It then must "negotiate" a price for a multimillion-dollar computer (the large ones cost about $7 million each) without any cost data or any way of determining whether the contractor's price is reasonable.

The Navy waived the requirements of the act in the purchase of a $10 million nuclear aircraft turbine from General Electric even though the price was substantially higher than for similar equipment provided earlier and although GE admitted the price included a 25 percent profit. When the Pittsburgh Plate Glass Company refused to comply with the act during the sale of windshields for the F-105 aircraft, the Pentagon threw away its rights to cost breakdowns by granting a waiver. The Eastman Kodak Company withheld cost data in the sale of aerial film, so the government issued a waiver. The act has been waived for Western Electric Company (a subsidiary of AT&T), the Studebaker Corporation and a number of foreign contractors. According to Rickover, suppliers of materials such as steel and nickel and forging suppliers are also not required to provide cost data.

WATCHDOGS FOR CONGRESS: THE GENERAL ACCOUNTING OFFICE

The General Accounting Office was created in 1921 by the same act that established the Bureau of the Budget. As an agency of the legislative branch, the GAO was intended to serve as an independent auditor of all branches and all agencies of government. The head of the GAO, the Comptroller General, is appointed by the President for a 15-year term. The term cannot be renewed and the Comptroller General can be removed from office only by Congress, not by the President, an arrangement that is supposed to assure the independence of the agency. However, while the Bureau of the Budget has played a key role in increasing the power of the President, the GAO has not had great success in either materially enlarging the influence of Congress or checking the growth of the executive, especially with regard to the military establishment.

In the early years of the GAO its major concern was the auditing of vouchers. Practically every government expenditure no matter how small required a voucher approved by the GAO prior to a disbursement. There were literally tens of thousands of vouchers including the travel vouchers of federal employees, and during World War II, when government expenditures skyrocketed, about 15,000 GAO employees were kept busy mostly by shuffling around tons of vouchers. Until 1951 its duties were routine. But in that year Congress, concerned over potential contractor abuses and profiteering during the Korean War buildup, modified the GAO's statutory authority to permit it to examine contractors' books and records. For the first time the GAO became an investigative arm for Congress, with the primary responsibility for auditing defense contractors.

As the GAO's competence and confidence grew, it probed deeper into military procurement, issuing reports of its investigations to Congress with increasing frequency. Its power to suspend and disallow illegal payments of public funds was extended to include illegal contracts. It exercised this power to a small extent, more often referring cases to the Justice Department for further investigation or recommending that the Pentagon attempt to collect voluntary reimbursements from contractors guilty of overcharging the government. Cumulatively GAO's reports of the late 1950s and early 1960s were a devastating critique of military contracting. But it was ahead of its time. Only a few in Congress were impressed and disturbed over the revelations, notably Carl Vinson, the chairman of the House Armed Services Committee. The tide of opinion was in the opposite direction, and many began growing hostile to the GAO green-eyeshade military critics. Vinson retired in 1964, to be succeeded as chairman by Mendel Rivers. In 1965 a subcommittee of the House Government Operations Committee, headed by Chet Holifield, began an investigation of—guess who?—the GAO.

The Government Operations Committee has jurisdiction over the GAO in that it considers the legislation and authorizes the funds for the agency. In opening the investigation Holifield expressed "the great concern that has been shown in industry circles, and recently, in the Department of Defense, over the difficult and sometimes awkward situations created by the GAO audit reports," and he asked these questions:

Is the GAO, as some Government and industry parties believe, enforcing its own standards of procurement on Government and industry without authority of law or without the benefit of the intimate technical and business experience which resides in the parties to the procurement process? Is there developing a clash of procurement philosophies between GAO and DOD?[6]

This inviting tone was eagerly accepted by the Pentagon and its contractors, who queued up to testify.

It was an inquisition, and before it was over, Joseph Campbell, the Comptroller General, resigned, under a barrage of criticism, from the military, industry and Congress, for reasons of "health." The basic complaint was all those GAO reports on defense contracts. The lead-off witness was Paul R. Ignatius, Assistant Secretary of Defense, who stated the case for the prosecution: the GAO's reports on the Pentagon went up from 206 in 1962 to 544 in 1964. Ignatius did not believe that the increase in the number of reports indicated the number of deficiencies in procurement, and he further maintained that the GAO was in effect violating the integrity of the government's contracts by recommending and therefore coercing contractors into voluntary refunds. The Pentagon, Ignatius said, did not intend to seek voluntary refunds in a number of cases where the GAO had recommended them. Assistant Secretary of the Air Force Robert H. Charles expanded these views. "The sanctity of contracts," he testified, "is the bedrock of our commercial system. You nibble away at this and you nibble away at something far bigger than an occasional refund out of the millions of transactions in which we are involved." To which Hollifield replied, "The Chair is in complete concurrence with your statement."

Ignatius also explained the reorganization of the Defense Department contract-audit function, formerly performed within each of the military services, into a centralized body called the Defense Contract Audit Agency (DCAA). What may have appeared at the time to be merely one of the endless changes in Pentagon organization charts, affecting the unexciting subject of accounts and audits, represented an important power grab by the Pentagon and a demotion for the GAO tacitly approved by Congress. Hereafter, most audits of defense contractors would be performed by the DCAA,

[6] Eighty-ninth Congress, first session, Military Operations Subcommittee of House Government Operations Committee, "Comptroller General Reports to Congress on Audits of Defense Contracts" (1965), p. 3.

and gradually it would push the GAO aside. The rationale was that as each of the executive agencies improved its ability to audit individual contracts and exercise surveillance over contractors, the need for the GAO to do so diminished. In reality the idea was to get the GAO out of the Pentagon's and the contractors' way. In good military bureaucratese Ignatius said that the DCAA's responsibilities would "allow for continuation of the use of GAO reports as one of the audit management tools for evaluating the effectiveness of the contract audit function and for disclosing significant contract audit matters needing improvement or greater emphasis." In other words, the Pentagon considers the GAO a useful "tool" as long as it can control its use.

The contractors and their representatives, Boeing, Lockheed, United Aircraft, Honeywell, Grumman Aircraft, Aerospace Industries, Inc., the Western Electronic Manufacturers' Association, the National Security Industrial Association, and others identified the GAO's sins more specifically. The GAO, they charged, used colored and sensational language in the titles and the substance of its reports. Words like "overcharges, unnecessary costs, wasteful practices, improper charges, failure to protect the Government's interest" encourage wide publicity in the news media and create the distorted impression that most military procurement is unsound. They may even create the impression that there is profiteering, asserted Karl G. Harr, the president of Aerospace Industries, Inc. Titles of reports such as "Overstated Cost Estimates Included in Target Prices Negotiated for B-52G Airplanes Produced by the Boeing Co., Wichita Branch, Wichita, Kansas" and "Excessive Prices Negotiated for Installation and Test of Radar Systems Under a Negotiated Fixed-Price Contract with Avco Corp., Electronics Division, Cincinnati, Ohio" were inflammatory and unfairly singled out individual contractors for public censure.

Moreover, argued Lockheed, over 90 percent of whose total business was with the government, comments by the GAO imply that contractors whose business is primarily with the government are in reality agents of the government rather than private businesses dealing with the government. The GAO was leaning dangerously toward the theory that the defense industry is analogous to a regulated industry, alleged the spokesman for the Machinery and Allied Products Institute. According to the National Security Industrial Association, a "nonprofit and nonlobbying" group created by former Secretary of Defense James Forrestal and supported by contributions from defense contractors, the GAO was creating chaos, disregarding due process of law and eroding the free-enterprise system.

Campbell, the Comptroller General, testifying for the first time on the day following the appearance of Secretary Ignatius, was immediately asked to comment on Ignatius' testimony, which amounted to asking the defendant to answer an indictment one day after it is read. Of course, he could not, although he returned one week later with a prepared response, especially to Ignatius' assertion that the GAO was violating the integrity of the Pentagon's contracts. By this time, however, the committee was not interested in Campbell's reply, and they questioned him on other matters. Nevertheless, the statement, which was inserted into the record of the hearings (in extra-small type), does contain some interesting facts.

For example, Ignatius had complained about the 1964 report on the *USS Bainbridge,* which the GAO concluded was a case of overpricing on the part of the contractor, the Bethlehem Steel Company, and recommended a refund of about $5 million. Ignatius testified that the Pentagon did not agree there was any overpricing and would not seek a refund because it would violate the integrity of the contract entered into by the government. Campbell pointed out that Bethlehem began work on the ship under a letter contract providing for reimbursement of costs until final terms could be worked out. Negotiations to finalize the contract were fruitless for three years, until the Navy's Bureau of Ships gave in to Bethlehem's demands for a fixed price of $87 million. At the time of the agreement 75 percent of the work on the ship had been completed. But the Navy's contract-approval authority refused to approve the contract on the grounds that the price was too high. The matter was then referred to the Assistant Secretary of the Navy, who approved Bethlehem's offer a year later.

The GAO found that it was improper to enter into a fixed-price contract at a time when relatively little work remained to be done on the ship. Under a fixed-price contract the contractor is supposed to assume the risk of a cost overrun inasmuch as he is paid only the fixed price, and if the costs exceed the fixed price, he must pay the difference out of his pocket. But the risk consists of not knowing at the outset what the final job will cost. Here the work was almost completed when the fixed price was agreed to, and there was no risk, because the contractor had already incurred most of the costs. In addition, the GAO's analysis of the incurred and estimated costs submitted by Bethlehem to support its demands showed over-charges totaling $5 million. Finally, despite Ignatius' assertion that the government would not seek a refund, Campbell showed that the Navy had once unsuccessfully tried to get a voluntary refund prior to the signing of the final contract, after the GAO pointed out that Bethlehem was improperly charging costs to the government for the *Bainbridge* that should have been charged either to Bethlehem's commercial work or to other government contracts.

Ignatius had testified that the Pentagon would not withhold payments from the Raytheon Company, as recommended by the GAO in another 1964 report. Campbell explained that in this case the Army had purchased over a million dollars' worth of unnecessary spare parts for Hawk missile test equipment after the test equipment had been replaced. Not only were the spare parts useless and obsolete, but the Army made the purchase after Raytheon had offered them knowing the test equipment had been replaced and that the parts were therefore worthless.

On another case Ignatius stated no refund would be sought even though the contractor was wrong in adopting a take-it-or-leave-it attitude with the government. This case involved the purchase of Klystron tubes from Varian Associates, which developed and held a monopoly on Klystron. Varian refused to furnish cost data or even negotiate prices and established the price of its product uni-laterally. The GAO's examination showed that the prices exceeded actual production costs by from 36 to 279 percent. Varian claimed its costs were proprietary, yet as the sole-source supplier virtually all Klystron had been sold for military use.

Another case referred to in the previous chapter, about which Ignatius again complained that the integrity of contracts was being eroded, concerned the rent-free use by Pratt and Whitney of government-owned facilities for nine years while using the facilities to produce 10,000 engines that it sold to commercial customers. The contract provided that if Pratt and Whitney benefited from the commercial use of the government-owned facilities, its prices to the government would be reduced. According to the GAO, there were no price reductions or other benefits received by the government. Here, too, Ignatius maintained that the government would not seek a refund.

Following the testimony of the defense-industry spokesmen, the committee recessed for about a month, then resumed for one last day, to hear from Campbell's acting replacement. As Campbell had been on two occasions, the acting Comptroller General was badgered by a hostile committee, and the hearings were ended. A year later the committee issued a report announcing a complete reorganization of the defense division of the GAO and a new audit approach to defense contracts. In the future, rather than pinpointing individual cases of weaknesses, reports would be "broadened" to cover "major subject matters." Instead of reporting on separate contracts, a series of related problems would be bunched together in a single report, and the names of the contractors would often be withheld.

The hearings had whacked the GAO in the head, and in some ways it has still not recovered. Its reports, never considered permanent contributions to the world of literature, have been purged of most of the "colored" and "sensational" language that the contractors complained of. Now the reports bear titles like "Need for Improving Administration of the Cost of Pricing Data Requirements of Public Law 87-653 in the Award of Prime Contracts and Subcontracts." Nothing sensational about that, and further, one can read that particular report from cover to cover without finding a trace of a contractor's name. In a 1968 report the Holifield Committee, discussing the improvements that it had brought within the GAO, stated, "There has been, in fact, a definite shift of GAO personnel from direct contract auditing to other defense areas," and Comptroller General Staats testified that this was due primarily to the improved work that has been performed by the Defense Contract Audit Agency.[7] Ironically, within a year many other voices in Congress began criticizing the GAO for not paying enough attention to defense contracts.[8]

[7] Ninetieth Congress, second session, House Report No. 1132, "Defense Contract Audits."

[8] For example, see opening statement by Sen. Abraham Ribicoff and statement of Sen. Richard S. Schweiker in Ninety-first Congress, second session, Subcommittee on Executive Reorganization of the Committee on Government Operations, U.S. Senate, "Capability of GAO to Analyze and Audit Defense Expenditures," pp. 1–2, 168–175 (1969); and testimony of Elmer Staats, Comptroller General, in Ninety-first Congress, second session, Subcommittee on Economy in Government of Joint Economic Committee, "The Military Budget and National Economic Priorities," Part 2, pp. 721–41 (1969).

THE BUREAU OF THE BUDGET, THE
COUNCIL OF ECONOMIC ADVISORS
AND FISCAL IRRESPONSIBILITY

Two civilian executive agencies that could have in the past, but
did not, exercise a restraining influence on defense spending in general and on the distorted relationship between the Pentagon and the
defense industry in particular are the Bureau of the Budget (now the
Office of Management and Budget) and the Council of Economic
Advisors. The bureau's function was to review the budgets of the executive agencies and make recommendations to the President. Each
year the individual agencies were required to submit their new budget requirements to the bureau. The bureau examined the requests
agency by agency, holding informal hearings at the bureau's offices
to determine how the agency had spent its funds in the previous
year, whether it was carrying out the program of the White House
and by what amount, if any, its funds needed to be increased for the
following year. For any agency this was an excruciating process, for
it knew that the bureau's recommendations to the President could
vitally affect manpower levels, the ability to carry on and initiate
new programs, and bureaucratic growth and status. If an agency was
unhappy with the bureau's recommendations, it could appeal them
directly to the President. The tendency, however, was for the President to rely on the bureau, and, in any event, an adverse recommendation placed a severe burden upon the agency. The recommendations of the bureau were eventually incorporated into the President's
annual budget and transmitted to Congress. In theory Congress reviews the budget and may change, up or down, any item before
making appropriations.

The question is how this process works when it comes to the
Pentagon's budget. The fact is that the process summarized applied
only to the civilian agencies throughout the Kennedy and Johnson
administrations, not to the Defense Department. The bureau once
did have substantial influence over military spending, so much so
that the military began complaining bitterly that it had become a
super-agency and was overriding the collected wisdom of the Joint
Chiefs of Staff and the Secretary of Defense. Of course, it was designed as a kind of super-agency to coordinate planning and pro-
gramming for the chief executive. A military establishment properly
controlled by the civilian government would not be expected to

succeed with an argument that it ought to be exempt from central civilian planning. A peculiar set of circumstances permitted this exemption to come about.

During the panicky reactions to Soviet space achievements, Lyndon B. Johnson was available as chairman of the influential Preparedness Committee to accelerate a shift in bureau procedures in favor of the Pentagon that had begun to take place in the Cold War. In the 1959 hearings on "Major Defense Matters," two days were set aside to inquire into "The Role of the Bureau of the Budget in Formulation and Execution of Defense Budget."[9] Said Johnson to Bureau Director Maurice H. Stans, "We hear member after member of Congress state that they are under the impression that the budget dictates this dollar straightjacket to the Joint Chiefs of Staff." And "Military witnesses often imply that they are limited by the Bureau of the Budget's arbitrary decisions."

Stans assured the committee that the bureau was not interfering with the military; in fact, he revealed, the bureau did not even review the Pentagon's budget requests the way it did those of other agencies. Instead of the usual independent review the bureau engaged in a "joint" review of the Pentagon's budget with the Pentagon. The bureau does not eliminate military requests in the joint review, although it does make cuts in its reviews of the other agencies. Stans testified:

We do make eliminations and review them with [civilian] agencies, with the understanding that if they are not satisfied with them, they can appeal to the President. But in the case of Defense, we do not make eliminations or determine a budget figure.

Even Johnson seemed a little puzzled at the fact that the bureau had already surrendered its authority to the Pentagon, and he asked, "How do you justify the difference in treatment between the Defense Department and other agencies?" Stans gave four reasons: (1) the very large size of the defense budget; (2) "the basic significance of our defense posture"; (3) there isn't time enough for the bureau to review the defense budget after the Secretary of Defense reviews it; and (4) "the relationship of the President as Commander in Chief of the armed services."[10]

---

[9] Eighty-sixth Congress, first session (1959).

[10] Eighty-sixth Congress, first session, Senate Armed Services Committee Preparedness Investigating Subcommittee, "Major Defense Matters," Part 2, p. 242.

Now, that explanation does not make sense and, in fact, should have been interpreted as an insult to the intelligence of the committee. In the first place, it is patently ridiculous in an age of computers to assert that part of the federal budget is too large to review, especially when the rest of it is being reviewed. If the Budget Director did not have sufficient personnel to do the job, he should have said so. The same could be said about his argument that there isn't time enough to review defense requests. Second, his other reasons—the basic significance of defense and the relationship of the President to the military—are meaningless. One could just as well use the same reasons to support the opposite conclusion: defense is too important to allow the Defense Department to write its own budget.

Six years later Johnson was in the White House and his Secretary of Defense was testifying before the House Armed Services Committee under Chairman Rivers on the same matter. Why, Rivers wanted to know, is the Budget Bureau allowed to make decisions that affect the Pentagon? Secretary McNamara responded that it just wasn't true, the bureau made no decisions for the Pentagon. He, McNamara, and the President made all the decisions: "The Bureau of the Budget has absolutely no authority to determine in any way the budget of the Defense Department." The bureau, he assured the committee, is "not in the chain of command with respect to the Defense Department." Rivers, obviously pleased, did not ask for any further explanation, and McNamara did not offer any. It must have been one of the few occasions when Rivers and McNamara agreed on anything.

Not until 1969 did members of Congress, outside of the few committees with jurisdiction over military affairs, begin to appreciate the significance of the hands-off treatment given to defense spending by the Bureau of the Budget. In its annual hearings on the President's Economic Report, members of the Joint Economic Committee, concerned over the impact of military expenditures on the economy, raised questions about the role of the bureau. President Johnson's outgoing Budget Director, Charles J. Zwick, conceded that the bureau's analysts did not get into the Pentagon's budget in so great detail as they did with other budgets. A few weeks later Senator Proxmire raised the question again with President Nixon's incoming budget director, Robert P. Mayo, who revealed that only about 10 percent of the bureau's professional staff were assigned to defense analysis, although defense spending comprised about 80 percent of relatively controllable federal spending; that is, of the roughly $100 billion in the federal budget over which there is relative government control through the appropriations process, about $80 billion goes for defense (relatively controllable funds do not include that part of federal spending, such as the trust funds, which is spent automatically without requiring an annual appropriation). Thus in the bureau 10 percent of the analysts are assigned to 80 percent of the budget.

The facts should have come as no surprise, given the existence of the hands-off policy. The real question, which Mayo glossed over for Johnson in 1959 and which McNamara did not bother to go into for Rivers in 1965, is why the bureau had a double standard, one for civilian agencies and one for the Pentagon, and why the Pentagon was able to write its own ticket. The explanation came from an unexpected source: Phillip S. Hughes, Deputy Director of the Bureau and a longtime career civil servant. Testifying before the Holifield Committee in March 1969 and prodded by Representative William S. Moorhead (also a member of the Joint Economic Committee), Hughes gave a rare bureaucrat's insight into the way political decisions are made and, to be specific, why the military gets favored treatment from the bureau.

The most relevant consideration [he testified] is, in blunt terms, sheer power—where the muscle is—and this is a very power-conscious town, and the Secretary of Defense, and the defense establishment are a different group to deal with, whether the Congress is dealing with them or whether the Budget Bureau is dealing with them.

It is of some interest that Hughes slightly altered his oral statement for the printed version. He changed what he actually said, "The *most* relevant consideration," so that it reads, "I think one of the relevant considerations . . ." Only a matter of emphasis, perhaps. But in government it is the emphasis that counts. Hughes resigned later that year after 20 years of government service.

A second important revelation of how decisions are made came in the spring of 1969 from Charles L. Schultze, a former budget director under President Johnson. In testimony during the Proxmire Committee hearings on "The Military Budget and National Economic Priorities," Schultze offered his opinion that although the process of reviewing the military budget might be improved, it would not make much difference in the amount of military spending. The procedural matter is of modest importance, he said, because the President can have the Budget Bureau dig into military requests under any procedure. The real question, according to Schultze, is whether the President feels that he can effectively question military judgment.[11]

Schultze's analysis contains an ominous note. Why wouldn't the President, as Commander in Chief and with all the resources and professional expertise at his disposal, feel that he can effectively question military judgment? Could it be that Schultze was referring not to the President's technical capability to question military judgment, but to his *political* strength to oppose the Joint Chiefs of Staff? In this light Schultze's next statement is instructive. "The fact is that we are dealing primarily with the problem of public attitudes, public understanding and with the need to generate informed discussion." It sounds as if Schultze were saying the President needs greater public support before he will feel capable of questioning military judgment, that is, before he will be strong enough to resist military demands for government funds.

This interpretation is reinforced by Schultze's later testimony. The former budget director had disclosed what he considered to be erroneous decisions to procure some of the more advanced and costly weapons systems. For example, the decision to replace three conventional aircraft carriers with three nuclear carriers seems to have been based not on what was necessary for national security, but on the unquestioned assumption that the United States needs to maintain a force of 15 attack aircraft carriers (in addition to smaller carriers for antisubmarine warfare). The number 15 is derived from the Naval Disarmament Treaty of 1921, in which the United States was allotted 15 "capital" ships, then battleships. Until World War II proved them obsolete, the Navy maintained 15 battleships. Since 1951 the Navy has had 15 carriers, except during the Korean War, when the number went up temporarily. To the cost of purchasing a nuclear carrier, about $600 million, must be added the cost of operation and maintenance, the cost of the aircraft that go with it and the cost of the ships and men that supply and provide logistical support for it. The cost of all that, a carrier task force, is about $1.8 billion. In addition, because of the need to overhaul and provide

11 Ninety-first Congress, first session, Joint Economic Committee, Subcommittee on Economy in Government, "Hearings on the Military Budget and National Economic Priorities," Part 1, pp. 54–55.

crew leave, carriers are rotated between on-station combat assignments and off-station backup roles. On an average there are two carriers in port for every one on-station. Thus, 15 carriers permit five on-station and ten in port. But whether military requirements—ancient treaties and the desires of admirals aside—can be served as well with 14 or 12 or ten or no carriers is a question the Budget Bureau never raised. Others have, however, in view of the fact that no other nation, including the Soviet Union, has any attack carriers.

For another example, the Poseidon program to convert about 30 Polaris submarines to equip them with MIRV (multiple independently targeted reentry vehicles—capable of carrying five to 15 warheads instead of the usual one) was originally justified as a response to what was assumed to be a Russian ABM. This assumption proved to be an error when the Russian Tallinn turned out to be an antiaircraft system, not an antimissile system. The military then altered the justification for Poseidon, claiming that it was necessary anyway to defend against a new Russian ICBM, the SS-9. Then, when the Sentinel-Safeguard ABM proponents needed a justification for a nonurban-oriented program, they too latched on to the Russian SS-9 for justification. Thus the decision was made to go ahead with Poseidon on the basis of a threat that never materialized, then justified on the basis of a completely different threat, the SS-9, which also provided the justification for an entirely different system, the ABM.

When Schultze was asked how he explained the failure of the bureau to raise questions about multibillion-dollar expenditures, he replied with another illustration. The SAGE air-defense system cost about $18 billion to build. It was justified on the assumption of a Soviet bomber threat that also never materialized. Recently the decision was made to replace SAGE with another system, called AWACS, at a cost of additional billions despite the fact that Russia still does not have a sizable intercontinental-bomber force. Schultze explained that when the program was analyzed in the bureau, the conclusion was made that the new system did indeed represent an improvement over the existing system. However, no one asked whether either system was necessary. No one questioned the basic assumptions made by the Pentagon, although the bureau regularly questions the basic assumptions of agencies like Health, Education and Welfare, Housing and Urban Development, the Office of Economic Opportunity and other civilian agencies.

Then Schultze made this statement: "But it seems to me the real problem has to do with general political attitudes, with respect to what is politically possible to do and what it is not possible to do in terms of questioning basic military decisions." Senator Proxmire asked what Schultze meant by "when the President feels that he can effectively question military judgment." Schultze replied, "Question military judgments, yes, but in the basic environment of the Cold War and the post-war era, question military judgments to the point where the President will possibly face a major attack on grounds of undercutting the security of the United States, no."

Phillip Hughes' observations about the "sheer power" of the Pentagon should be considered in light of Schultze's remarks. One can only ponder what the consequences might be if the President antagonized the Joint Chiefs of Staff by contravening their judgment on military affairs.

Despite the reorganization of the Bureau and the establishment of the Office of Management and Budget there were few signs of any significant change in the review of agency budget proposals. OMB has continued the practice of jointly reviewing the Defense Department's budget with the Defense Department. It seemed to have lost whatever influence it once had over military spending to the National Security Council, and there was little promise of increased scrutiny of the Pentagon as a result of the reorganization.

Similarly the Council of Economic Advisors, which is supposed to assist the President in evaluating the impact of government programs on the economy and offer advice on economic decisions, has dealt itself out of the game of defense analysis. Although it has spoken out frequently about the need for exercising "fiscal restraint" with regard to domestic spending programs, it has closed its eyes to unrestrained military spending and has paid little if any attention to the impact of defense expenditures on local and regional development, on employment and unemployment patterns, on the shift of highly skilled manpower from civilian to military and space industries, on price stability and inflation, and on the state of the economy generally. Typically the annual Economic Report barely mentions these issues. In the 1969 Report fewer than two pages were devoted to the problems of military spending, including procurement; in the 1970 Report there were none, although the chairman of the Council, Paul W. McCracken, indicated on one occasion that the subject might be dealt with in the 1971 Report. The Council's conclusions in 1969 that an innovation in military contracting, called "total-package procurement," would increase the level of competition and give the government greater control over defense purchases, were ludicrous in view of the experience with the C-5A cargo aircraft, the first total-package procurement program.

CONGRESS AND THE C-5A

Congress, like the civilian agencies of the executive branch, has done a poor job of monitoring the defense establishment. The Johnson Preparedness Committee, the Holifield Military Operations Subcommittee, the Rivers Armed Services Committee and other committees with jurisdiction over defense matters now and in the recent past have shown little interest in regulating the defense industry or scrutinizing military spending. The tendency of the military committees not to be critical of the military, to approve most or all requests for funds and sometimes to authorize and appropriate more funds than requested by the Pentagon has given rise to legitimate charges that the committees, and the entire Congress, for that matter, have behaved like a rubber stamp for the Defense Department. Until the Vietnam war buildup it was McNamara, the Secretary of Defense, who at times had to restrain the Congress from funding unnecessary programs, such as the abortive B-70. In 1961 Congress voted to buy 100 additional B-52 and B-58 bombers at a cost of $525 million, although McNamara had pleaded with it not to do so. In 1969 the House authorized $400 million for ship construction not requested by the Pentagon.

The propensity of the powerful military committee chairmen to be the most vociferous advocates of larger and ever larger defense budgets has exposed some of those chairmen to accusations of currying favor with the military in the form of facilities and defense plants for their districts, and junkets and military transportation for themselves and their staff. In 1964 Senator Proxmire wrote:

The most important Defense "lobby" is so obvious it is often overlooked since it consists of members of Congress, both Senators and Representatives. In an understandable zeal to aid industry and workers in home states and districts, many Congressmen in effect act as highly potent lobbyists for military spending.[12]

---

[12] In Henry M. Christman (ed.), *Peace and Arms* (New York: Sheed and Ward), p. 6.

The fact that a number of congressmen and senators on the military committees hold reservist commissions does not contribute to the eagerness of those committees to exercise the legislative oversight function with the Defense Department, or to Congress' ability to make decisions about defense spending with complete objectivity.

But there is a deeper-rooted fault in the way Congress has approached its Constitutional mandate to provide for the common defense, other than the occasional excesses of some of its members. Congress has failed to develop the analytical capability necessary for the entire Congress fully to understand the annual defense requests and has therefore lacked the confidence to interpose its judgment for the Pentagon's. This lack of capability, as much as the pressures generated by the Cold War, has been responsible for the loss of congressional control over military affairs. The committee system has not been adequate to the needs of Congress. The military committees have not been able to reduce waste and inefficiency, to resist demands for superfluous and gold-plated weapons systems, to ferret out violations of the law, to take corrective action against programs in difficulty or even to keep the rest of Congress informed about the status of major weapons programs so that it might know how the public's money is being spent.

A classic example of almost all the problems discussed so far in this chapter, as well as a few not yet mentioned, is the C-5A cargo-plane program. The C-5A was originally justified as one part of a two-part plan involving the improvement of our airlift and sealift forces. The second part of the strategy was the fast-deployment logistic ship (FDL). Together, the new airplanes and ships were to provide a "rapid-deployment" capability, that is, the ability to maintain a central reserve of highly mobile forces that could be deployed promptly wherever they might be required. The C-5A was advertised by the military as the world's largest cargo plane, able to airlift all items of equipment—no matter how large—of an Army division, and to land on short and relatively primitive airfields. The FDLs would be stationed overseas with heavy equipment ready to support troops airlifted to points of conflict.

In 1967 Secretary of the Navy Paul H. Nitze explained how important it was to the strategy of rapid deployment for both programs to go forward. Secretary Nitze said:

The Joint Chiefs of Staff have advised the Secretary of Defense that a rapid deployment capability is a requirement for our forces. If one accepts this, we see no practicable solution other than the FDL/C-5A combination. If one does not accept the necessity for a rapid deployment capability, the numbers of C-5A required come under question.[13]

McNamara, too, had always presented the concept of rapid deployment with the C-5A and FDL in tandem.

The FDL, however, came under heavy fire within Congress, especially from Senator Richard Russell, the chairman of the Senate Armed Services Committee until 1969 when he stepped down to become the chairman of the even more powerful Appropriations Committee. Russell's major objection, aside from the costs of building the giant ships which would not be available for any peacetime use and which would be sitting ducks for submarines, was his fear that they would tend to draw us into new wars. On one occasion he told McNamara and General Earle G. Wheeler, Chairman of the Joint Chiefs of Staff, "If we build anything like this, we are just going to be handed more and more of this business of fighting everybody's wars everywhere."[14] Although considerable money was spent for research and development on the FDL, its purchase had not been authorized as of this writing, and the program was deleted from the 1970 procurement act.

The Air Force, undaunted by the fact that at least half of the justification for the C-5A was sunk with the FDL, has gone forward with the C-5A. Of course, the objections to the FDL apply with equal force to the C-5A. Some have suggested that the major distinction is the fact Richard Russell represents the state of Georgia, where the C-5A is being built.

In 1964 the Air Force selected five rivals for the program: Boeing, Douglas, Lockheed, Martin Marietta, and General Dynamics. Each was given $375,000 to submit "concept-formulation studies." After their submission a second round of awards, totaling $6 million each, was handed out to the three finalists—Boeing, Douglas and Lockheed. These sums were supposed to cover the costs of preparing "technical proposals." Lockheed's proposal contained the lowest price, $2.2 billion, approximately $400 million lower than Boeing's price and over $100 million lower than Douglas'. Lockheed was awarded the contract in 1965. Although it was to build only the

---

[13] Ninetieth Congress, first session, Subcommittee on Department of Defense of Senate Committee on Appropriations, "Military Procurement Authorizations for Fiscal Year 1968," p. 646.

[14] *Ibid.*, pp. 359–60.

airframes, under the unique contract entered into it would have total program responsibility for integrating the engine with the airframe and delivering the final product. A similar rivalry brought the engine contract to General Electric.

The contract for the C-5A was the first of its kind, called a "total-package procurement." It also incorporated a fixed fee, incentive provisions and a strange repricing formula that has been dubbed the "golden handshake." The contract invented for this program was a direct outgrowth of the F-111 (TFX) controversy. McNamara, deeply wounded by the failure of the F-111 contractors to keep the costs from rising to scandalous proportions, was determined not to let the next major weapons-system program get out of control. In 1967, discussing the C-5A program, he told the Senate Armed Services Committee:

> The cost estimates for this airplane [the F-111] were not satisfactory. This was known before the contract was let. This was typical of the way the airframe and engine manufacturers dealt with the government in the past. We believe that we have corrected it since this award was made. The C-5 contract was the first example of the new approach.[15]

The unique features of the contract were (1) that it combined the research and development phase with the production phase and (2) that it was supposed to contain firm price, delivery and performance commitments. In effect, according to the Air Force, it was saying to Lockheed, we will give you a multibillion-dollar, multi-year contract to do both the research and development and the production, if you will obligate yourself to the price, delivery schedule and performance specifications. Thus, it was thought, the buy-in and the cost overrun would be avoided.

The program called for 120 planes. Work was to begin on the first 58—three squadrons—and, according to the contract, the government could exercise an option by the end of January 1969 as to three additional squadrons. In other words, until 1969 the government was obligated to buy only the first 58 planes.

The total cost for 120 planes was estimated at $3.4 billion in 1965. In this program, as in most others, it has been hard to extract the true early estimates from the Pentagon, but $3.4 billion is the figure that McNamara and others familiar with the program have

15 Ninetieth Congress, first session, "Hearings on S. 666," p. 380.

used. For three years the reports from the Defense Department were that the program was going along just fine, no overruns, no schedule delays, etc. Early in 1968 McNamara testified before the Senate Armed Services Committee that all was well with the C-5A. The government got a good price, there has been efficient production by the contractor, the program has proceeded very satisfactorily, and "We have been very pleased with the entire approach." Later that spring Pentagon officials also sang everything was coming up roses in the C-5A program for the benefit of committees in the House and Senate. In November 1968 an Air Force official told the Proxmire Committee that there was a $2 billion cost overrun in the C-5A program, that it would cost not $3.4 billion but approximately $5.3 billion.

The Air Force had been concealing the existence of the overrun for three years and, it was learned, McNamara had known about it since at least 1967. This was disclosed in the release of a memorandum from the then comptroller of the Defense Department, Robert N. Anthony, dated November 24, 1967, to McNamara which contradicted an earlier memorandum about the C-5A from the Air Force Chief of Staff, General John P. McConnell. McConnell's memo to McNamara asserted that there was only a moderate overrun on the C-5A, about what the Air Force had predicted at the time the contract was signed, and it was under control. But Anthony warned McNamara in his memo that the Air Force chief was misleading him. An overrun of $420 million had already been identified, he said—far greater than the Air Force was admitting—and it was growing worse.

The Proxmire Committee was later to learn from a witness, A. E. Fitzgerald, Air Force Deputy for Management Systems, that the overrun was first discovered in November 1966. At that time Fitzgerald and an Air Force team uncovered the disturbing facts about the costs in two visits to the government-owned plant at Marietta, Georgia, where Lockheed was building the C-5A. Fitzgerald also revealed what up until the 1968 hearing had been kept a close-held secret by the Air Force and its contractors, the repricing formula in the Lockheed contract.

The repricing formula provided a built-in price increase for all airplanes built after the first 58. In other words, the higher the costs on the first 58, the higher would the price go on subsequent planes. In the event the Air Force elected to go ahead with four or more squadrons it would be obligated to renegotiate the price with Lockheed on the basis of the costs of the first 58 aircraft. As the costs of the first three squadrons had skyrocketed, additional squadrons would automatically escalate, thus creating an even greater overrun. The key was the government option. Its exercise would trigger the repricing formula. Air Force assurances that the costs were being controlled by the "firm" price commitments entered into by Lockheed seemed a bit hollow once the "golden handshake" repricing formula was exposed. How could there be firm price commitments if the contract provided a formula to increase the price?

Following the November 1968 hearings, Senator Proxmire demanded immediate investigations into the program by the General Accounting Office and the Defense Department. He also requested that the Pentagon not exercise the option to buy the additional planes, due to expire at the end of January 1969, until the investigations were complete and the proper reports made to Congress. The hearing was recessed until January 16, 1969, when they were resumed for the testimony of the General Accounting Office and the Air Force. Testifying for the GAO was Frank H. Weitzel, Assistant Comptroller General, the same official who had testified as acting Comptroller General in the 1965 Holifield hearings after Campbell resigned. Coincidentally, Weitzel announced at the outset of his testimony that he was now resigning.

He might have done so one day earlier and saved the committee the bother of hearing his report. In short, that dauntless band of investigators, the watchdogs of Congress, could find out practically nothing. Lockheed refused to give the GAO its cost overrun estimates and told the government auditors to go see the Air Force. Not until two days prior to the January hearing did the Air Force give the GAO any information about the costs, and by that time it was too late for analysis or verification. At the hearing the GAO could only transmit to the committee what the Air Force had seen fit to let it know, and that wasn't much. In addition to the cost-overrun issue, Proxmire had asked the GAO to find out whether Lockheed was using any of the C-5A progress payments to finance development of Lockheed's commercial version, the L-500, some of the work for which was being done at the Marietta location. Weitzel could only state: "In the limited time available, we were not in a position to determine whether all costs related to the commercial work were properly recorded." The five-page "report" tendered by the GAO was more pathetic for its content than its size, and the members of the committee present, Senators Proxmire and Symington and Representative Martha Griffiths, were notably annoyed at the failure of the GAO to investigate fully.

Assistant Secretary Robert H. Charles testified for the Air Force. Charles, the "father" of the total-package procurement concept, who believed the C-5A buy was a "miracle procurement," insisted there was nothing wrong with the program, that the cost overrun was due mainly to economic inflation and that the important thing was that except for the cost problem the contractor's performance in all other respects was excellent. Charles denied that the Air Force had concealed the overrun. He even denied that Air Force officials had given assurances less than a year earlier that there were no significant overruns. One of the Pentagon assurances, given on March 5, 1968, to the House Appropriations Committee by Air Force Secretary Alexander Flax was later inserted in the record. Said Flax about the C-5A costs,

> We believe it is within the range between the target and ceiling costs at the moment. . . . According to the best estimate of our people in the program office the contractor is in the range where it should be between the target and ceiling costs.

A few weeks after Charles' testimony the Air Force announced a six-month delay in the scheduled delivery of the first operational C-5As.

In the weeks that had passed between the November and January hearings, another equally serious procurement problem surfaced. Less than two weeks from the day he disclosed the $2 billion overrun, in response to questions asked by Proxmire, A. E. Fitzgerald was told by the Air Force that his job had been reclassified. He had been stripped of tenure and could now be dismissed without cause and without Civil Service protection. In addition, the Air Force, it was learned, had tried to prevent him from testifying in the first place (he was permitted to testify only because of Proxmire's insistence) and then had actually tried to doctor his written testimony by changing the figures relating to the cost overrun. Proxmire had asked Fitzgerald during the November hearings to supply the committee with a written breakdown of the C-5A cost overruns. Fitzgerald compiled the figures and gave them to his superiors for transmittal to the committee. The figures found their way to Charles' desk, where they lay for several weeks. After prodding by the committee, the Air Force finally delivered the figures to the committee on Christmas Eve under the heading "Insert for the record/Testimony of A. E. Fitzgerald." But a routine check with Fitzgerald showed that the figures had been altered by someone to show a smaller overrun. The document was returned to the Air Force and a few weeks later (the day before the January hearing) Fitzgerald's true testimony was transmitted.

Charles denied that any disciplinary action had been taken against Fitzgerald as a result of his congressional testimony or that any was contemplated, even when confronted with a copy of a memorandum that had been prepared for Secretary of the Air Force Harold Brown by his administrative assistant, detailing the ways that Fitzgerald could be dismissed. One method outlined was a reduction in force, abolishing his job. Since he no longer had tenure, he would have no recourse and would be out. Of another method (an inscrutable bureaucratic procedure), the author of the get-Fitzgerald memo commented that "this action is not recommended since it is rather underhanded and would probably not be approved by the Civil Service Commission." Charles' only explanation was that the wording of the memo "may have been unfortunate."

Soon after Charles' testimony it became known that Fitzgerald had lost all his major program responsibilities in addition to his job protection. Formerly he had systems-management responsibility for practically every major Air Force weapons system including the C-5A, F-111 and the Minuteman. After his November testimony he was relieved of all those duties and given a new assignment, to look after the construction of a bowling alley in Thailand. There, too, Fitzgerald displeased the Air Force hierarchy. He wondered about a serious overrun problem in the bowling-alley project—and asked why the Air Force was building it, anyway—and was quickly reassigned to check into costs at Air Force mess halls. A few months later, in November 1969, he was fired. The Air Force explanation was that his job had been abolished through a reduction in force for the purpose of achieving economy.

But it soon became known that on the same day Fitzgerald was fired for economy the Air Force had hired a partner of the Arthur Young and Company accounting firm to do part of his job. Arthur Young and Company was also the auditor for Lockheed. Embarrassed by this revelation and in the face of a minor congressional uproar, the Air Force dismissed its $104-a-day consultant three days later.

Throughout 1969 the C-5A controversy stood out like a flying sore thumb whenever military spending became the subject of a congressional debate or congressional hearings. Senator Symington cited it as the kind of cost escalation that has come to typify major weapons-systems purchasing and used it during the ABM debate as an example of the real costs that could be expected of that program. At least four committees in addition to the Proxmire Committee held hearings devoted in part to the C-5A. One of the most enlightening was the hearings of the Holifield Committee, despite the efforts of its chairman to keep the C-5A out of what was intended to be a series of discussions designed to develop support for Holifield's proposed blue-ribbon Commission on Government Procurement. Because of the interest of Representative Moorhead the C-5A question was raised.

It was in the course of those hearings that one of Fitzgerald's most damaging charges against the Air Force received corroboration from an Air Force colonel. Fitzgerald had told the Proxmire Committee that after the cost overruns became known to the Air Force, the evidence of their existence began disappearing from the internal government reports. Fitzgerald alleged that the internal reports "had been changed by direction from higher headquarters."

During the Holifield hearings, Colonel K. N. Beckman, the Air Force System Program Officer in charge of the C-5A, admitted that the Air Force had intentionally deleted evidence of the overruns from internal documents because "they might put Lockheed's position in the common market in jeopardy." According to Beckman, information about overruns was reported from the field to headquarters verbally, instead of in writing, to prevent the possibility of leaks. In other words, the Air Force, in sympathy with Lockheed's need to maintain a strong financial image, decided to falsify its written reports on the C-5A program in order not to jeopardize its contractor's financial reputation.

The trouble with this friendly and cooperative manner on the part of the Air Force is that (1) it concealed the truth about the C-5A from the Congress, which has a right to the facts in order to decide whether it is worth continuing its support of the program with public funds; (2) it concealed the truth about Lockheed's financial condition from Lockheed's stockholders and from investors who may have been misled into purchasing the company's securities. Although it is true that the Pentagon has always been able to find a way to get sick contractors well, a company in as large an overrun position as Lockheed does theoretically stand to lose a great deal of money. The Air Force had estimated that Lockheed could lose about $670 million because of the C-5A cost overruns, much more than the net worth of the corporation. It is also a fact that in 1967 Lockheed marketed bonds worth $125 million, to mature at four and one-half percent in 25 years. That is, it was borrowing that amount of money from private investors. Had those investors known about Lockheed's C-5A problems, some might have decided not to buy the bonds. And (3) the suppression of the overrun together with the filing of Lockheed's statement with the Securities Exchange Commission for registration and sale of the bonds may have constituted violations of the Securities Exchange Act or other federal criminal laws.

In 1970 the SEC and the Justice Department were acting on requests by Proxmire for investigations of potential violations of law. The SEC staff investigation, which took a full year to complete, found that both the Air Force and Lockheed had concealed the cost overruns. Lockheed's annual reports and other submissions to the SEC regularly failed to mention the overruns caused by rising costs and technical problems in meeting the contract specifications. As a result of the staff investigation the Commission itself opened public hearings into public disclosure of cost overruns by defense contractors. The SEC also investigated charges that Lockheed officials had illegally sold large blocks of Lockheed stock because of inside information about the C-5A overruns. Although the Commission announced that the investigation "did not disclose evidence of unlawful trading," the staff report showed that Lockheed officers had sold thousands of shares while the overruns were being concealed. A spokesman for the SEC later told a congressional committee that whether or not a violation of law had been committed by one of the officers was a close question.

In the face of the controversy over the C-5A cost overruns, disclosure of the repricing formula that would automatically add new costs to the optional portion of the program, and an imminent changing of the White House guard with the inauguration of President Nixon only a few days away, the Pentagon, on the morning of the January 16, 1969, hearing by the Proxmire Committee, announced its decision to exercise its option and purchase at least the fourth squadron, 23 new planes. This meant that in addition to the initial 58 planes purchased in 1965, comprising three squadrons, the Air Force would buy a fourth squadron, making a total of 81 planes. The question of whether to buy a fifth and a sixth squadron was deferred.

In the summer of 1969 Proxmire introduced an amendment to the Military Procurement Authorization Act to delete the funds for the fourth squadron, $481 million plus $52 million for "long lead-time items," a sort of down payment for the fifth squadron. His position was that while nothing could be done about the 58 planes already under construction and mostly paid for, the enormous over-runs were a red light signaling the need to pause and reconsider the government's options. Should the fourth squadron be purchased from Lockheed at the enormous costs indicated, and then a fifth and a sixth at possibly higher costs? Would it be possible for another contractor to produce the C-5A cheaper? Boeing had used its rejected C-5A designs to build the 747, a plane similar in size to the Lockheed's C-5A. Significantly the 747 was being sold for about $22 million each, the price advertised by Boeing at the outset of its construction, while the C-5A had gone from its early advertised price of $28 million to an estimated $53 million or more. Did the Air Force need a fourth squadron at all?

In August the contents of two documents dealing with the C-5A, prepared by the Systems Analysis Division of the Pentagon, became known to Proxmire.[16] One was prepared in November of 1968, one in June of 1969. The November paper, observing the large cost increases, questioned whether it was wise to push forward for a fourth squadron in view of the fact that the three authorized squadrons, if used more intensively than originally planned, could provide the same amount of airlift. In addition, the study estimated that the airlift capability of the equivalent of six squadrons could be achieved by intensive use of the three squadrons plus the use of the existing C-141s, a smaller cargo plane, at a ten-year savings of $2 billion.

The June study likewise concluded that the most efficient airlift program to support military requirements would be the three exist-

---

[16] See article by Bernard Nossiter, "C-5A Limitations Data Withheld by Pentagon," *Washington Post*, August 31, 1969.

ing squadrons plus the C-141's. This study, much more detailed than the earlier one, analyzed the probable use of the C-5A and found that the Army, whose equipment would be transported in the planes, would not be able to utilize more than three squadrons effectively. The principal advantage of the C-5A is rapid deployment, the ability to move equipment to a crisis point fast. But the only time that this capability is useful is in the few days following the outbreak of a war. It is at that point, in a Korean type situation, when rapid deployment can make a difference, according to the military strategists. The findings of the June study were that the military could effectively utilize no more than three squadrons of C-5As in a ten-day period. After ten days C-141s and sea transport can move cargo far more cheaply and just as quickly as the C-5A. In addition, the June study argued that because of cost increases, the C-5A was no longer an economical replacement for the C-141.

These arguments, of course, were not conclusive. The C-5A had been a controversial program within defense circles since its inception. Proxmire's point was that, considering the huge cost increases and in view of the Air Force's concealment of information and its deception, Congress needed to reconsider before pouring good money after bad. In any event, a delay of a few months or a year in the authorization of the fourth squadron would not be harmful, and Proxmire proposed in his amendment that the General Accounting Office study the cost effectiveness of the fourth squadron and report its findings to Congress so that a decision could be made at a later time.

Of the many arguments that were made during the Senate floor debate of the Proxmire amendment, the one that seemed to carry the most weight with the supporters of the C-5A—principally John Stennis, Strom Thurmond and Barry Goldwater—was one that had been originally set forth by the Air Force in a memorandum to Stennis. This was briefly that Lockheed would suffer such great losses if the program were cut off after 58 planes that the company would be forced either to go into bankruptcy or to default on its contract. In either event, it was argued, the Air Force would not get more than a few C-5As. It would be small consolation that the government would have a legal action against a possibly defunct corporation. Therefore it was necessary to authorize the fourth squadron and the spending of about one-half billion dollars so that Lockheed could continue to perform its contract.

What this argument meant was that because of the overruns the program had run out of funds, even though none of the planes had yet been delivered, and Lockheed could not afford to finance the remaining work with its own funds. Thus the government had to salvage what it could by advancing the money for a fourth squadron in order to be assured of receiving at least the first three squadrons. The Air Force asserted that Lockheed's projected losses of $670 million on the first three squadrons would be reduced to about $500 million if it could build the fourth squadron.[17] (Lockheed denied it would suffer any substantial losses.)

Proxmire countered that the government was being forced to fund a program that was of doubtful military value because of the financial difficulties of a defense contractor. In effect, the Air Force was threatening the Congress with the loss of the billions of dollars already spent on the C-5A program and the delivery of no or few C-5As if it did not go along with the request for a fourth squadron. The fact that no C-5As had yet been delivered because of the schedule slippage punctuated the point. The warning being conveyed was that a lot of senators might find themselves embarrassed with their constituents if they had to explain how billions were spent for a plane that the government did not get. This, Proxmire concluded, was political extortion and the Senate ought not to participate in it. His amendment was defeated 64 to 23.

A second Proxmire amendment, to eliminate all funds for a fifth squadron, was also rejected. This amendment would have terminated the program at 81 planes. That was in September. In November, two weeks after firing Fitzgerald, the Air Force announced its decision not to buy a fifth squadron. The C-5A was the second Lockheed program against which Congress forced drastic action in 1969. (The Cheyenne helicopter was the other.) On the plus side for Lockheed, however, was the fact that it would spend as much or more on the 81 planes as it had promised to spend for 120. It had been awarded another multibillion-dollar contract from the Navy, for a new antisubmarine aircraft, in August, and it had moved up in 1969 from second-largest to largest defense contractor.

[17] Proxmire predicted during the debate that if the funds were approved for a fourth squadron Lockheed would come back within a year to ask for more money to bail it out from the projected $500 million loss. Early in 1970 Lockheed told the Pentagon it needed $500 million for "interim financing" in order to continue work on the C-5A and over $100 million for three other programs. See Chapter Eight.

Chapter Six

THE MEANING OF
MILITARISM

Militarism, Alfred
Vagts wrote in his classic work, *A History of Militarism: Civilian and Military,* is the domination of the military man over the civilian, an undue preponderaͳce of military demands, an emphasis on military considerations, spirit, ideals and scales of value; and it means the imposition of heavy burdens on a people for military purposes, to the neglect of welfare and culture, and the waste of the nation's best manpower in unproductive army service. Vagts made two distinctions. First, not all military establishments are militaristic. There is a difference between the military way and militarism. The military way is a scientific method of combining men and materials to win specific objectives of war with efficiency and a minimum expenditure of blood and treasure. Militarism transcends military purposes, permeates society, may become dominant over

industry and the arts and may hamper and defeat true military objectives. For example, the acid test of the military and the only justification for its existence is war. Yet nations under the heel of militarism, mesmerized by caste, cult, authority and belief, have often lost their wars.

Second, imperialism and militarism are not the same, though they often go hand in hand. Imperialism looks to increase size and territory; militarism covets more men and more money. The former is outward-looking, the latter inward-looking. An imperialistic nation seeks to dominate foreign peoples. A militaristic nation seeks to control its own people. Joseph Schumpeter's description of Rome illustrates how militarism and imperialism work together. Rome, Schumpeter said, was a classic example of that policy

which pretends to aspire to peace but unerringly generates war, the policy of continual preparation for war, the policy of meddlesome interventionism. There was no corner of the known world where some interest was not alleged to be in danger or under actual attack. If the interests were not Roman, they were those of Rome's allies; and if Rome had no allies, then allies would be invented. When it was utterly impossible to contrive such an interest—why, then it was the national honor that had been insulted. The fight was always invested with an aura of legality. Rome was always being attacked by evil-minded neighbors, always fighting for a breathing space. The whole world was pervaded by a host of enemies, and it was manifestly Rome's duty to guard against their indubitably aggressive designs.[1]

The account suggests certain contemporary analogies, but it is not necessary to analyze a nation's foreign relations to detect its militaristic tendencies. Militarism and imperialism can be studied separately.

Neither must we speak only of absolutes. The historical panorama of the most extreme forms of militarism runs from ancient Rome, and Persia and Sparta before it, to Nazi Germany, Fascist Italy and the Japan of World War II. But even those states were something else before they embraced militarism. For a period each was in the process of becoming militarized, and the question is whether the United States has entered such a period.

By almost any standard the answer is that it has. The burden of

[1] Joseph Schumpeter, *Imperialism and Social Classes* (New York: Augustus M. Kelly, 1951), p. 66.

THE ECONOMIC BURDEN

carrying a military establishment, though always substantial, has never been so heavy as in the recent past, and claims of the military and other guardians of national security for public resources have been growing larger. The apologists for military power have grown fond of comparing military expenditures with gross national product for selected years in order to show relative constancy in the percentages. Thus the argument was made by Robert Moot, Assistant Secretary of Defense (Comptroller), before the Proxmire Committee in 1969 that as a percentage of GNP, military outlays reached their post-World War II low in 1948, when they were 4.5 percent, a Korean War high in 1953, when they were 13.4 percent, and a Vietnam high in 1968, when they were 9.5 percent, and that they would be somewhat lower in 1969 and 1970. There are several difficulties with this line of reasoning. In the first place, GNP is an awfully sloppy and vague number to compare anything to. It is defined as the value of all goods and services produced annually in the nation. Included in GNP are the values of all manufactured end products, such as bread and steel, and services, such as maid services and gardening. It is literally a gross attempt to measure national economic activity in the form of output, and it can be useful when comparing one nation's GNP with another's, assuming the statistics are comparable, and when measuring the economic growth of a nation from one year to the next. But to compare one portion of governmental activity, defense spending, to GNP is as misleading as comparing profits to sales.

Even so, a comparison of military outlays to GNP can be illuminating if done fairly and not with an intent to minimize the importance of the long-range trend. For example, the fundamental fact is that in the 1930s military outlays were about 1.3 percent of GNP. (In the 1920s they were under one percent.) During the war, of course, the percentage was very high, but afterwards it came down again, not for a single year, as Moot implied in his testimony, but for four consecutive years, from 1947 through 1950, when it ranged from 4.5 to 5 percent. The truth, then, is that military outlays as a percentage of GNP are 7 times the pre-World War II level and about twice the relatively peacetime postwar levels of 1947–1950, even accepting the narrow official definition of defense spending.

A better indicator of the load that the military establishment has imposed on the backs of the people is seen in the dominant position that defense and defense-related programs occupy in the federal budget. Because the federal government's role in the total economy has increased greatly over the years, this fact takes on added significance. The largest single item in the budget is defense. As shown earlier, military spending went from under $50 billion in 1965 to about $80 billion in 1968. If the costs of war, past, present, and future, were added together they would total over $100 billion. Over 85 percent of all federal purchases of goods and services are accounted for by defense and defense-related outlays. As Murray Weidenbaum has pointed out, in the aggregate, purchases of all other federal agencies are at about the same level as in 1940. (Spending by federal agencies in the form of grants in aid and transfer payments, as distinguished from purchases of goods and services, has increased substantially.) Virtually the entire increase in the federal government's role as a purchaser and consumer since before World War II is a result of the expansion of military programs.

Another way of looking at the costs imposed by military spending is to compare federal tax revenues to outlays for military purposes. In 1969 the federal government took in $188 billion through all types of taxes, retirement payments and customs duties. Of this sum, $87 billion was taken in individual income taxes—the bulk of all federal revenues, including the war surtax. National defense outlays were $81 billion in 1969. An additional $4 billion was spent for the space program, bringing the total for defense and space to over $85 billion. Now, if we take out of total government receipts unemployment and other insurance and retirement contributions and trust-fund collections, we are left with $143 billion. About 60 percent of this amount was used for defense/space, not including veterans' benefits and interest on the national debt, which can justifiably be classified as part of the cost of national security. Looked at in this way, defense/space outlays absorb the equivalent of 98 percent of individual income-tax payments. This gives a somewhat uneven picture because the government has other sources of revenue and it uses all its receipts to pay for national security, but as far as the individual taxpayer is concerned, he would not be unjustified in saying that 98 cents of every dollar he paid in individual income taxes in 1969 went for military or military-related purposes. A stricter comparison of individual income taxes with military-related activities would show that in 1969, 53 percent of the total tax dollar (income taxes plus other revenues) was used to support the military establishment.

The United States experienced three inflationary marches from 1950 to 1970. The first accompanied the Korean War, the second occurred in the period 1955 to 1957, when there was a significant increase in military-contract awards, and the third began with the 1965 buildup for Vietnam. While it is true that no single factor, such as military spending, can be identified with scientific precision as the single cause of inflation, the correlation between defense spurts and price spurts is too strong not to be considered an important, if not *the* important, contributing cause.

A number of economists are of the belief that the crisis brought on by the war was essentially a financial one, that is, a problem of financing the war effort, and that had taxes been increased early enough, say in 1966, the round of inflation could have been prevented. The better view, in my judgment, is that it might have been possible to finance the war in a less inflationary way than was done, but, given the amount of money being spent on the total military effort, including Vietnam, there was no way to avoid serious economic dislocations.

This is so because the use of massive resources for military purposes is massively uneconomic. Military spending uses up resources in a wasteful way by destroying them or by employing them in a manner that is less productive than other ways in which they could be used. Materials and manpower diverted to the military are no longer available, as Arthur F. Burns has pointed out, for making consumer goods or for adding to the stock of industrial equipment or for public uses in education, health or urban development. The funds we pour into defense represent labor, materials and capital that can no longer be used for other things. "The civilian goods and services that are currently forgone on account of expenditures on national defense are, therefore, the current real cost of the defense establishment."[2] Referring to the costs of the war in Vietnam, Harvard economist Wassily Leontief told the Joint Economic Committee:

The rising costs of the steadily expanding war are usually described in terms of so many billions of dollars. They can more meaningfully be

[2] Arthur F. Burns, "The Defense Sector: An Evaluation of its Economic and Social Impact," Moskowitz Lecture, 1967, New York University.

expressed in millions of man-years, millions of square-yards of planet space filled with all kinds of industrial equipments, millions of barrels of oil pumped from the earth. In short, the real costs of the war are measured in terms of human and natural resources and stocks of productive capital accumulated over a period of many years, absorbed in production, transportation, maintenance and replacement of weapons, equipments and supplies of all kinds now shipped in a steady stream to distant battlefields. To these we have to add the hundreds of thousands of man-years of military and civilian personnel, directly engaged in military operations and their direct support.[3]

The entire defense budget, not only the incremental expense of a particular military adventure, should be costed out in the manner outlined by Leontief.

It is in the sense of opportunities for productive use forgone that the numbers of military and civilian personnel employed by the Pentagon, the goods it purchases from the private sector, the real estate it ties up and the technology devoted to warfare that military spending ought to be considered. Not only do we lose the opportunity for civilian use of goods and services, we also lose the potential economic growth that these resources might have brought about. For example, the production of a missile may entail the same amount of economic activity as the production of a school or machinery for a textile factory. But the missile will eventually be exploded and will add nothing to the nation's productive capacity, while the school or textile machinery will continue to enhance productive capacities. No amount of tax tinkering can compensate for the real costs of military spending, especially when the costs have been sustained at so high a level and for so long a period as it has in the United States since World War II.

THE MILITARY BUREAUCRAT AS PROFITEER

As if to prepare for its new role as guiding force of the American order, the military establishment has been gradually reorganizing itself and taking on added responsibilities, some quite foreign to traditional concepts of military activity. Ironically, centralization, from the bringing together of the separate services under the umbrella of a single Defense Department in the 1940s and 1950s to the

---

[3] Ninetieth Congress, first session, Joint Economic Committee, "Hearings on the Economic Effects of Vietnam Spending" (1967), p. 242.

combining of auditing functions under the Defense Contract Audit Agency (DCAA) in the 1960s, has brought about less, not more, efficiency. But such steps have an effect more important to the militarist than efficiency in the use of resources. They create excuses for claiming more resources and for increasing the size of the military establishment, such as creating a need for additional civilian employees, always under the control of military superiors, and they reduce the possibility of surveillance from the outside, as when the DCAA pushed the General Accounting Office out of much of the government auditing business.

The military bureaucrat, like the private entrepreneur, seeks to maximize his profits, which to him means control over resources. One way the private entrepreneur, including the defense-industry entrepreneur, maximizes his profits is by becoming a monopolist. His monopoly position allows him to charge more for his product than would otherwise be charged and to enjoy excess profits. The military bureaucrat similarly strives for "excess profits," by enlarging the role of his bureaucracy in the political and economic system and by monopolizing the knowledge necessary to operate within the system. J. A. Stockfish, a senior analyst with the Institute for Defense Analysis, has written that

the bureaucrat/monopolist is motivated to maximize the size of his agency or bureau, and in this fashion to derive personal fulfillment. . . . What would be "excess profits" to a private monopolist are used by the bureaucratic monopolist to enlarge the size of his agency or service.[4]

Hence the fetish with secrecy and classification. Hence the exaggeration of the enemy threat so as to justify new military requirements and a larger budget.

The ultimate purpose of bureaucratic-inspired change and bureaucratic action is to increase the power of the bureaucracy, to serve what John Kenneth Galbraith calls the "bureaucratic truth" as distinguished from the larger public interest and the reality of life. This tendency holds for all great bureaucracies, Galbraith states, "but the most spectacular examples of bureaucratic truth are those that serve the military power—and its weapons procurement."[5]

[4] J. A. Stockfish, *The Sociology and Politics of Military Cost-Effectiveness Analysis*, Research Paper P-535, Institute for Defense Analysis, p. 9.

[5] John Kenneth Galbraith, "How to Control the Military," *Harper's Magazine*, June 1970.

DOMESTIC PROPAGANDA

To spread its gospel of military truth and to combat the heresy of criticism and opposition, the Pentagon has come to rely increasingly on its domestic propaganda program, euphemistically called "public relations," and its system of internal surveillance. Propaganda is diffused through concerted efforts of the Office of the Secretary of Defense and each of the service branches and, in a less formalized fashion, with the assistance of the military auxiliary organizations such as the Navy League and the American Legion. The techniques include the kinds of briefings, tours, sideshows, pamphlets, planted magazine articles and industry-coordinated advertising recommended in the Resor-Starbird memoranda (examined in Chapter Seven) as well as speeches by military officers, press releases and management of news, distribution of audiovisual material, press and VIP junkets, and the use of Hollywood and TV productions.

It should be clear that the program to sell ABM to the American people outlined by Resor-Starbird is in general part of the approach used by each of the services. On January 20, 1970, Senator Fulbright criticized the Air Force for sending a team of officers from the North American Air Defense Command to Albuquerque to drum up support for a more costly air defense system. The three-man team, addressing the Albuquerque Press Club, used scare tactics to warn of missile and bomber attacks by the Soviet Union and China and the inability of present defenses to stop them. Fulbright said, "This propagandizing for public support of higher military spending typifies the problem of the Defense Department's public relations program."[6] During the same month the Army dispatched a sergeant to Arkansas, Texas and Oklahoma to give a series of talks on why the United States should continue the war in Vietnam, an interesting policy for the Army to be following in light of President Nixon's stated commitment to end the war.[7]

Propaganda, defined in modern times as the dissemination of questionable facts from a concealed source or with a concealed purpose, is not new to this country. The successful use of propaganda methods in the United States, especially by advertising through the

[6] *Congressional Record,* January 20, 1970, p. S 196.
[7] *Congressional Record,* February 3, 1970, pp. S 1099–1100.

mass media, during World War I became a model for other nations to emulate and helped form the basis for what became in the pre-World War II period the German *Angstkrieg*, the war of nerves, precursor to the Cold War. Military propaganda became a matter of concern to Americans when, during the late 1940s and 1950s, interservice rivalry among the Army, Navy and Air Force reached some sort of peak and was used to advance the interests of one at the expense of the others.

When spending ceilings were imposed on the Defense Department by the Eisenhower administration, the struggle for slices of the military money pie was stepped up, and each of the services launched major campaigns hawking the virtues of its wares and proving beyond any reasonable doubt that national security would immediately collapse if its budget was not maintained or enlarged, or if it was not given responsibility for the latest weapons system.

One of the most celebrated cases involved the contest between the Army's Nike-Hercules and the Air Force's Bomarc, a slugfest for the title of antiaircraft missile-system king. In the Army's corner was Western Electric Company; with the Air Force was Boeing. Their strategies were similar: Advertise extensively in the newspapers, buttonhole members of Congress and advise those from districts where sites and contractors' plants were located of the unemployment effects of cutbacks. Representatives of both industrial protagonists told the House Armed Services Special Investigations Subcommittee headed by Congressman F. Edward Hébert in 1959 that the newspaper advertisements were part of long-term "information" programs, and Western Electric testified that its ads had been suggested to it by the Army. The happy solution in the Nike-Bomarc case, as in the Thor-Jupiter case before it, and many others before and since, was to buy both systems.

In 1960 President Eisenhower criticized the services for "noisy trumpeting about dazzling military schemes or untrustworthy programs." Earlier he had stated that "political and financial considerations" rather than strict military needs were influencing the defense program and he warned that unless such forces were curtailed, "everybody with any sense knows that we are finally going to a garrison state." Turning to the industrial side of the propaganda coin, President Eisenhower issued one of his strongest statements at his last press conference, January 18, 1961, in which he denounced the intensive advertising of defense contractors for creating "almost an insidious penetration of our own minds that the only thing this country is engaged in is weaponry and missiles."

Because of these and similar practices, Congress placed limits from time to time on the amounts of money that the Defense Department could spend on public relations and public information, the last time in 1959, when a $2,755,000 ceiling was placed on this category of expenditures. Ten years later, in 1969, the Pentagon's publicity efforts were reported by it to total $27,953,000. The tenfold increase for promotion of a budget that had not quite doubled during the same period indicates the heightened importance the military places on propaganda and the fact that funds diverted for this purpose are considered a good investment. Moreover, there is reason to believe that the amounts are vastly understated. Senator Fulbright, at whose request the figures were provided, pointed out in a speech December 1, 1969, that they omit the cost of using military aircraft, aircraft carriers, destroyers, other investments and overhead. They also leave out the costs of all personnel other than career public affairs officials trained for such duty.

The operations of the Navy's public affairs program typifies the way the military services and the Office of the Secretary of Defense exceed the bounds of responding to the public's need for facts and information about the Defense Department. In fiscal year 1969 the Navy spent, according to it, $9,901,000 on public relations. A full-time staff of 1,086 and an additional 1,600 to 1,800 men were employed at the task. The Navy sets forth its public affairs objectives in a series of memoranda that promulgate the "Department of the Navy Public Affairs Plan" annually and in similar directives issued by each of the 31 Navy Reserve Public Affairs companies located throughout the country. The annual plan for the Chicago Naval Reserve lists among its objectives the following:

—Increase awareness of need for keeping a powerful Navy, both for wartime and peaceful purposes.
—Broaden the concept of the carrier strike force.
—Increase support for expansion of nuclear fleet.
—Publicize Navy-Marine Corps efforts in Vietnam.

The audience to which the Chicago operation is to direct its attention is described as the general public within a 500-mile radius of Chicago, the business community, and other civic, government and religious leaders including Navy League, young men and women

of high school age and above as potential active and reserve re-
cruits, media representatives, active-duty Navy and other military
personnel, and active and retired reservists, Navy and other services.
The memo goes on to state that "every available communications
medium" is to be used "to bring the story of the Navy and Navy
reserve to the targeted audiences": newspapers, trade magazines,
Sunday supplements, direct mail, personal contact, TV and radio,
advertising, brochures, outdoor billboards, and something called
"electronic devices," and it then specifies the types of projects and
activities that will be or are being employed to meet the program
objectives. Some of the more than 40 activities scheduled by the Navy
for the Chicago area involve arrangements for the singing of the
"Navy Hymn" in 4,000 churches, establishment of a special project
in conjunction with the *Chicago Tribune* to give special attention
and awards to people and organizations displaying the American
flag, setting up cruises for media representatives on Navy ships in
the Great Lakes, planning a program at the Navy League's request
to improve the Navy's image, and promotion of the need for an improved merchant marine.

Multiply the Chicago public affairs program 31 times, for each of
the Naval Reserve Public Affairs companies; add the hundreds of
speeches made to national and local groups by admirals and high-
level civilian officials, the numerous seminars and short courses
conducted for civic and industrial leaders at the Navy War College
and other locations, the youth-oriented indoctrination through the
Navy League Cadet Corps for boys twelve and thirteen years of age,
the Naval Sea Cadet Corps and other youth organizations, and the
extensive advertisement of the newest major weapons systems; throw
in several cruises to Hawaii on aircraft carriers for "top media
executives," Navy contractors, union leaders, educators and other
VIPs; consider the huge inventory of Navy films on over 850 subjects distributed for public and television showings, and the fact
that over a thousand news releases and 39,000 news photos are distributed to the press in a single year, and one begins to understand
how comprehensively and insidiously the Navy pursues its "public
affairs" objectives and why $10 million is a conservative estimate of
the actual annual costs.

In addition to the well-thought-out programs of the Army, Navy,
Air Force and Office of the Secretary of Defense, the military trans-
mits its message with the enthusiastic assistance of its satellite citizens' organizations, superpatriotic groups and industrial associa-

tions, including the Association of the U.S. Army, the Air Force Association, the Navy League, the National Guard Association, the Reserve Officers Association, the National Rifle Association, the American Legion, the Veterans of Foreign Wars, the Aerospace Industries Association, the National Security Industrial Association and others. These groups provide forums for the military point of view to be expressed in practically every community in the nation, show military-prepared films and other audiovisual presentations to their members, and publish and distribute numerous press releases, pamphlets, magazines, books and films for general consumption that, among other things, provide outlets for the heavy advertising conducted by military contractors. They also help bridge the gap between propaganda and direct lobbying efforts by inspiring letter-writing campaigns and through direct contacts with members of Congress and officials in the Executive Branch, thus forming an important part of what was described earlier as the informal polity.

The military, for its part, maintains on Capitol Hill a lobby force without peer among its sister agencies in the government or among the private lobbies registered under the Federal Regulation of Lobbying Act. In 1967 the various Pentagon operations classified as congressional relations or legislative liaison spent close to $4 million, more than ten times the amount reported by the largest spender reporting under the lobbying act. Much of the activities of the military lobby, as with other lobbies, are not covered by the reported costs. Visits by generals, admirals and civilian officials to the offices of senators and congressmen, testimony before congressional committees, foreign junkets, tours of domestic installations, ship launchings and other official ceremonies, and extending to members of Congress and their staffs courtesies and favors such as the use of military transportation for trips back home, are all part of the concerted and expensive program for winning friends and influencing people in the legislative branch.

Propaganda is not simply advertising or publicity. It is devious advertising or publicity, the circulation of facts that may be only half factual, for a hidden purpose. Propaganda may contain distorted information, falsified statistics, lies or rumors. It is special pleading marked by falsification. In a democracy propaganda is abhorrent because it attempts to persuade the people through deception. Not all of the public information activities of the military should be classified as propaganda. Doubtlessly some of the activities described above are perfectly legitimate and in any case should not be prohibited. There is no need to muzzle the military. But there is a deeply disturbing dimension to public relations in the Department of Defense that goes beyond the question of why it needs $28 million to communicate with the people and that suggests it is engaged in a massive propaganda effort. It is one thing for military personnel to tell the public of their experiences in Vietnam; it is something else for the military to organize speaking tours so that its official representatives can argue for continuation of the war, particularly when it is official policy to end it, and publicly to accuse those critical of United States policy in Vietnam of contributing to the deaths of Americans killed in the war, as General Lewis Walt of the Marines did in a speech to the Pensacola, Florida, Rotary Club on October 21, 1969, and to question the patriotism of members of Congress such as Senator McGovern, and to charge newspapers such as the *Washington Post* and the *New York Times* with arming the Vietcong with material that breaks the morale of American prisoners.[8] It is one thing for the military to explain the facts about individual weapons systems, ours or those of any other nation; it is something else for one of the services to create war scares and to thump its tub for its newest weapon by claiming it is the key to peace. It is one thing for the military to want to maintain harmonious relations with communities in which its facilities are located; it is something else to take the leaders of those communities on cruises to Hawaii, trips to Las Vegas and tours around the country. It is one thing for the military to want to have a good image and to reply to criticism; it is something else to plant newspaper stories and magazine articles, to insinuate its beliefs into Hollywood and TV productions and to use places of worship for image building.

As Senator Fulbright has observed, "There is something basically unwise and undemocratic about a system which taxes the public to finance a propaganda campaign aimed at persuading the same taxpayers that they must spend more tax dollars to subvert their independent judgment."[9]

[8] See story by Bernard D. Nossiter, "Major Held 5 Years by Vietcong Wages Fight on Doves in Congress," *Washington Post,* November 23, 1969, *Congressional Record,* December 5, 1969, p. S 15843; Orr Kelly, "Defense Chiefs Carry Message to Citizenry," *Washington Star,* November 12, 1969, *Congressional Record,* December 1, 1969, p. S 15151.

[9] *Congressional Record,* December 2, 1969, p. S 15333.

CIVILIAN SURVEILLANCE

To an authoritarian government practically all citizens are considered potential troublemakers, requiring a large national police force to carry out the policy of closely watched people. The United States does not have a national police force, but we are heading in that direction. Moreover, modern technology has made available to government the capability of maintaining a kind of constant guard over the public beyond any monarch's or Fascist dictator's dream. Electronic eavesdropping devices, computers, data-processing equipment and such mundane things as the teletype, camera and tape recorder have made it possible for everyone's name, Social Security number, conversations and daily activities to become part of some federal agency's dossier.

It is not surprising that a certain amount of surveillance is exercised in the name of national security and law enforcement. There is evidence, however, that the extent of surveillance has gone far beyond what is reasonably necessary for any legitimate purpose. For example, on August 26, 1969, the United States Secret Service promulgated its "Guidelines for Reporting Information," which has been distributed to agencies through the federal government. Its purpose is to encourage federal employees to supply the Secret Service with information about private citizens who engage in acts considered dangerous. The official rationale for the guidelines is that the Secret Service has the responsibility to protect the President and other high-level government officials. This might justify a request for information relating to any threat, plan or attempt to *harm physically* the President or other high officials. But does it justify an instruction, and the guidelines so instruct, that federal employees should report any threat, plan or attempt to *embarrass* those officials? Here are some of the citizen activities that the Secret Service wants to know about:

—Information pertaining to a threat, plan or attempt by an individual, a group or an organization to physically harm or embarrass the persons protected by the U.S. Secret Service, or any other high U.S. Government official at home or abroad.
—Information on persons who insist upon personally contacting high government officials for the purpose of redress of imaginary grievances, etc.

—Information on any person who makes oral or written statements about high government officials in the following categories: (1) threatening statements, (2) irrational statements, and (3) abusive statements.
—Information on professional gate crashers.
—Information regarding anti-American or anti-U.S. Government demonstrations.
—Information regarding civil disturbances.[10]

Amusing as it might be to contemplate the tortuous thinking and efforts that went into this document, the brutal fact is that a group of men did compose the guidelines and that federal employees are duly supplying the information desired, in the written form prescribed, and that it is being processed, filed and stored on computer tape.

Equally threatening is an Army project that in spirit, at least, bears some relationship to the Secret Service guidelines. Until recently, the project was known as Conus Intelligence Branch, Operations IV ("Conus" is military jargon for "Continental United States"), and was based at the Investigative Record Repository, Fort Holabird, in Baltimore, Maryland. Its function was to collect information, to be stored in files, on civilian political activities in the United States. In other words, it was a program of military surveillance of American citizens.

It was manned by about 1,000 plainclothes investigators operating out of numerous offices throughout the country and was an outgrowth of the Pentagon's interest in civil disturbances. There was, however, a separate organization, called the Army Operations Center, sometimes known as the "domestic war room," located in the Pentagon that dealt exclusively in riot control by dispatching and coordinating the use of troops. The Conus Intelligence investigators, acting as undercover agents, filed reports on meetings and protests of national, regional and community activist organizations such as the American Civil Liberties Union, the Southern Christian Leadership Conference, Clergy and Laymen United Against the War in Vietnam, Women's Strike for Peace and the Black Christian Nationalist Movement. The reports were distributed through a nationwide teletype service daily to all major troop commands in the United States

[10] The text of the guidelines may be found in the *Congressional Record*, November 10, 1969, pp. S 13983–84.

and to riot-control units on standby alert. Weekly summaries of the reports were sent to Army commands throughout the United States and headquarters in Europe and Panama. The Investigative Records Repository at Fort Holabird, where the data bank was maintained, was made available to the FBI, the Secret Service, the CIA, the Passport Office, and other intelligence agencies and the Army and Navy.

The following example of a report is from the Conus Intelligence summary for the week of March 18, 1968:

B. Rev. Albert Cleage, Jr., the founder of the Black Christian Nationalist Movement in Detroit, spoke to an estimated 100 persons at the Emmanuel Methodist Church. Cleage spoke on the topic of Black Unity and the Problems of the Ghetto. The meeting was peaceful and police reported no incidents.

Here is another:

Philadelphia Pa: Members of the Vietnam Week Committee composed largely of professors and students of the University of Pennsylvania will conduct a "sleep-in" to protest the scheduled appearance of Dow Chemical Company recruiters on campus. The next day, March 19, the same organization will sponsor a protest rally on campus.[11]

It should be apparent from these examples, which are typical, that the Army has not been investigating possible violations of national security through such operations as Conus Intelligence, nor does the project seem to bear on any military responsibility of the Army. What the Army's activities do bear on, like those of the Secret Service, are Constitutionally guaranteed rights, in this case of assembly and free speech, being exercised by groups of citizens in meetings and in demonstrations of their dissent from the policies and practices of the government and its military contractors.

Senator Sam J. Ervin has compared the Army's program to other government computer-facilitated threats against Constitutional rights. In a Senate speech he said of Conus Intelligence, "Clearly, the Army has no business operating data banks for surveillance of private citizens; nor do they have any business in domestic poli-

[11] The quotes are from Christopher Pyle, "CONUS Intelligence: The Army Watches Civilian Politics," *Washington Monthly*, January 1970.

tics."[12] The framers of our Constitution, Ervin recounted, considered the Army necessary, though dangerous to liberty, and therefore an institution that ought to be "confined within its essential bounds." The profound fear and distrust of the military was embodied in the Constitution, which made the military subject to the law of the land and the servant to civilian rule and which gave the Congress the sole power to appropriate money and make rules and regulations for the armed forces. These Constitutional principles, Ervin said, "will be devastated beyond repair if the collection of unwarranted files and development of data banks for surveillance purposes is not halted."

Senator Ervin's objections to military surveillance are similar to Senator Fulbright's objections to military propaganda. In both cases the military has insinuated itself into areas formerly considered off-limits for the government, much less its military arm. In both cases, whether or not one agrees that the activity ought to be conducted, there can be little doubt that it ought not be conducted by the military. In both cases there is an extension of military authority over the civilian.

THE MILITARIZED UNIVERSITY

The spread of weapons-development production throughout industry, itself a form of militarization, has brought about a similar infiltration of important civilian institutions. The university is a prime example. The military alliance with the university can be traced back to World War II, when the academic world enlisted in what was considered a just war. Efforts such as the Manhattan Project, which began at Columbia University and later involved the University of Chicago, the University of California and other schools, proved to be of inestimable value to the military, although the Army had to be dragged into the project three years after it was begun. The lesson was plain: The university was a gold mine of scientific and technical talent that needed only to be tapped to enrich the field of weapons research and development. Ever since,

12 *Congressional Record,* February 3, 1970, p. S 1085. Following Senator Ervin's and other outcries from Congress, the Army announced it had destroyed the data bank at Fort Holabird. However, it later admitted, in a suit filed by the American Civil Liberties Union, that it was continuing its surveillance program.

the payoff has gone both ways: to the military, which benefits by picking the brains of the academic world, and to university administrators and faculty members, who take in hundreds of millions of dollars annually in defense and defense-related contracts.

In the process the academic world and the rest of civilian society have become poorer. The Manhattan Project was started by scientists who were also humanitarians, such as Niels Bohr and Albert Einstein, many of whom were political refugees from Europe and who feared world conquest by Germany. Since World War II it has been the prospect of profit, not the prospect of a totalitarian takeover, that has spurred the universities into the arms of the military. For example, the largest of the university military contractors, the Massachusetts Institute of Technology (MIT), was awarded $119 million for weapons research in fiscal year 1968 and a similar amount in 1969, representing about half of MIT's total budget and several times the amounts of the operating budgets of many smaller colleges and universities. When student and faculty protests against the diversion of university talent and resources into weapons research, much of it classified, flared up in the late 1960s, MIT was thrown into a financial as well as philosophical crisis. The possibility of losing such a large source of funding was something no school could look forward to without fear for survival. A university placed in such a position of dependence upon the Pentagon has lost its most important asset, its ability to function as an independent force for learning, scientific investigation and social criticism, including criticism of the military, and all of society pays the price.

MIT, of course, is not alone. In fiscal year 1968 its fellow university military contractors included Johns Hopkins University ($57.6 million), the University of California ($17.4 million), Stanford University ($16.4 million), the University of Rochester ($13.1 million), Pennsylvania State University ($10.5 million), Columbia University ($9.9 million), Michigan State University ($9.5 million) and the University of Illinois ($8.6 million), to name a few. The Navy alone awards about 1,100 contracts each year to colleges and universities. In 1968, 143 colleges and universities were occupied, if not preoccupied, with Air Force research projects.

Fed by the same rich supply of defense contracts, the milk of human unkindness, a variety of hybrid educational institutions has grown up to serve the needs of weapons and other military research. These are the research institutes, think tanks, laboratories and other centers that owe their existence to the defense budget. Some operate in loose association with the universities out of which they sprang, such as the Stanford Research Institute–Stanford University and Cornell Aeronautical Laboratory–Cornell University relationships. Others, such as Rand and the Logistics Management Institute, were created by the Pentagon. One of the largest, the Institute for Defense Analyses (IDA), got its start from a consortium of universities put together by James R. Killian, Jr., MIT's Chairman of the Board. All maintain ties with universities because they are sources of trained manpower and respectability.

But the university tradition, whatever is left of it in America, of independent scholarship hardly persists beyond that point, with the exception of a few dissident researchers who are attempting to reclaim their academic birthright. The primary function of "nonprofit" institutions such as IDA, as James Ridgeway has pointed out, is to serve as an adjunct to the Pentagon where bright university scientists can be enticed into its service without the tedium and low pay of Civil Service government work.[13] The same point can be made about the university-based military projects. There, too, defense work is a lucrative source of income to scientists who would be paid on a lower scale for doing the same research in a government laboratory. The contract system thus operates in part as a scheme for the Pentagon and its workers to evade Civil Service salary limitations.

In 1968 over $665 million in military prime contracts were awarded by the Pentagon to colleges, universities, think tanks, and other nonprofit institutions (see Table 6). In addition, NASA awards to this class of contractors amounted to over $165 million, and Atomic Energy Commission awards were another $163 million, making a total of close to a billion dollars in defense and defense-related contracts to universities and other nonprofits.

Much ado has been made by all sides over the classified projects on campuses, as if their elimination would remove the chief source of friction between the military and the universities. This, in my opinion, is a shortsighted view of the problem. Classified research represents a relatively small percentage of university projects, a percentage that could be easily reduced further if the Pentagon wanted to declassify those projects which ought not be classified in the first place. For example, in 1968 the Air Force had 1,090 contracts with

13 James Ridgeway, *The Closed Corporation: American Universities in Crisis* (New York: Random House, 1968), p. 132.

university scientists. Of those only 88 were classified, 22 of which were classified only because the principal investigator had access to classified information, not because the work itself was of a classified nature. An Air Force regulation permits declassification in such instances. Although the secrecy involved in classified work militates against the intellectual environment that ought to exist in schools of higher learning, the corrosive effects of military influence would persist through the bulk of the nonclassified projects.

The problem is the loss of independence, and the difficulty lies as much in the attitudes of university administrators and faculty contractors as it does in the Defense Department. Universities that have gotten used to steady flows of money from the military have learned to bathe comfortably in them. They like being dependent upon the Pentagon, although they may delude themselves with notions of their essential independence, just as industrial contractors delude themselves about being free enterprises while enjoying their dependence upon military contracts. Nor have the universities, now addicted to the habit-forming doses of money, been shy about coming to the Pentagon to ask for more. Senator Stennis observed in 1969 that "at some of our Appropriations Committee hearings, we see where these universities come down here fighting tooth and nail to get that money."[14]

A scholar working on a defense contract must apply his scholarship within the narrow bounds of his contract; for most practical purposes he is no longer a scholar, he is a military-contract employee. His allegiance has now been diverted away from the university and society at large. A billion dollars buys a lot of scientific talent, talent that becomes obligated to the purposes of its military and military-related benefactors, the effects of which are to deny its use for other purposes.

A scientist on a government contract, whether in a university or a think tank, has moved within the Pentagon's sphere of influence and is subject to military control. He is no more free to be openly critical of military programs or military policies than he would be were he employed in a government laboratory or for a defense contractor, which is to say not at all. The fear of falling out of favor with the Pentagon, of having a contract terminated, of being blacklisted from obtaining future contracts or from receiving a high-level appoint-

---

[14] Ninety-first Congress, first session, "Hearings on Authorization for Military Procurement, Research and Development, Fiscal Year 1970," p. 1553.

TABLE 6. Excerpt from Department of Defense Listing of 500 Contractors According to Net Value of Military Prime-Contract Awards for Research, Development, Tests and Evaluation Work

SECTION II—NONPROFIT INSTITUTIONS
Fiscal Year 1968

Name of Contractor and Location	Thousands of Dollars	Name of Contractor and Location	Thousands of Dollars
Massachusetts Institute of Technology	119,175	Rand Corporation	19,139
Cambridge, Mass.	31,662	Santa Monica, Calif.	19,139
Lexington, Mass.	87,513		
		California, University of	17,393
Aerospace Corporation	73,339	Berkeley, Calif.	5,767
El Segundo, Calif.	73,307	Davis, Calif.	127
San Bernardino, Calif.	32	Irvine, Calif.	65
		La Jolla, Calif.	5,510
Johns Hopkins University	97,614	Los Angeles, Calif.	1,471
Baltimore City, Md.	2,713	Point Mugu, Calif.	12
Silver Spring, Md.	54,901	Riverside, Calif.	89
		San Diego, Calif.	3,182
Mitre Corporation	35,712	San Francisco, Calif.	256
Bedford, Mass.	35,712	Santa Barbara, Calif.	870
		Santa Cruz, Calif.	44
Stanford Research Institute	28,716		
Ethiopia	198	System Development Corporation	17,372
Thailand	58	Huntsville, Ala.	414
Homer Village, Alaska	18	Lompoc, Calif.	700
Menlo Park, Calif.	27,687	Los Angeles, Calif.	61
Stanford, Calif.	323	Santa Monica, Calif.	13,120
Mercury, Nev.	437	Washington, D.C.	363
Cheyenne, Wyo.	75		

Name of Contractor and Location	Thousands of Dollars
Belleville, Ill.	350
Lexington, Mass.	375
Rome, N.Y.	191
Dayton, Ohio	303
Falls Church, Va.	1,226
Hampton, Va.	234
Norfolk, Va.	35
Stanford University	16,422
Palo Alto, Calif.	218
Stanford, Calif.	16,204
Rochester, University of	13,182
Rochester, N.Y.	13,182
Cornell Aeronautical Laboratories, Inc.	12,500
Edwards, Calif.	86
Buffalo, N.Y.	11,889
Wright Patterson, Ohio	37
Falls Church, Va.	488
ITT Research Institute	12,172
Chicago, Ill.	7,017
Annapolis, Md.	5,130
Wright Patterson, Ohio	25
Institute for Defense Analysis	11,691
Arlington, Va.	11,691
Pennsylvania State University	10,513
University Park, Pa.	10,513
Research Analysis Corporation	10,067
Iran	155
Vietnam	398
McLean, Va.	9,273
Various Domestic	241
Columbia University	9,929
New York, N.Y.	9,929
Michigan, University of	9,478
Honolulu City, Hawaii	1,600
Ann Arbor, Mich.	6,947
Willow Run, Mich.	734
Ypsilanti, Mich.	197
Illinois, University of	8,583
Chicago, Ill.	89
Urbana, Ill.	8,494
Battelle Memorial Institute	8,322
Germany	57
Washington, D.C.	114
Columbus, Ohio	8,036
Richland, Wash.	115
United States National Aerospace Academy	7,026
Edwards, Calif.	25
Moffett Field, Calif.	40

Name of Contractor and Location	Thousands of Dollars
Pasadena, Calif.	19
Washington, D.C.	77
Houston, Tex.	155
Ridgeley, W. Va.	6,710
Riverside Research Institute	6,315
New York, N.Y.	6,315
Washington, University of	5,552
Seattle, Wash.	5,552
Texas, University of	5,386
Alamogordo, N.M.	10
Austin, Tex.	4,598
College Station, Tex.	68
Dallas, Tex.	43
El Paso, Tex.	502
Galveston, Tex.	135
Houston, Tex.	30
Woods Hole Oceanographic Institute	5,143
Woods Hole, Mass.	5,143
Utah, University of	4,356
Dugway, Utah	283
Salt Lake City, Utah	4,073
Syracuse University Research Corporation	4,172
Burlington, Mass.	94
Syracuse, N.Y.	4,078
Dayton, University of	3,610
Dayton, Ohio	3,358
Wright Patterson, Ohio	252
Cornell University	3,595
Arecibo, P.R.	1,585
Ithaca, N.Y.	1,949
New York, N.Y.	61
George Washington University	3,306
Washington, D.C.	3,295
Alexandria, Va.	11
Southwest Research Institute	3,149
Wright Patterson, Ohio	226
Dallas, Tex.	35
San Antonio, Tex.	2,888
Denver, University of	2,982
Denver, Colo.	2,982
Ohio State University Research Foundation	2,958
Columbus, Ohio	2,686
Wright Patterson, Ohio	272
American University	2,944
Washington, D.C.	2,944
National Academy of Sciences	2,838
Washington, D.C.	2,756

Name of Contractor and Location	Thousands of Dollars
Watertown, Mass.	47
Dover, N.J.	35
Duke University	2,812
Durham, N.C.	2,812
New Mexico State University	2,787
Alamogordo, N. Mex.	24
Las Cruces, N. Mex.	640
University Park, N. Mex.	1,612
White Sands Missile Site, N. Mex.	511
Alaska, University of	2,695
College Village, Alaska	2,695
Miami, University of	2,602
Coral Gables, Fla.	1,161
Miami, Fla.	1,461
Carnegie Mellon University	2,575
Pittsburgh, Pa.	2,575
Harvard University	2,524
Boston, Mass.	182
Cambridge, Mass.	2,182
Fort Davis, Tex.	160
Minnesota, University of	2,507
Minneapolis, Minn.	2,507
California Institute of Technology	2,487
Pasadena, Calif.	2,487

Name of Contractor and Location	Thousands of Dollars
Texas A&M Research Foundation	2,475
College Station, Tex.	2,475
Purdue Research Foundation	2,455
Lafayette, Ind.	2,442
West Lafayette, Ind.	13
New York University	2,304
Bronx, N.Y.	731
New York, N.Y.	1,513
Syracuse, N.Y.	25
University Heights, N.Y.	35
Maryland, University of	2,100
Baltimore, Md.	703
College Park, Md.	1,397
New Mexico, University of	1,986
Albuquerque, N. Mex.	934
Sandia, N. Mex.	1,052
New York, State University of	1,982
Albany, N.Y.	1,538
Buffalo, N.Y.	318
New York, N.Y.	115
Stony Brook, N.Y.	11
Oregon State University	1,969
Corvallis, Oreg.	1,969
Florida, University of	1,842

Name of Contractor and Location	Thousands of Dollars	Name of Contractor and Location	Thousands of Dollars
Gainesville, Fla.	1,842	Stillwater, Okla.	1,422
Princeton University	1,803	Iowa State University of Science and Technology	1,372
Princeton, N.J.	1,803	Ames, Iowa	1,372
Midwest Research Institute	1,762	Chicago, University of	1,360
Kansas City, Mo.	1,615	Chicago, Ill.	1,320
Wright Patterson, Ohio	147	Lemont, Ill.	40
Louisiana, State University of	1,754	Florida State University	1,338
Baton Rouge, La.	1,754	Tallahassee, Fla.	1,338
Georgia Tech Research Institute	1,725	Colorado State University	1,329
Atlanta, Ga.	1,725	Tallahassee, Fla.	1,329
Stevens Institute of Technology	1,596	Kansas State University of Agriculture	1,321
Hoboken, N.J.	1,559	Manhattan, Kans.	1,321
New York, N.Y.	37		
Wisconsin, University of	1,591	Brooklyn Polytechnic Institute	1,304
Madison, Wis.	1,591	Brooklyn, N.Y.	1,274
		Farmingdale, N.Y.	30
Hawaii, University of	1,568	Catholic University of America	1,304
Honolulu, Hawaii	1,568	Washington, D.C.	1,304
Analytic Services Inc.	1,495	Research Triangle Institute	1,254
Falls Church, Va.	1,495	Iran	296
Cincinnati, University of	1,446	Durham, N.C.	606
Cincinnati, Ohio	1,446		
Oklahoma, State University of	1,422		

Name of Contractor and Location	Thousands of Dollars
Triangle Park, N.C.	352
Georgia Institute of Technology	1,221
Atlanta, Ga.	1,221
New Mexico Institute of Mining and Technology	1,210
Chino Lake, Calif.	200
Socorro, N. Mex.	1,010
Syracuse University	1,197
Syracuse, N.Y.	1,184
Utica, N.Y.	13
Pennsylvania, University of	1,125
Philadelphia, Pa.	1,125
Rhode Island, University of	1,084
Kingston, R.I.	1,084
Smithsonian Institute	1,082
Washington, D.C.	1,067
Cambridge, Mass.	15
Indiana University	1,044
Bloomington, Ind.	1,044
Kansas, University of	1,044
Kansas City, Kans.	18
Lawrence, Kans.	1,026
American Institute of Research	1,038
Palo Alto, Calif.	93
Silver Spring, Md.	145
Camp Lejeune, N.C.	54
Pittsburgh, Pa.	746
Case Western Reserve University	1,011
Cleveland, Ohio	1,011
Rensselaer Polytechnic Institute	1,001
Troy, N.Y.	1,001
United States Atomic Energy Commission	995
Washington, D.C.	175
Germantown, Md.	39
Las Vegas, Nev.	270
Albuquerque, N. Mex.	451
Oak Ridge, Tenn.	40
Richland, Wash.	20
Illinois Institute of Technology	988
Chicago, Ill.	988
United States Commerce Department	985
Boulder, Colo.	540
Washington, D.C.	324
Gaithersburg, Md.	46
Rockville, Md.	10
Suitland, Md.	65
Rutgers University	983

Name of Contractor and Location	Thousands of Dollars	Name of Contractor and Location	Thousands of Dollars
New Brunswick, N.J.	983	Eugene, Oreg.	531
Southern Research Institute	965	Portland, Oreg.	315
Birmingham, Ala.	965	Oklahoma, University of	840
Colorado University	964	Fort Sill, Okla.	100
Boulder, Colo.	706	Norman, Okla.	335
Denver, Colo.	258	Oklahoma City, Okla.	405
Northeastern University	952	Virginia, University of	787
Boston, Mass.	952	Charlottesville, Va.	787
Washington University	933	Tennessee, University of	751
St. Louis, Mo.	933	Knoxville, Tenn.	520
Brown University	932	Memphis, Tenn.	64
Providence, R.I.	932	Tullahoma, Tenn.	167
Pittsburgh, University of	921	Southern California, University of	749
Washington, D.C.	195	Los Angeles, Calif.	735
Pittsburgh, Pa.	726	San Diego, Calif.	14
Missouri, University of	876	Southern Methodist University	735
Columbia, Mo.	798	Dallas, Tex.	735
Kansas City, Mo.	50	Delaware, University of	732
Rolla, Mo.	28	Newark, Del.	732
Notre Dame, University of	855	Georgetown University	714
Notre Dame, Ind.	855	Washington, D.C.	714
Oregon, University of	846	Yale University	709

Name of Contractor and Location	Thousands of Dollars	Name of Contractor and Location	Thousands of Dollars
New Haven, Conn.	684	Northwestern University	590
Alamogordo, N. Mex.	25	Evanston, Ill.	590
Houston, University of	680	American Institute for Research	569
Houston, Tex.	680	Vietnam	26
Auburn University	657	Washington, D.C.	62
Auburn, Ala.	657	Pittsburgh, Pa.	481
University Corporation for Atmospheric Research	635	Mississippi State University	564
Boulder, Colo.	−40	State College, Miss.	564
Sunspot, N. Mex.	695	Travelers Research Center	561
Dartmouth College	652	Hartford, Conn.	561
Hanover, N. H.	652	North Carolina State University	551
Arizona State University	649	Raleigh, N.C.	551
Tempe, Ariz.	649	Massachusetts, University of	511
American Society for Engineering	621	Amherst, Mass.	493
Washington, D.C.	621	Waltham, Mass.	18
Lowell Technical Institute	618	Arizona, University of	504
Billerica, Mass.	40	Tucson, Ariz.	504
Lowell, Mass.	578	National Society of Professional Engineers	493
Lovelace Foundation	613	Washington, D.C.	493
Albuquerque, N. Mex.	613	Michigan State University	464
Ohio University	608	East Lansing, Mich.	464
Athens, Ohio	608	Boston College	455

Name of Contractor and Location	Thousands of Dollars	Name of Contractor and Location	Thousands of Dollars
Chestnut Hill, Mass.	318	Tufts University	380
Weston, Mass.	137	Boston, Mass.	41
South Dakota School of Mines and Technology		Medford, Mass.	339
Rapid City, S. Dak.	454	Arctic Institute of North America	354
	454	Canada	75
Nevada, University of	426	Washington, D.C.	279
Reno, Nev.	426	Alabama, University of	351
Flight Safety Foundation	423	Birmingham, Ala.	176
Phoenix, Ariz.	423	Huntsville, Ala.	102
North Carolina, University of	390	University, Ala.	73
Chapel Hill, N.C.	390	Utah State University of Agriculture	344
United States Interior Department	387	Bedford, Mass.	162
Denver, Colo.	50	Logan, Utah	182
Washington, D.C.	37	Iowa State University	342
Bartlesville, Okla.	85	Iowa City, Iowa	342
Albany, Oreg.	50	Lehigh University	341
Pittsburgh, Pa.	165	Bethlehem, Pa.	341
Presbyterian Hospital	384		665,365
Chicago, Ill.	384		

ment to the Defense Department is always present. Thus, for example, he will probably not agree to testify before a congressional committee unless the Pentagon gives its permission, and if it gives its permission, it may reserve the right to review his prepared statement in advance. The Pentagon has actively discouraged experts from appearing before committees of Congress that it believes are unfriendly to it, and for the most part the experts have complied with the Pentagon's wishes. The problem of resisting the military planners over the years has been compounded by the fact that most of the military experts in the physical and the social sciences have been rounded up, corralled and broken by the military establishment, either directly by employing them in the Pentagon or defense industry or indirectly by awarding contracts to universities and think tanks.

Chapter Seven

MOVING INTO THE 1970S

No sooner had Lyndon Johnson announced his decision not to seek re-election early in 1968 than did the consequences of his lame-duck Presidency reverberate against the swollen defense budget. The antiballistic missile system, to be specific, came under a sustained semi-organized attack for the first time in 1968. The year before, Senator Joseph Clark, mostly by himself, tried to raise the issue with notable failure. Clark's efforts against the ABM and other weapons systems were ineffective, drew little support and contributed to his political undoing. In 1968 Senator Hugh Scott, Clark's fellow Pennsylvanian, chided him for his "careless and cavalier attitude toward national defense and vital military needs." It was still unpopular and politically dangerous to suggest that weapons programs, no matter how outlandish in their conception or outrageous in their purpose, were wasteful and bad for national security. The unhappiness over the war in Vietnam was responsible for increasing criticism of Johnson, the Pentagon and the government in the most general way, not against individual weapons or defense spending. The fineness of Scott's sensitivity to this distinction may be seen in the fact that Clark was defeated in his bid for reelection, while Scott went on as a moderate opponent of Johnson's Vietnam policy to succeed Senator Everett Dirksen as Minority Leader in 1969.

Still, with war dissent growing and Lyndon Johnson going, some members of Congress took heart, screwed up their courage and paused to think about ABM before voting on it. The chief opponents were Senators Phillip A. Hart, a Democrat, and John S. Cooper, a Republican. Their argument was that there was no assurance the system would work, that is, intercept virtually all of an enemy's incoming nuclear missiles and destroy them in midair before they could do any damage, and that the mere decision of this country to set up an ABM system would provoke the Soviet Union to take countermeasures and precipitate a new round of nuclear-arms escalation. The amendment they jointly sponsored aimed to delete the funds earmarked for construction of ABM sites, then intended to be placed around a number of cities. The effect would be to delay that part of the program for a year so that, in the words of Cooper, "we might find out more certainly whether the system has any value."

That was the ostensible reason. Less conspicuous was the rising disaffection with and lack of confidence in the military, the awareness that Johnson was becoming less of a force to be reckoned with and the spreading concern that the Pentagon with its seemingly boundless budgets was leading the nation toward militarism. Senator Charles Percy said on June 24, 1968, that the decision to begin site construction for the ABM should not be made by a lame-duck administration, and he hinted at his own belief that the military budget was too large and ought to be reduced. Senator Clark stated the issue more bluntly. The 10 percent surtax had just been passed to pay for the war. It had also been decided by Congress to cut federal expenditures by $6 billion as an anti-inflation measure. "In my judgment," Clark said, "the $6 billion cut could be made up entirely out of the swollen defense budget," and that was reason enough to stop ABM. It was an odd sort of debate for the Senate to be carrying on, because deliberations over weapons systems had almost always been within the exclusive province of the Armed

Services and Appropriations committees, and prior attempts to reverse the judgments of those powerful bodies had been easily beaten down. There was thus a good deal of surprise when 34 senators voted for the Hart-Cooper amendment, including several members of key committees such as Allen J. Ellender, Margaret Chase Smith and Stuart Symington.

It was also an odd sort of learning process for the Congress to be going through. The elected representatives were beginning to understand the limitations of the executive branch, its inability to halt what McNamara had termed the "mad momentum intrinsic to the development of all new nuclear weaponry," a phenomenon that the Nye Committee had identified three decades earlier as intrinsic to the development of any major weapon, such as a warship. That Nye was more nearly correct about the nature of arms production would start to become clear later in 1968, when the C-5A imbroglio first made news, for that giant aircraft was intended for use in conventional warfare and yet the impetus for its development was as irrational as for any nuclear device; and the same could be said about the F-111, the Main Battle Tank and the attack aircraft carrier, to name a few. Congress was moving into a mood of self-awareness and a mode of confrontation with the executive branch.

NEW ECONOMICS, OLD FEARS
AND MILITARY SPENDING

The 1968 vote against ABM was an audacious gesture, in keeping with the times perhaps, but seemingly in hopeless opposition to the tides of events that throughout the twentieth century had been carrying political power to the national executive from the legislature, especially in the area of national security. For Congress to question the wisdom of the military and to presume to exercise its own independent judgment about a new weapons system was anachronistic and against the weight of accepted authority.

Neo-Keynesian Presidential advisors had helped incorporate into federal policy the conventional wisdom that government spending, whether for military or civilian programs, conferred the same benefits on the economy. James Tobin, writing in 1958 and later to become a member of John F. Kennedy's Council of Economic Advisors (Arthur Schlesinger, Jr., referred to him in *A Thousand Days* as

"Kennedy's conscience"), chastised the Eisenhower administration for not spending enough on defense and pointed an accusing finger at Secretary Wilson for being so backward as to reduce the rate of Pentagon expenditures. In that year spending by the Department of Defense amounted to $40 billion, nearly one-half of total federal outlays. The year before it had been a billion dollars less. In 1954, however, it was $40.6 billion and, one supposes, according to the Pentagon's principle of perpetual expansion, by 1958 it should have been much greater. Tobin was incredulous: "At a time when the world situation cried out for accelerating and enlarging our defense effort, the administration *released* money, labor, scientific talent, materials, and plant capacity"[1] (emphasis in original). The basic question, Tobin went on, is whether the released resources are to be put to a higher use. Hardly, he concluded. Defense reductions would bring about unemployment, and the resources not expended would be frittered away "for research and development of new consumer luxuries, for new plants in which to produce more consumers' goods, old and new, all to be marketed by the most advanced techniques of mass persuasion to a people who already enjoy the highest and most frivolous standard of living in history." It was wasteful to divert funds that might support public programs, defense or nondefense, to private consumption, and this belief was held firmly by many liberal economists throughout much of the 1960s.

The more orthodox and conservative thinkers justified high-level defense expenditures on the simplistic grounds that the Reds would get us if we abandoned a wartime economy. In 1958, the same year that James Tobin railed against the Republican administration for not spending more on defense, the Committee for Economic Development, a nonprofit organization composed of corporation presidents and board chairmen and presidents of universities, railed against the idea that the military budget should be contained beneath any ceiling. It is timid to suggest, stated James F. Brownlee, a CED trustee and Chairman of the Subcommittee on Economic Policies for National Security, that defense expenditures might lead the country to economic stagnation or collapse, nor must we "hobble ourselves with the notion that there is some arbitrary limit on what we can spend for defense or a limit that we can exceed only

---

[1] B. H. Wilkins and C. B. Friday (eds), *The Economists of the New Frontier* (New York: Random House, 1963) p. 45.

with disastrous consequences."[2] There is very little risk, Brownlee said, that the American way of life would be ruined by a defense budget of 10 or 15 percent or a larger portion of the gross national product. "We live in a situation of constant danger. . . . *We can afford what we have to afford*" (emphasis in original).

This climate of opinion—a mixture of indiscriminate pump-priming theory, a de facto concession that the capitalist system requires an arms race to sustain economic growth, and fear of the Red Menace—prevailed until the late 1960s. Even the Friedmanite monetarists, devastating critics of government spending, shied away from the issue of defense outlays, minimized their magnitude and made comforting pronouncements about the ability to contain inflationary pressures through adjustments of the money supply. In Congress conservatives remonstrated for fiscal morality and a balanced budget, without bothering to explain how their double standard regarding civilian and military spending—austerity for one, indulgence for the other—served either. The guns-and-butter consensus of the Johnson administration, only mildly opposed on Capitol Hill and generally for the wrong reasons, was articulated by the President in his 1966 Budget Message ("We are a rich nation and can afford to make progress at home while meeting obligations abroad") and echoed by Secretary McNamara in his assurances to Congress that the enlarged defense program would not contribute to inflationary pressures. On one occasion, in 1967, Senator Symington asked McNamara how long the nation could afford to continue paying the gigantic costs incident to the war, and the Secretary replied,

I think forever, and I say it for this reason: that there are many things, many prices we pay for the war in South Vietnam, some very heavy prices indeed, but in my opinion one of them is not strain on our economy."[3]

2 Brownlee's statement, a summary of CED's "Statement on National Policy," is reported in Walter F. Hahn and John C. Neff (eds.), *American Strategy for the Nuclear Age* (Magnolia, Mass.: Peter Smith, 1960), pp. 398–405.

3 Ninetieth Congress, first session, Senate Committees on Armed Services and Appropriations, "Supplemental Military Procurement and Construction Authorizations" (1967), pp. 96–97. Afterward, as President of the World Bank, McNamara called for defense reductions and accused the major nations of "incurable folly" for spending annually 20 times more on military activities than the $7 billion devoted to foreign economic development assistance. *Wall Street Journal*, September 25, 1970.

THE MILITARY DEBATE OF 1969

With the attack against the ABM the dogmas of national security began to come under question, and by the spring of 1969 the opposition had grown to approximately half the members of the Senate. Several significant events had occurred in the intervening months since the 1968 effort. One was the disclosures concerning the C-5A. These revelations popularized the waste-and-inefficiency criticism of weapons programs, introduced the term "cost overrun" into everyone's vocabulary, cast doubts about the veracity of the testimony given by Pentagon officials to congressional committees, and created a widespread revulsion against this incompetently managed weapons-procurement program. For the first time a major weapons-system contract was examined in public hearings and shown to be a complete sham. As a practical matter, there was no contract in the common-law sense of an agreement imposing rights and duties on both parties. It was more in the nature of an informal arrangement to facilitate placing public funds and property into the hands of the contractors in return for which the contractors would deliver to the Air Force at some uncertain time in the future a number of aircraft of unspecified design and performance characteristics for an unknown price. Whether the planes would be delivered six months or a year late, or would perform in accordance with the original contract specifications, or would cost $2 billion or more above the agreed-upon price seemed matters of little consequence to the Air Force.

The case represents the ultimate corruption of government. The written agreement between the parties involves a *quid pro quo,* something for something, but the government's something constantly depreciates in value with the delivery delays and the degradation of performance standards, while the contractor's something appreciates with the cost increases and the amount of government capital he is able to obtain. The government not only agrees to a clause, the repricing formula, designed to abrogate whatever price commitment on the part of the contractors may have seemed apparent from the face of the agreement, it waives or chooses not to enforce its own rights, such as the right to require that the Federal Aviation Administration certify the quality and airworthiness of the plane and the right not to accept delivery of defective aircraft.

The concealment of facts from the Congress, false testimony, changing of internal cost reports, reprisals taken against an Air Force official for telling the truth, and the farcical nature of the contract all reflect the decay, if not the actual violation, of the law so far as the Pentagon is concerned. The government promotes lawlessness by rendering the law meaningless.

The C-5A revelations made the public and Congress more aware of the deficiencies of military contracting where the large contractors are concerned, and the lack of credibility of the military establishment. As the vulnerability of the Pentagon and its contractors to public criticism was made plain, the ranks of those determined to look into the business of acquiring new weapons, including ABM, grew more numerous and bold.

NATIONAL PRIORITIES

Another important development in 1969 was the rising concern in Congress with "national priorities." The cumulative effects of unsolved social and economic problems, unsatisfied demands by low income and minority groups for a share of the general affluence, and widespread resentment by the low and middle classes against tax increases and tax inequities drew attention to the federal budget and the way it was being used. It took no more than a cursory review of federal spending to see that the largest single outlay was made by the Department of Defense and that total national security expenditures literally dwarfed the rest of government spending. The massive waste in weapons procurement demonstrated by the C-5A and related investigations of the Proxmire Committee, the cancellation of the Manned Orbiting Laboratory program, the suspension of the Cheyenne Helicopter, and an outpouring of speeches in the House and Senate pointing to numerous earlier programs canceled after billions of dollars were spent gave needed substance to the long-standing criticism that the nation was misallocating its resources to areas of low priority and neglecting the problems of the people. What was new about this argument was that attention had finally focused on the military rathole in the federal budget.

In June of 1969 the Proxmire Committee shifted its attention from the narrow area of weapons contracts to the broader questions implicit in excessive defense spending and conducted hearings on

"The Military Budget and National Economic Priorities." Perhaps the most eloquent and pointed testimony of the many witnesses who appeared was given by Senator William Fulbright, who contrasted military with civilian expenditures as a measure of the government's relative priorities. The budget, he stated, reflects the sense of values of the dominant political leadership, and a reading of it tells us whether America is modeling itself after ancient Sparta, a city dedicated to the arts of war, or Athens, which at one time at least was democratic and peaceful; whether we place a greater value on trying to mold foreign societies than on eliminating the inequities of our own society. What, Fulbright asked, does the defense budget mean in terms of dividing up the national pie? One could scarcely improve on his own reply:

It means that, outside of trust fund spending, about 55 cents out of every dollar the Federal Government spends goes to the military.

It means that 70 cents of every dollar from general revenue will go for paying the cost of wars—past, present, and future.

It means that over $400 per capita will be spent on the military—an increase of 60 percent in each citizen's bill for the military over the last 5 years.

He then compared the $80 billion defense budget with what is left to take care of civilian needs:

Education is an example of such a need. Schools from kindergarten to graduate school are overcrowded and underfinanced. Nine billion dollars is authorized for the various programs of the Office of Education in the next fiscal year. Only about one-third the amount authorized, $3.2 billion, is included in the budget.

Less is proposed for elementary and secondary education than it costs to assemble an attack carrier task force; we have 15 such carriers.

More is budgeted for chemical and biological weapons than is to be spent for vocational education.

More will be spent on the ABM, taking the military estimate at face value, than will be invested in higher education.

The unhappy comparisons, of course, could go on almost indefinitely. To Fulbright only one conclusion was possible. The disparity in spending between military and civilian programs was an accurate reflection of the distribution of power among the Washington bureaucracies, not of the real desires of the people: "Our system of priorities is cockeyed." This thought occurred to more than one member of Congress, although some were quick to point out that simply transferring funds out of the military into the civilian budget was no guarantee that civilian needs would be better served, in view of the disappointing experience with federally assisted civilian programs such as highways, urban renewal and welfare.

THE ANTI-ABM MOVEMENT

When the ABM debate resumed in the Senate over the 1969 request for funds (three-quarters of a billion dollars), the opponents had the advantage of an unprecedented hostile public reaction to the new weapons system. President Johnson's ABM plan, named Sentinel, called for the system to be deployed around metropolitan centers for the protection of those populations. When the Army began site construction in a number of communities, citizens in Boston, Chicago, Los Angeles and Seattle angrily protested the dubious distinction of becoming neighbors to deadly antimissile missiles. The citizens, joined by an impressive array of scientists, scholars and former government officials, including many from the State and Defense Departments, who intensified the skepticism that already existed about the technical performance of the weapon and its impact on the nuclear arms race, formed a grass-roots lobby against the ABM that defied the bugaboo of Cold War anti-communism and the taboo of military planning.

The public opposition and private doubts of senators about the wisdom of going forward with a new multibillion-dollar weapons system resulted in an unusually mixed reaction to administration witnesses appearing before the normally friendly Armed Services Committee, which in late June approved the program by the slim margin of 10–7. Voting against were Democrats Stuart Symington, Daniel Inouye, Howard W. Cannon and Stephen M. Young, and Republicans Margaret Chase Smith, Edward W. Brooke and Richard Schweiker (who had beaten Clark for his Senate seat).

THE RESOR-STARBIRD MEMOS

The military's performance on ABM in the preceding months had been particularly inept. In February, for example, two damaging Army memoranda leaked out of the Pentagon and were reported in the press. Written by Army Secretary Stanley R. Resor and General Alfred D. Starbird, manager of the ABM, they had been forwarded several months earlier in classified form to Defense Secretary Clark Clifford as a proposed massive public relations campaign in behalf of the beleaguered project. The plan was to counteract the arguments made by those notable scientists who had spoken out against ABM, including Hans Bethe, George Kistiakowsky and Jerome Weisner, by encouraging other nongovernment scientists to answer publicly the questions that had been raised. The Army, according to Resor, would contact scientists familiar with the program "and who may see fit to write articles for publication supporting the technical feasibility and operational effectiveness of the Sentinel system." To those scientists the Army would extend "all practical assistance." Starbird's memorandum included an instruction for personnel affiliated with the ABM public affairs program to "cooperate and coordinate with *industry* on public relations efforts by *industries* involved in the Sentinel program" (emphasis added).

In addition, the Army would undertake a much broader effort to win political support for the program by arranging, among other things, visits and classified briefings from high-level officials to members of Congress, meetings with local officials in areas where citizen protests had developed, calls to editors and publishers in the cities where there had been difficulties as well as all others scheduled for Sentinel sites, a traveling sideshow of taped commentary, visual aids and mockups to show how ABM would work, and an information packet to be mailed to interested persons. The Resor-Starbird plan became the basis for Army regulations setting up guidelines for the flow of information on ABM in order to "gain public understanding of the necessity of a Communist Chinese-oriented antiballistic missile (ABM) system," and to "establish a favorable public attitude toward the locating of Sentinel system facilities in or near civilian communities and industrial complexes." At a press conference shortly after these matters were reported, Secretary Laird conceded the facts but denied that the Pentagon was spending large amounts of money for pro-ABM propaganda.

Nevertheless, the Army's public information tactics can hardly be interpreted in any way other than a covert effort to propagandize the American people into accepting ABM. What was particularly disconcerting about the episode, aside from the unanswered ques-

tion as how much the propaganda was costing, was the stealth of
the Army's movements and the complicity of the contractors. The
Resor-Starbird memoranda would have been kept secret were it not
for the leak. Apparently even the Army regulations on the subject
were to be hidden from public view had not inquiries to the Pentagon brought about their release. The Army planned secretly to
inspire and assist in the preparation of scientific articles for magazines and technical journals, and it is likely that some were published in this manner. What was meant by the instruction for military personnel to "cooperate and coordinate with industry on public
relations efforts by industries involved" in ABM is a little more
difficult to understand. Was the Army to write advertising copy for
the ABM contractors, or vice versa?

Paraphrasing the words of James Tobin, who feared the public's
susceptibility to Madison Avenue—type merchandising of consumers'
luxuries, ABM would be marketed by the most advanced techniques
of mass persuasion to a people who already enjoyed the highest and
most frivolous defense budget in history. Within a few months a
new organization, calling itself the Citizens' Committee for Peace
with Security, placed a series of full-page advertisements in leading
newspapers hawking the attributes of ABM. Of the 355 signers of
the ad, 64 were directors of or employed by ABM contractors and
subcontractors, and at least one had high military connections,
retired Army General Lucius Clay, who was the chairman of the
Republican National Finance Committee at the time. Another
organization, the American Security Council, also bought newspaper space and radio time to plug the ABM. One of the signers of
its newspaper ads was Robert W. Galvin, Chairman of the Board
of Motorola, Inc., supplier of electronic components for the ABM.
The disclosure of the Resor-Starbird memoranda raised serious
doubts about the legitimacy of published articles favoring it and
focused attention on the fact that those who stood to gain from
the program were most active in its behalf and that contractors were
being encouraged by the Army to use their marketing resources to
promote it.

PACKARD, PANOFSKY AND FULBRIGHT

Another example of the Pentagon's fumbling attempt to manipu-
late the facts relating to the ABM occurred when Deputy Secretary

of Defense David Packard, testifying in March before the Senate Foreign Relations Committee, asserted that Wolfgang Panofsky of Stanford University was one of the independent scientists consulted by the Defense Department when it was deliberating over whether to go ahead with the program. Panofsky (formerly of the Institute for Defense Analysis), it so happened, was present and quickly stated that his consultantship consisted only of a chance meeting with Packard at the San Francisco airport at which time the subject was briefly discussed. He asked permission to straighten out the record and, when he testified a few days afterwards, strongly opposed deployment.

Further, Packard was sharply criticized in May by Fulbright, Albert Gore and other senators for permitting site acquisition and procurement for ABM to proceed contrary to Packard's assurances in the March hearings that work would not begin until Congress gave its permission. President Nixon by the time of Packard's testimony had announced his own modified plan for ABM, now called Safeguard. The senators took the position during the hearings that a new authorization by Congress would be necessary before the Army could deploy the system, in view of the Nixon changes, and Packard agreed. The following exchange occurred with Packard:

SENATOR FULBRIGHT: . . . I hope you are not proceeding on the theory that because the Congress has already approved the former Sentinel system that you are entitled to go ahead with the new one as if we were committed. I do not consider that we are. I hope we are not.
MR. PACKARD: I do not, Senator Fulbright.
SENATOR FULBRIGHT: Good.
MR. PACKARD: We are recommending a new funding schedule.
SENATOR FULBRIGHT: Good.
MR. PACKARD: In this funding schedule in the fiscal year 1970 budget, it will be necessary for us to proceed in such a way that the Congress will have ample opportunity to look at the whole program.
SENATOR FULBRIGHT: Good. The program you are talking about must now await the authorization; is that right?
MR. PACKARD: Yes.
SENATOR GORE: So, unless the Congress approves, this will not proceed.
MR. PACKARD: I do not see how it can be any other way.[4]

4 Ninety-first Congress, first session, Committee on Foreign Relations, U.S. Senate, "Hearings on Strategic and Foreign Policy Implications of ABM Systems," Part 1, pp. 221–92. Panofsky's testimony begins on p. 326.

A few weeks later Packard admitted that procurement of ABM components was in progress despite the fact that Congress had not yet authorized the Safeguard version. Packard stated on May 13, 1969: "Part of the work which has been done under the authorized Sentinel program has been to start construction and manufacture of missile components which will go into an actually deployed system."

Packard and the Pentagon were caught in a clear contradiction with the earlier testimony. As Fulbright acidly commented, Packard's later statement ran "directly contrary to the understanding of all of us at that time." The Pentagon lamely explained that missiles were being purchased for research, not to be deployed on sites until Congress approved Safeguard.

COOPER-HART

Given these facts—the C-5A overruns and other weapons mishaps, the concern over misplaced priorities in the federal budget, the popular outrage against the ABM and the general dissatisfaction with the war and the military establishment——one might have expected the 1969 vote on the ABM itself to turn on the more significant issues involved, namely, whether building the system was a reasonable way to strengthen national security and whether it would be worth the costs in terms of its probable effectiveness and the alternative uses to which the ABM funds could be put. Unfortunately Congress, like the Supreme Court, often manages to sidestep or postpone taking up the most controversial political issues, and ABM was no exception. The thrust of the opposition in the congressional debates and hearings as well as the numerous studies prepared for the members of Congress by outside experts once again emphasized the technical problems of doing what the ABM is supposed to do and the arms race consequences of deployment, and once again the argument was made that there were so many unanswered questions and doubts about the program that it needed to be slowed down and reexamined. The issue pressed by most of the opponents in 1969 as in 1968 was whether to delay deployment for a year to allow for further research and development, rather than whether to cancel it altogether.

The Cooper-Hart amendment again proposed that only the funds for research and development be approved and that construction of sites, production of missiles and deployment be postponed for a year. It was on this proposal that the debate raged, until the day on which the vote was scheduled to take place, when Senator Margaret Chase Smith dismayed almost everyone by offering her amendment to delete *all* Safeguard funds. If, she argued, the program was as technically deficient and likely to heat up the arms race as the critics maintained, then why spend the hundreds of millions contemplated even under the Cooper-Hart approach? "Why waste funds on research and development of a system in which you have no confidence?" Safeguard, she said, "is too vulnerable and too costly and would be a waste of resources at a time when we must carefully determine our national priorities."

Only 11 senators voted for the Smith amendent, while Cooper-Hart was barely defeated, 51–49. The difference in the two votes was a good measure of the difficulty of stopping any individual major weapons system. The fact is that even had Cooper-Hart won, Safeguard would have received most of the money requested for it by the administration, and although it would have disappointed the military establishment not to have gotten all it asked for, it would have been in a good position to come back for the rest in the following year, considering the resources at its disposal. Over $5 billion had been spent on ABM prior to 1969 and, short of a demonstrable failure, such as the crash of the Cheyenne Helicopter that brought about its cancellation, or a decision on the part of the executive to terminate a program, such as Kennedy's decision to discontinue the B-70 bomber and Nixon's decision to discontinue the MOL, the overwhelming tendency is for programs once funded to stay funded. As for the constraint on deployment that Cooper-Hart would have imposed, the Army had already demonstrated how far it could go under the guise of research and development in the Fulbright-Packard affair a few weeks earlier. The best that could be said, then, is that when the Senate critics of military spending obliquely confronted the ABM in 1969, they almost succeeded in temporarily setting it back. When they challenged the program directly with the Smith amendment, they got clobbered.

On the other hand, the ABM clash succeeded in providing a rallying point for large segments of the public, the scientific and academic communities, ex-officialdom and Congress against a weapons system that promised to diminish rather than enhance national security. It gave many persons inside and outside of Congress their first lessons in defense analysis, and they found the discipline accessible to ordinary reason and reading skills. The closeness of the Cooper-Hart vote was interpreted as a moral victory against the military juggernaut, and with the confidence that moral victories bring and the discovery that reducing defense spending was a popular political issue, the Senate critics were encouraged to continue their efforts against the military authorization act, of which ABM was just a part.

Much of the remainder of the legislative year was taken up with debates over a succession of amendments directed against military spending, first in the Senate and later in the House. The proposals varied from attempts to delete part of the funding for specific weapons programs, such as the C-5A and the Main Battle Tank, to studies to be made by the General Accounting Office, to new legal requirements having the effect of tightening military spending practices. There were some minor successes and some major defeats. In general all the amendments to delete funds for major weapons systems failed. Proposals for studies and changes in the law not affecting the dollar amount of the authorization bill succeeded. A few minor spending cuts were accomplished, Fulbright's amendment to remove $45 million from the Pentagon's social science and foreign policy grant program being one. In the end Congress authorized approximately the amount of funds recommended by the Armed Services Committee.

MILITARY SPENDING IN THE 1970s

Only a modicum of hope was offered in 1969 to those concerned with the runaway military budget and the growth of the defense industry. The pressures generated in Congress forced the executive to reduce its military budget requests, to terminate or cut back a few weapons programs and to announce plans for reducing military manpower. Congress itself, while it did not materially alter the authorization or appropriation bills once they came out of committee, did sharply reduce both the authorizations and, more importantly, the appropriations in committee. The Stennis Committee, for example, reduced the research and development authorization by a billion dollars. In the House the Appropriations Committee, headed by George Mahon, recommended an appropriation $5.3 billion below the amount requested by Nixon and $4.4 billion below the amount actually appropriated the year before. The appropriation finally enacted was $5.6 billion below Nixon's request and was the first to decline from the previous year since the post-Korean War year of 1954. The Mahon Committee also served notice that military requests would be more closely scrutinized by it in the future. The year 1969, it stated in its report, was the year of the cost overrun: "No single year stands out in which inordinate escalations in costs for defense weapons systems developments and procurements have been surfaced to the extent they have been this year in the hearings." And it debunked the Pentagon's usual excuse for cost overruns, inflation, finding that it accounted for only 11.4 percent of the total increases identified. "It can be said that cost overruns in fact have contributed to inflation."

But the defense budget was hardly rolled back in 1969, an unlikely feat to have expected after so lengthy a military buildup. It would be more accurate to say that it leveled out in that year. Whether it would be reduced or increased in the early 1970s was yet to be determined. The lag between appropriations actions and spending actions made it difficult to judge what the effects of the appropriations reductions would be. Congress, of course, appropriates funds, while the executive does the spending. On some items, especially procurement of weapons, there is a sizable time gap between congressional appropriation and Pentagon spending, so that a substantial delay can be anticipated before any congressional action is translated into a spending cut. Thus defense spending for fiscal year 1969 (which ended June 30, 1969) actually *increased* slightly over 1968, and actual military outlays by the Department of Defense for fiscal year 1970 were only about 1 percent below fiscal year 1969.*

The noticeable reluctance on the part of Congress and the executive to stop the existing major weapons programs and to withhold approval of the newly proposed ones was a cause of deep concern for the long-range prospects of reducing military expenditures. With the costs of individual weapons systems rising, there could be no substantial permanent reductions in the overall budget unless the number of systems or the number of units per system were reduced. There was no evidence in 1969 that either was likely. The go-ahead signal was given to two new fighter aircraft, a new supersonic bomber, a

---

* Military outlays for the Pentagon were $77.4 billion in 1968, $77.9 billion in 1969, and $77.1 billion in 1970 (fiscal years). In real terms, however, taking inflation into account, the figures indicate a somewhat larger reduction than at first appears.

new tank, several new missiles and torpedoes, a new antisubmarine aircraft, the landing helicopter assault ship (LHA), Minuteman III (with MIRV), ABM, and a new bomber defense system (AWACS). These programs were carried forward into 1970 with what Representative William S. Moorhead termed a "Camel's Nose Budget." Moorhead estimated that the costs of six weapons programs for which $2.2 billion was being requested (the Camel's Nose) would end up costing from $136 to $152 billion (Nose, Humps and all) (see Table 7). Almost all of the older programs, including the F-111,

TABLE 7.   Estimated Costs of Selected Weapons

Weapons System	The 1971 Camel's Nose Budget	Estimated Total Systems Cost or Nose, Humps and all
F-14 (Navy Fighter)	$938 million	$ 26–36 billion
F-15 (Air Force Fighter)	370 million	25 billion
AMSA (or B1A) (Advanced Manned Strategic Aircraft)	100 million	15–20 billion
ABM (Antiballistic Missile)	600 million	50 billion
AWACS (Air Warning Control System)	87 million	15 billion
CVAN-70 (Third Nuclear-Attack Carrier)	152 million	5–6 billion
	$ 2.2 billion	$136–152 billion

Poseidon, the destroyer program, and the nuclear-powered guided-missile frigates, were continued at more or less their same levels. The single exception was the C-5A, whose numbers were cut back from 120 to 81, but in 1970 the Air Force and Lockheed began hinting at possible new uses for the C-5A, such as a tanker, a bed for an airborne Minuteman, and a nuclear-powered plane, one of the Air Force's old dreams; and a subcommittee of the House Armed Services Committee issued a report recommending an increase in the number of C-5As to be purchased. In 1970 it also became known that the costs of Safeguard ABM had been seriously understated. The official estimate for building the 12 sites contemplated in Phase I and Phase II was increased from $9.1 billion to $10.7 billion. The Pentagon attributed the increase to inflation, a stretchout of deployment, design changes and "more detailed estimates for the work earlier contemplated." Not included in the $10.7 billion figure were operating costs estimated at $350 million per year, Atomic Energy Commission costs related to ABM estimated at $1.2 billion, and the cost of warheads, range support, and integration of the system, none of which had yet been estimated. In addition, the Army had been spending about $100 million per year on hardsite defense of the ABM Sprint missiles, but not including those costs as part of the ABM. Estimates for the hardsite defense program ranged from $5 billion to $10 billion. Just over the horizon, funded at levels so low (a few million dollars each) they did not merit enumeration in the budget requests or the appropriation bills, were proposals for a laser-beam ABM to replace Safeguard, an undersea long-range missile system to replace Poseidon, a mobile Minuteman to replace those in silos, and something that General William C. Westmoreland called the "automated battlefield," on which $2 billion had been spent by the end of 1969 by hiding funds in numerous projects, some of whose titles were classified.[5]

Viewed in this light the defense-spending plateau established in 1969 and 1970 could be seen as a launching pad a few years hence for a renewed series of military spending takeoffs. For, despite the appropriation actions, the cuts announced with great fanfare by Secretary of Defense Melvin Laird and the probability of a dip in outlays in the early 1970s, the weapons programs continued to carry the bulk of the defense budget forward, and there was great confidence within the Pentagon and in the defense industry that the congressional demands for reductions would soon subside. In 1970 spokesmen for the military establishment began speaking openly of new gaps into which our national security was falling. John S. Foster, Director of Defense Research and Engineering, voiced concern "because this country is in danger of losing its technological superiority," and the *Air Force/Space Digest* (January 1970) described the optimism shared within the aerospace industry and made a prediction: "There will be an equipment gap—Defense Sec-

[5] See "The Pentagon Plays Electronic War Games," *Business Week*, January 31, 1970.

retary Melvin R. Laird says our capabilities will be reduced and defenses weakened—and the gap will persist until it is filled by production lines." The defense industry, having suffered through temporary budget squeezes before, kept a knowing eye on the reality of market trends. For example, an article in *Electronic News'* annual "Guidelines to Government Electronics" edition of February 1970 advised "companies willing to invest money necessary to keep their technology sharp while riding out Defense Department decision delays, however, may reap big profits beginning in the mid-70s." Any effort to contain military spending would be doomed to failure without a direct confrontation with the question of whether the Pentagon and its industrial allies were to be given the right to commit the nation to every weapons system that could be conceived and produced, regardless of its cost and real contribution to national security.

Chapter Eight

CONCLUSIONS

THE FAILURE OF THE CONTRACT SYSTEM

Our knowledge of defense profits is not complete, but it is considerable, based on investigations of individual contracts, such as McClellan's "Pyramiding of Profits and Costs," and the M-16 hearings, select studies of certain aspects of the problem and the testimony of individuals such as Admiral Rickover with experience in military contracting.

We know, for example, that in modern corporate practice the concept of "profit" has been expanded to take into account benefits that do not show up on the profit-and-loss statement—such as the opportunity to maintain "standby pools" of technical employees, the use of government equipment on commercial production, the benefit of interest-free funds supplied by the government, the transference to nondefense business activities of technical know-how gained in military research and development programs, and government reimbursement for a share of general and administrative expenses and overhead.

The average citizen, hampered by textbook ideas of how capitalism works, might think it strange that business can be so wasteful and inefficient, yet so profitable. Why, he might ask, would defense contractors want to be inefficient in the first place, and if they are, why isn't something done about it? Those are normal questions which do not apply in the abnormal world of defense production.

The real question is, Why should a defense contractor be efficient? Efficiency does not come naturally to any business establishment. It requires managerial skills, foresight and constant effort to coordinate a firm's resources so that it might produce a high-quality product at the lowest possible cost. It is not easy to acquire and retain a highly trained work force properly motivated to put forth their best effort. A mistaken judgment can lead to disaster in the marketplace. A product priced too high might not sell. An inferior product might not be able to compete. When an ordinary businessman miscalculates his costs or the volume of sales, he must be able either to absorb his losses, to borrow against future profits or to go out of business. The reason most businessmen are efficient is because they cannot afford not to be.

If you are a giant corporation, like General Motors or General Electric, or a conglomerate of a number of acquired corporations, like Litton or LTV, you may be able to control many of the variables associated with a market economy—for example, through the administered-price technique. If, in addition, you deal with the Defense Department, the economic uncertainties of doing business are virtually eliminated, and what remains is the political problem of wheeling and dealing within the informal polity, perfecting the art of brochuremanship so that proposals for new weapons will be received in the best possible light, and knowing and being able to influence the right decisionmakers. The only efficiency really necessary is in the sales department, not in production. That is why the rainmaker is so important in the tribal life of the defense community. The most important employees to a large contractor are the rainmakers, the ones who prepare and present proposals—and win contracts—for new weapons systems. The next most important employees are the ones who negotiate with the Pentagon's contract negotiators over the terms of the contract. Once the contract is signed, the first team, the rainmakers and the negotiators, moves on to another contract.

Defense production is a secondary problem. After the contract is signed, there is really no reason to cut costs, prevent waste or be efficient. The higher the costs, the higher the profits, both direct and indirect. Whatever the costs, the Pentagon will pay. Whatever the difficulties, the military will come to the rescue—with more money. If the delivery schedule can't be easily met, it will be extended. And if, when the product is ready for delivery, it does not perform in quite the way the contract requires it to perform, it will be accepted as is. If necessary, the performance standards in the contract will be degraded so that technically the contractor has fully complied.

The Pentagon's response to poor performance reinforces the contractor's behavior. The formal apparatus of government controls and government regulations turns out to be like a piece of modern electronic sculpture that whirrs, blinks and emits the noise of a half-tuned-in radio, but has no function to perform. The contractor is unimpressed, except for the mountains of paperwork he is required to do to give the appearance of complying with the rules, for the costs of which he is reimbursed anyway. The Armed Services Procurement Regulations in the final analysis are a massive collection of requirements and restrictions useful mainly for harassing the small contractor who can't even afford to hire a lawyer to read them. As far as the large contractor is concerned, he is a member of one or several of the business-advisory groups, and if he does not like a particular requirement, he can more than likely change it or make sure it is not enforced. To him the gears in government machinery have no teeth, except for those which grind within the federal mint.

As for the Joint Chiefs of Staff, the military leaders, their objective is to modernize and expand their arsenal as rapidly as possible. They are not really interested in the costs, which are considered merely the bookkeeper's problem. They are interested in getting new weapons. If they do not have the funds at hand to buy everything they would like to buy—and they never do, because their wants are unlimited—they expect the public to provide them through Congress without question or complaint. They are more or less convinced that the defense industry can produce whatever they need if given enough time and money. Their devotion to the contract system is based on the wonders of science and technology and the accomplishments of industry, buttressed by the fact that many former fellow officers work for the major contractors. Their attitude toward the contractor is therefore one of generosity, liberality and camaraderie. The contractor is a member of the defense-industry "team." It does not seem to concern the military that its teammate might be throwing the game by selling it things it does not need and that do not contribute to national defense, or that his performance in the manufacture of weapons systems is incredibly bad. Some military leaders believe that some waste and inefficiency is good, that it is necessary to support the "industrial base" of defense so that it will be available when needed for all-out war. In this sense industrial inefficiency is a national policy.

The military bureaucrat who manages weapons programs, like his counterpart in industry, has a heavy hand on the decision-making process and occupies a monopoly or near-monopoly position. He controls the use of enormous public resources with little, if any, public accountability and helps shape the budget from which he derives the excess profits of a bureaucratic empire. His efforts on his own behalf more than likely also serve the interests of the contractors with whom he does business, and the effect is to create opportunities for obtaining a job in the defense industry that might later become a stepping stone to a more powerful position in the bureaucracy.

Given this relationship and the belief in the infallibility of the large contractor, it is perhaps natural for the Pentagon to consider private criticism of the defense industry blasphemy and public criticism of any weapons program sinful. The worst transgressors are those within—the employees of the defense establishment, military or civilian. It may be pardonable to argue about problems within the confines of the establishment so long as one does not insist that they be solved. What is unpardonable is to try to *do* something about inefficiency or any other shortcoming of the system.

This is a terrible problem for some honest people who take their responsibilities seriously. If your job is to eliminate wasteful practices from weapons programs and your superiors in the Defense Department refuse to do anything to correct the problems that have been uncovered, do you bite your tongue and look the other way or speak out and risk the loss of your job? This was the dilemma of A. E. Fitzgerald, who did not agree with his military superiors that defense contracts ought to be considered a kind of WPA for the power élite and who realized that the Air Force was going to allow the public to be taken for a $2 billion ride on the C-5A cargo-plane program. If you are a career military officer in charge of the purchase and installation of highly complex and costly components of nuclear submarines and you know the contractors are using their oligopolistic position unnecessarily to hike costs and profits with the blessing—sometimes the encouragement—of your superiors, do you play the part of the "good" German or protest? This has been Admiral Rickover's dilemma. Only because of his status and unique relations with Congress has he been able to do his job conscientiously and not get transferred to Addis Ababa or fired, although he is subjected to constant criticism and backbiting by the Navy hierarchy.

The point has been made by Admiral Rickover that any military person can speak out, provided he is prepared to be transferred the next day to a station distant from Washington. The humiliation of General Meyer during the LOH incident underlines the point, as do the actions taken against countless others whose stories will never be told. The reprisals take many forms, from lost promotions to lost contracts, depending upon whether you are an employee or a small contractor. The discovery that Pratt and Whitney was 50 percent inefficient in the production of the F-111 engines was first made by a small consultant firm, the Performance Technology Corporation, which had been hired by the Pentagon to look into the program. Unfortunately for it, the company looked too far and found too much. The defense establishment did not like what it found and proceeded to drive it out of business by blacklisting it so that contracts were no longer available for consulting work from the government or industry, even though its efforts in the Pratt and Whitney case resulted in substantial savings to the government.

This ruthlessness toward the wavemakers is matched only by the military's timidity toward its large contractors. In contrast to the Pentagon's vicious treatment of anyone who gets out of line by insisting on doing his duty is its cringing, scraping and bowing before the defense industrialists. The Army, which humiliates its own at the drop of a contractor's hat, wears AT&T's nose ring.

The defense establishment's usual response to exposure of cases that illustrate defects in the contract system is to label them "horror stories." No system is perfect, it is maintained, and the Defense Department will admit to its faults; on the whole its record is a good one despite the isolated mistakes that can be located, they say. The point, though, which I hope has been made by this book is that literally every major weapons system is a "horror story." The troika of contract troubles—cost overruns, late delivery, poor technical performance—is so pervasive that it would take an indefatigable researcher to locate even one program free of them.

The issue is not whether we should have a defense program. The issue is whether the present contract system serves the public interest in a defense program. For the sake of preserving "the industrial base" the Defense Department has abdicated much of its responsibility and authority in the weapons acquisition process.

What the Pentagon means by "the industrial base" that must be preserved at almost any expense is the elite group of giant contractors who are deemed to have the unique capabilities of producing advanced weapons systems. This industrial base is maintained, first, by seeing to it that each major contractor gets a turn at the trough. Contracts are carefully rotated so that no one is left without a big one for too long.

Second, the industrial base is preserved by protecting contractors against "catastrophic losses," that is, by not allowing them to lose a great deal of money on any contract. But if you cannot do anything to cause the large contractor to lose money for fear that he will go bankrupt and erode the industrial base, what kind of corrective measures are possible when his performance is lousy, which it almost always is? If, in other words, it is not feasible to take punitive action against the contractor who is part of the industrial base, what good is the contract and what good is the contract system? When one party to a contract gives up the right to enforce it against the other, there is no contract. There is only a one-way commitment to do what the other side wants. It is a form of unilateral disarmament.

The situation is much more serious than when, as James B. Conant said, the Defense Department sprang onto the horse of military technology and rode madly off in all directions. Today any major weapons system is a multibillion-dollar affair. The economic and political power wrapped up in such projects cannot be overestimated. The defense contract is a cascade of money that circulates throughout communities, universities, states and regions, creating tens of thousands of jobs and instant voting blocs. The corporate manager, the military officer and the politician whose interests depend on the stream will do whatever they can to prevent it from drying up.

The two imperatives in the weapons business are: Get the contract and get the funds. Providing those funds is the burden imposed upon all of society whose support and tacit consent make possible the diversion of public resources into the military budget.

The weapon, once built at the cost of billions, must be operated and maintained at the cost of additional billions, while its replacement is already in some stage of development and testing. Before one generation of weapons is worn out, another supplants it. They get more complex, more "effective," more costly and more numerous. At the same time, we seem to get less security.

Just how close the contract system is to total collapse became clearer in 1970 when the Pentagon made public a request from Lockheed for about $640 million for "interim financing" on four of its major programs: the C-5A, the Cheyenne Helicopter, the SRAM missile (for which it is a major subcontractor to Boeing), and various shipbuilding projects. On each of the four programs Lockheed had filed large claims or was involved in contractual disputes with the government. According to the contractor the dollar magnitude of the disputes was so great that it could not afford to await administrative review and resolution. An immediate infusion of money was required to assure continued performance on the programs. In other words, Lockheed would go out of business or shut down production on the four major weapons systems if the government did not pay it the $640 million. As Rep. William S. Moorhead put it, Lockheed was threatening the government with corporate suicide: "This is like an 80-ton dinosaur who comes to your door and says, 'If you don't feed me I will die and what are you going to do with 80 tons of dead stinking dinosaur in your yard?' "[1]

Although Lockheed's request hardly told the whole story, a tremor was sent through the Pentagon, much of the rest of the government and the entire aerospace industry. Lockheed emphasized its financial difficulties and blamed them on the ill-conceived total package type of contract and what D. J. Haughton, Chairman of the Board, termed "a breakdown in the procurement process." But it was no secret that Lockheed had experienced severe technical failures on many of its programs. The Cheyenne helicopter had been canceled by the Army largely because of difficulties with the rotor mechanism and the C-5A had wing cracks and radar problems, to name two examples. And most, if not all, of Lockheed's major programs, other than the four specified as the source of its cash shortage, were also in trouble. Even the S-3A antisubmarine warfare aircraft contract, awarded to Lockheed in 1969, already appeared to be about $100 million overrun. One question raised was whether $640 million would be enough to bail Lockheed out of its financial crisis for more than a few months (Lockheed later increased its demand to $1 billion).

[1] Peter D. H. Stockton, "Lockheed Threatens to Die," *The Nation*, April 6, 1970.

A second question was whether the Lockheed syndrome could be kept from spreading. Within a few days of the Pentagon's release of Lockheed's appeal the Air Force was flooded in a sea of tears from other contractors, said by the *Armed Forces Journal* to number over 400, seeking the same treatment; and several other large contractors were getting set to file claims of their own, a technique perfected by the shipbuilding industry. The Pentagon's inclination was to grant Lockheed relief either by making a lump sum settlement of the claims, guaranteeing a loan on the contractor's behalf, or both, or other administrative and contractual contrivances.[2] One suggestion was to transform Lockheed's fixed price contracts into cost-plus arrangements, a step that would confirm what many had long suspected, that all negotiated contracts with the large military contractors were *de facto* cost-plus, that "fixed" price contracting was a myth. Indeed, anything done for Lockheed which had the effect of bailing it out of its contractual commitments to produce and deliver the aircraft, missiles, and other weapons for the prices agreed upon would reinforce that suspicion. It would also tell the rest of the industry not to take its contracts too seriously. The line behind Lockheed would extend clear around the Pentagon.

A different kind of solution would be for the government to behave as if there really were a free enterprise system, to insist on adherence to the contractual commitments. Enforcement of the government's rights under the contracts would require Lockheed to perform or go into default. If it could not perform, the government's recourse would be to terminate the agreements and collect damages. The programs could then be transferred to Lockheed's competitors or if Lockheed went bankrupt a receiver could be appointed to operate the business until all claims were settled. An alternative possibility would be for the government to take over the company to make sure the weapons programs entrusted to it were completed, while the disputes were being resolved. If Lockheed had to go out of business it would be doing what thousands of small firms in the

2 The "solutions" were outlined by Deputy Secretary of Defense David Packard in testimony before the House and Senate Armed Services Committees, March 9 and 10, 1970. At the same time Senator Proxmire asked the GAO to investigate Lockheed's financial condition and began a campaign to prevent the Pentagon from acting unilaterally in the matter, insisting that the issues should be decided by Congress. See speeches by Senator Proxmire, Ninety-first Congress, Second Session, *Congressional Record*, March 10, 1970, pp. S 3307–08; March 16, 1970, pp. S 3763–66; and March 31, 1970, pp. S 4690–97.

commercial world are forced to do each year. In the marketplace the prospect of going broke is supposed to weed out the inefficient from the efficient. What was troubling the Pentagon, however, was the likelihood that many other large contractors could be forced up against the same wall and then where would the contract system be? On one point there was widespread agreement: the procurement processes had broken down.

The contract system has failed. Only the self-serving interests of its operators and the vested interests of its beneficiaries preserve its momentum and give it the semblance of viability. The billions of dollars it wastes could be more wisely used. Many of the weapons it rings around us we could well do without. The sooner it is replaced, the better.

WEIDENBAUM AND DISENGAGEMENT

There are several ways of altering the present arrangement. One, advocated by Murray Weidenbaum, would be to preserve the contract system while restoring the traditional relationship of government and industry—to disengage the defense industry from government.[3] Weidenbaum's point is that the convergence of the military and the defense industry is leading to the "arsenalization" of the private sector and that industry would be better off in the long run to forgo some of the advantages of military subsidies in order to shake loose from the red tape and interference with the prerogatives of management. Disengagement would mean less government support and fewer government requirements. Government-owned equipment and government financing through progress payments would be withdrawn, but contractors would be able to charge the government for interest costs on money borrowed to carry out their contracts.

Competition under Weidenbaum's plan would be encouraged by the awarding of separate contracts on a competitive basis for the research and development, production and follow-on phases of weapons programs, rather than lumping together the research and development with the production in a negotiated contract and then awarding the follow-on contract to the same company. Lock-ins and other monopoly situations would be avoided by making parallel

[3] See Weidenbaum's testimony before the Proxmire Committee, Ninetieth Congress, second session, "Joint Economic Committee, Hearings on Economics of Military Procurement," Part 1, pp. 63–70.

awards and developing second sources. That is, contracts for a single weapons system would be awarded to two or several firms in the early stages of the program, before the government settles on a single contract for the major production work. This might be especially useful in aircraft and missile programs where it would be feasible for the government to pay for several prototypes that could then be tested before deciding on a final version. The government could also preserve the possibility for second sources by reserving to itself the right to distribute designs and production techniques developed by a contractor to any other potential contractors during the life of the contract.

The competitive base would be broadened by encouraging commercially oriented companies to diversify by doing some military work and by encouraging the defense-oriented companies to diversify into commercial markets. During the life of a program subsystems would be broken out for competition. It is already common for some subsystems, such as engines in aircraft programs, to be supplied by a contractor other than the one supplying the airframe. This principle can be extended by breaking out smaller subsystems for separate contracts. Participation in subcontracts would also be widened so that small contractors would have a greater opportunity to get work. Presently much subcontracting is done by companies that are prime contractors on other programs.

Weidenbaum's hope is that forcing contractors to fall back on their own resources through the restoration of competition will help bring about a reconstitution of the self-regulating mechanism of free enterprise, which according to the theory of capitalism is the best guarantor of innovation, efficiency and lower costs. Extensive government regulation would thus be unnecessary. Two things, however, make fulfillment of this hope improbable. One is the fact that it is unrealistic to expect the marketplace to behave as a self-regulating mechanism, particularly in the area of defense purchases. Corporate power over prices, costs, capital sources and consumers in the major industries and the movement toward concentration, accelerated through conglomerate mergers and takeovers, indicates that the fundamental condition for a competitive marketplace—companies that can and are willing to compete with one another—is rapidly disappearing. Industrial giantism is a fact of life. This is especially true in the defense industry, where concentration is high. The ineffectiveness of the antitrust laws to prevent or even retard economic concentration is notorious, possibly because the government has been unwilling to enforce the laws properly. Consequently prices in the marketplace are not so much determined by competition, which hardly exists, as they are administered by the very large corporations, and it should not be expected that defense firms would act differently under disengagement.

In any event disengagement is unlikely because the defense contractors don't want to disengage. Why face the rigors of efficiency and the risks of competition when business can be generated through the art of brochuremanship and maintained through the informal polity of which the contractor is very much a part? The Pentagon has cooperated with the monopolistic propensities of the large contractors by systematically destroying most opportunities for competition, in the face of repeated urging by many members of Congress to halt this trend. Because of the power delegated to the Defense Department through the contract system and the practically unreviewable discretion it has over the way contracts are awarded, it is unlikely that any steps Congress might take would remove the bias that exists within the military establishment against competitive weapons procurement.

GALBRAITH AND NATIONALIZATION

More in keeping with the structure of the defense industry is John Kenneth Galbraith's proposal to nationalize the big defense contractors.[4] His suggestion is that any firm that has done more than 75 percent of its business with the Defense Department over a five-year period be made into a public corporation with all stock in public hands. The common stock of such a company would be valued at market rates, and the stock and the debt would be assumed by the Treasury in exchange for government bonds. Directors would then be named by the government and the company thereafter operated as a publicly owned, nonprofit corporation. Subsidiaries of conglomerates such as the Aerospace Corporation of Ling-Temco-Vought and the Bell Aerospace Corporation of Textron would also

---

[4] See Galbraith's testimony before the Proxmire Committee, Ninety-first Congress, first session, "Hearings on the Military Budget and National Economic Priorities," Part 1, pp. 3–9, and Galbraith, "The Big Defense Firms Are Really Public Firms and Should Be Nationalized," *New York Times Magazine*, November 16, 1969.

be subject to nationalization when the subsidiary does 75 percent of its business with the Pentagon over a five-year period. Defense divisions of predominantly civilian firms such as General Electric and AT&T would be excluded under Galbraith's plan "for practical, if not strictly logical reasons." Apparently sales for military purposes to NASA and the Atomic Energy Commission would also be excluded.

Galbraith argues that taking over the defense firms, in exchange for fair compensation to its stockholders, would merely be recognition of the big contractors for what they are, a part of the public establishment. He cites Weidenbaum for the proposition that these firms have already become "seminationalized" by having taken on the characteristics and mentality of the government arsenal. But, Galbraith points out, they have managed "to combine all the comforts, including the classic inefficiencies, of socialism with all the rewards and immunities of private enterprise." They do not possess the most important characteristics of the private enterprise, for a very large part of their fixed capital and working capital is owned and supplied by the government; they engage in little or no competition with one another; their success or failure is not dependent upon the success of their operations, and they are instructed extensively by the government on matters traditionally considered part of the responsibilities of management. On the other hand, the contractors participate in public policy making: They define the missions and the needs for the armed services, make proposals for new weapons systems for which they help develop and then fill the specifications, and their top officials occupy positions of authority within the Pentagon. "The defense contractors and the Department of Defense are, in fact, complementary bureaucracies."

To the argument that nationalization would not solve the problem of controlling the military establishment, that simply enlarging the bureaucracy will not make it easier to deal with, Galbraith has a ready response. His rebuttal is that the large defense contractors are already a part of the bureaucracy, although a hidden part. By hiding behind the facade of private enterprise they are left free to engage in lobbying and other political activity, to urge policies that inure to their benefit by sponsoring or signing advertisements, to make substantial campaign contributions to friendly legislators, to support the Air Force Association "and other custodians of the weapons culture," and otherwise to do "what would be entirely inappropriate for an officer of a public corporation." Nationalization would eliminate the defense industry's political role in the formulation of defense policy.

The economics of defense production would also be more rational once the large contractors were nationalized. It is uncivilized and obscene, Galbraith says, for contractors to be fighting in Washington for new weapons business. Transforming them into public corporations would substantially remove the incentive to produce ever larger amounts of instruments of mass production, because without the profit motive, earnings, sales and prospects for growth would no longer be the criteria for measuring their success. They might even be more efficient. At the least, the prospects of being taken over should provide a powerful inducement to diversification into non-defense work.

The chief virtue of Galbraith's proposal is that it raises for the first time since the Nye Committee made a similar recommendation the important issue of whether or not radically to alter the procurement system by reversing the policy of contracting out for the military's needs. In effect it would reestablish the government laboratory and the government arsenal as the primary sources for the research, development and production of weapons, assuming that most of the aerospace firms currently dependent upon defense contracts would not be able to diversify to avoid nationalization. Galbraith's difference with Weidenbaum is not a difference of analysis, as both are in substantial agreement on the facts and the convergence of public and private sectors in the area of defense, but of how to correct the present situation. His solution is quite consistent with his general view of the mature industrial corporation that, "as it develops, becomes part of the larger administrative complex associated with the state."[5] In the defense industry the large corporations have become overmature, so to speak, and because under the present arrangement an inordinate and dangerous amount of power has passed to the Pentagon, it is necessary to modify the arrangement as part of a program to reduce that power.

Aside from the vacuous attacks that have been made on the grounds that Galbraith's proposal is socialistic (it is the current situation that is socialistic), the most obvious criticism is the one that he

[5] J. K. Galbraith, *The New Industrial State* (Boston: Houghton Mifflin Co., 1967), p. 393.

tried to anticipate: that nationalization will not by itself solve the problem of excessive military power. Indeed, nationalization would increase the power of the military and its bureaucracy by increasing the number of employees, plant and equipment under its direct control, notwithstanding Galbraith's point that the large contractors presently constitute a disguised part of the bureaucracy. Placing the contractors' employees on the Pentagon's payroll and adding the contractors' property to the Pentagon's inventory would unquestionably represent an increase in the amount of resources under the command of the military unless there were some assurance that the military budget would be reduced simultaneously with nationalization. One must also be concerned with the kind of excess profits that motivate bureaucrats, namely, larger and more heavily funded bureaus. A partial solution to the dilemma would be to place the new publicly owned corporations completely outside the control of the military, for example, under a separate civilian authority independent of the Defense Department (several persons have recommended that all military procurement be placed under an independent civilian agency). Such an arrangement would not be satisfactory to those who would oppose any enlargement of the federal government, civilian or military, but here Galbraith would probably concede his preference for public ownership as a way to provide necessary public services.

THE PROXMIRE COMMITTEE AND MILITARY-INDUSTRIAL INDICATORS

The Proxmire Committee has recommended that steps be taken not so much as an ultimate solution to the multitude of problems revealed in its inquiries than as a prerequisite for gaining control over the military budget. One step is the establishment of an information system on defense programs.

The "Economics of Military Procurement" report states:

Good information is a condition precedent to the attainment of government control over military procurement. Presently we do not have sufficient information about much of the procurement process including profitability, status of program costs, overruns, subcontracting, military prices, cost allocation, performance, and number of retired military employed by defense contractors.

The report goes on to set out in some detail a series of recommendations that when taken together would comprise "military-industrial indicators" whose purpose would be to provide a nonclassified, ongoing report to Congress and the public on the status of military expenditures. Such a report, according to the Proxmire Committee, would remedy the failure of the Defense Department "to provide itself, the Congress, and the public with the information necessary for a proper accounting of the tens of billions of dollars spent each year."

For example, the military-industrial indicators would include a status report of weapons programs so that anyone having the report could tell at a glance whether a weapons system was in a cost-overrun condition, whether it would be delivered on time, whether progress payments matched actual work completed, and whether final performance would meet contract specifications. Presumably had such a reporting system been in effect several years ago, the cost overruns on the C-5A, for one, could have been detected and Congress would have been in a position to insist that corrective steps be taken or to terminate the program before it went too far. The indicators would also include information on defense profits, a procurement cost index and a personnel directory showing the number and places of employment of former military officers (colonel and above) and former Pentagon civilian officials (GS-16 and above) working for contractors and former contractor employees working for the Pentagon.

In its report "The Military Budget and National Economic Priorities" the Proxmire Committee recommended that the annual posture statement of the Secretary of Defense be improved by including five-year projections of the future expenditure consequences of current and proposed defense programs. Thus when the Secretary explains why a new bomber is necessary, he would also estimate its costs over the next five years. The Pentagon has not made such estimates available, although they exist and should not be classified. The same report recommended that the executive deliver an annual posture statement on foreign affairs and that the Bureau of the Budget identify all defense-related expenditures so that a more accurate tabulation of the costs of defense would be reflected in the annual budget document.

The assumption, of course, is that representative democracy can still be made to work, that the average citizen is entitled to know how his money is being spent in the name of national security so that he can exert influence on his representatives from an informed position, and that Congress can make intelligent decisions about military programs once it has the facts. Until recently, where defense is concerned, Congress and the public have been deprived of both the facts and an active role in the political process. As the priorities report states:

Congress, for its part, has played a passive, noncritical role. Fiscal restraint with regard to military spending has been almost entirely absent. One reason for this has been the reluctance of Congress to require the Executive to disclose sufficient information on which to base intelligent judgments.

Implicit is the belief that on the whole the elected representatives of the people can by exercising their Constitutional power over the purse and through the deliberative processes of the legislature make decisions about national security more wisely and more in keeping with the legitimate aspirations of the people than the military, its bureaucracy and its industrial allies.

Galbraith, Charles L. Schultze, Richard J. Barnet and others have made similar assumptions in suggestions they have offered for the strengthening of Congress' role in military affairs (the Proxmire Committee recommendations relating to the military and foreign affairs posture statements were adapted from proposals made to the committee by Schultze). Galbraith's Military Audit Commission, Schultze's "appropriate institution" and the Defense Review Office endorsed by Barnet (first recommended by the 1969 Congressional Conference on the Military Budget and National Priorities in which Barnet, Schultze and Galbraith participated),[6] all seek to add to congressional capabilities for the gathering and analysis of information concerning the Pentagon's budget. The Military Audit Commission and the Defense Review Office would exist outside of Congress but be responsible to it, not the executive, in the manner of the General Accounting Office, and would be staffed by experts to provide studies and advice to any member of Congress. Schultze's "appropriate institution" and the Joint Committee on National Priorities proposed by Barnet would operate within Congress as a new committee or a part of an existing committee and would "review the basic factors

[6] For a transcript of the conference, see *The Progressive*, June 1969.

on which the military budget is based, in the context of a long-term projection of budgetary resources and national priorities."[7]

The Proxmire Committee has tended to look to the General Accounting Office for the kind of independent military analysis and expertise the others would establish in a new institution on the theory that the GAO is already in being and could, if it were guided in the right direction, serve the desired purpose. The uncertainty and delay that would accompany the creation of a new body would thus be avoided. For this reason the committee recommended that the military-industrial indicators be put together by the General Accounting Office and not by the Defense Department. The response of the GAO by early 1970 was less than enthusiastic but, to a limited extent, positive. It had declined to construct the military price index and the personnel exchange directory on the grounds that either the Pentagon or some other agency ought to have those responsibilities, and declined to do the profits study on the grounds that it needed additional statutory authority. Congress gave it the additional authority to do the profits study and directed the Pentagon to compile the personnel exchange directory. The GAO did agree to do a feasibility study of the should-cost approach to weapons cost controls and in a report to the Proxmire Committee in 1970 indicated that the should-cost approach could be a useful tool for its weapons systems reviews as well as for the Pentagon.

There was little sign of progress toward a military price index, a regrettable fact in light of the Pentagon's insistence that general economic inflation and price increases were responsible for many, if not most, cost overruns. Senator Proxmire had argued that the Pentagon was exaggerating the effects of inflation on military costs and that, if anything, military costs were contributing to inflation. The 1969 report of the Mahon Committee, it will be recalled, supported Proxmire's argument. A price index showing the prices paid by the government for military end products, such as engines, airframes and avionics, and the cost of labor, materials and capital used to produce the end products could indicate where costs are rising and lead to discovery of the reasons.

On perhaps the most important of the Proxmire Committee's

[7] See Schultze's testimony before the Proxmire Committee, Ninety-first Congress, first session, "Hearings on the Military Budget and National Economic Priorities," p. 56; Barnet, *The Economy of Death* (New York: Atheneum, 1969), pp. 138–39.

recommendations, for a status report on weapons programs, the GAO moved toward partial implementation. The committee had urged that the GAO collect the data needed for the status reports through its legal power to investigate all government expenditures and to audit the books of all contractors entering into negotiated contracts with the Pentagon and to submit the reports to Congress in unclassified form. Instead of developing such an information system, the GAO decided to review a system belatedly established by the Defense Department and to summarize its findings for Congress. The first summary of the Pentagon's information system, called System Acquisition Reports (SAR), was transmitted by the GAO to Congress in 1970.

GAO pointed out that the Pentagon did not even maintain a central file on the total number of systems it had going or their costs.[8] Although the report confirmed much of the criticism that the Proxmire Committee and others had been making about military procurement, the GAO's decision to review the Pentagon's information system rather than to establish one itself meant that Congress was still without the independent source of facts about weapons programs envisioned by the Proxmire report. There could be little assurance that the figures passed on by the Pentagon would always be accurate or timely. Significantly the GAO complained in its report of the difficulties it had encountered in trying to gain access to the Pentagon's data and of the delays that had resulted, and of the costs of several programs that were understated by substantial amounts.

Nevertheless, on balance the General Accounting Office was zigzagging in the right direction and, barring an abrupt shift in the political wind, it was expected that it would continue to provide some assistance to those in Congress who were demanding that a lid be placed on the defense budget. If this arm of the legislative branch was not moving fast enough or far enough to suit all the military critics, it should be pointed out that the GAO is subject to rather strong and sometimes ugly pressures from the other direction, as shown earlier in Chapter Five. The fact that it is influenced by those members of Congress who favor high-level military spending is unfortunate and could conceivably prevent it from ever coming to

---

[8] The cost overrun aspects of the System Acquisition Reports were discussed in Chapter Four.

grips with the real issues. But it should also be seen that any newly created legislative body would be subjected to the same influences from the same political potentates within Congress.

This is not to say that a new committee or a new GAO-type agency would not be a useful addition to the legislative process or that Congress does not need to increase its capability to deal with military questions. Congress is at present seriously understaffed and without the resources necessary for it to function as it was intended to function. It needs to equip itself with better facilities and with improved capabilities.

NIEBURG AND POLITICAL PLURALISM

It would also be desirable, as H. L. Nieburg has suggested, to enhance political pluralism by creating a variety of institutions with stakes in the contract system so that they might act as countervailing forces against the military and the contractors. "Built-in conflicts," Nieburg has written, "between the various constituencies of public contracting are the best and most effective source of self-restraint, policing, and critical evaluation by policymakers and the general public." Thus Nieburg would create new auditing institutions like the GAO, a public contract ombudsman to act as investigator and public defender, bounties paid to individuals who initiate charges of wrongdoing leading to the recovery of damages against contractors or public officials, new judicial bodies modeled after the U.S. Court of Claims to test contract decisions and award bounties, and new public corporations supplied with government funds to conduct research and development for civilian purposes so as to create competing claims for military research funds and also to act as a yardstick to measure the costs and quality of research performed by military contractors.

In order for such countervailing political forces to operate effectively, there would have to be a reliable information system, uniform accounting standards (to facilitate detection of padded costs and hidden profits) for all contractors engaged in negotiated procurement and full public disclosures of conflicts of interest. In fact some progress has been made on each of these issues. In addition to the commitment to provide Congress with periodic reviews of the SAR system, the GAO also completed in 1970 a feasibility study of uniform accounting standards for defense contractors in which it concluded that uniformity would be feasible and desirable, although it remained for Congress to legislate the standards into existence. The military-industrial personnel exchange should make possible more nearly full, if not full, disclosures of conflicts of interest on the part of officials in the Pentagon and in contractors' plants.

Apparently Nieburg would leave the contract system itself intact, while surrounding it with public and private groups ready and able to challenge its actions and to keep the informal polity off balance. This approach could also be usefully imposed on the partially nationalized industry that Galbraith recommends, and much of it could be used under a plan for complete nationalization.

Reliable information, uniform accounting standards, public disclosure of conflicts of interest, improved fact gathering and analytical capabilities for Congress, and new institutions to act as countervailing forces against whatever method of weapons procurement is hammered out of the present contract system should be seen as a minimum program for the reconstruction of the military-industrial complex, whether or not the large contractors are taken over by the government or more closely regulated. Even if the large contractors were permitted to continue to operate, such a program would be an even-handed approach to bureaucratic and industrial profiteering and inefficiency, taking into account the mixed nature of the relationships between the military and the contractors and the fact that although it often appears that the Pentagon dominates the defense industry, in practice it is often the reverse.

THE SIZE OF THE MILITARY BUDGET

The remaining set of issues concerns the level of military spending: "What is adequate defense? Adequate to what and to whom?" These questions were posed by Charles A. Beard in 1931, along with the observation that the materials for answering them had not yet been assembled.[9] The questions remain unanswered, the materials still not assembled; but we know that $80 billion was highly excessive in the late sixties, even with a war on.

[9] Charles A. Beard, "Making a Bigger and Better Navy," *The New Republic*, October 14, 1931, reprinted in Charles A. Beard, *The Economic Basis of Politics*, William Beard (ed.) (Magnolia, Mass.: Peter Smith), p. 121.

In 1968 an analysis by James G. Phillips in *Congressional Quarterly* concluded that $10.8 billion could be cut out of the defense budget from programs considered excessive, overlapping, unnecessary or of doubtful combat effectiveness.[10] The cuts would not affect United States combat capabilities, according to the analysis, and the nation's defense would be retained or even improved. Cutbacks or cancellations were recommended for major weapons systems such as ABM, the Hawk, Nike-Hercules and Bomarc surface-to-air missiles, the Continental Air Defense, the A-7D aircraft, the Cheyenne Helicopter, the antisubmarine and attack aircraft carriers, and the Manned Orbiting Laboratory, and substantial manpower reductions were urged. Phillips' cut-the-fat-out approach has been followed by several analysts, most notably Robert S. Benson, formerly of the Office of the Assistant Secretary of Defense (Comptroller), who demonstrated how $9 billion per year could be eliminated.[11]

A second approach is to look forward to the end of the war in Vietnam and plan a defense budget on the assumption that it can be cut back accordingly. President Johnson's Cabinet Coordinating Committee on Economic Planning for the End of Vietnam Hostilities (made up of the Secretary of Defense and other Cabinet members) estimated in its 1969 report that if the war ended by mid-1970, military spending could be reduced to about $73 billion by 1972.[12] The committee assumed that although the costs of the war were about $29 billion annually, $10 billion of this amount would be needed in peacetime for deferred military programs, such as new weapons that have had to be postponed, and that inflation and pay raises would consume an additional part. Thus defense spending could not be reduced by the entire costs of the war. Interestingly the committee also assumed that declines in spending would occur for only two or three years after a truce, followed by renewed increases. Others have made similar projections, coming out more or less at the same place.

There are several limitations with this method. It assumes that weapons programs already approved will go forward, that the humps

---

[10] *Congressional Quarterly*, June 28, 1968, pp. 1605–10.

[11] Robert S. Benson, "How the Pentagon Can Save $9,000,000,000," *The Washington Monthly*, March 1969.

[12] The "Report of the Cabinet Coordinating Committee on Economic Planning" is printed as an appendix in the 1969 Economic Report of the President.

and all inevitable follow the camel's nose. Some of these analyses recognize this fact and are intended to demonstrate the consequences of current decisions to purchase new weapons.

A more serious problem concerns the estimates for the costs of the war itself. Until 1970 the executive published the official figures for Vietnam spending at least once a year in its annual budget and on numerous other occasions, as the circumstances warranted. These figures were used for two different purposes: (1) to justify requests for additional military appropriations from Congress, especially in 1966 and 1967, when the administration made supplemental requests of more than $12 billion for each of those years because of miscalculations in the costs of the war; and (2) to show that the non-Vietnam portion of the budget was not rising appreciably. In this way the administration was able to whip up support of the war when it needed it and beat down criticism, such as there was, of the inflated defense budget.

During this period a few observers began to wonder whether the war was costing as much as the Pentagon was claiming. The reason for the skepticism was that calculation of the incremental costs of the manpower, weapons and other materials being used in Vietnam indicated a total amount of roughly $20 billion during the peak war year, as opposed to the $30 billion alleged. Skepticism mounted when in 1970 the budget submitted by President Nixon omitted all mention of Vietnam costs, and spokesmen for the administration refused to estimate for congressional committees what the war was costing on the grounds that separating Vietnam from non-Vietnam military outlays was confusing and meaningless. Yet a few months earlier, in November 1969, Secretary of Defense Laird had stated publicly that the costs of the war had declined sharply and would be down to a rate of $17 billion per year by June 1970.[13] On the basis of Laird's statement and other announced military cuts, Senator Proxmire asserted that the defense budget proposed in 1970 should have reflected at least a $15 billion reduction instead of the $5

---

[13] In his testimony before the Subcommittee on Department of Defense Appropriations of the Senate Committee on Appropriations, Ninety-first Congress, second session (1970), Assistant Secretary Robert C. Moot, comptroller of the Pentagon, gave new figures for the cost of the war, revising sharply downward the Johnson administration figures and Moot's own estimates given in congressional testimony the year before.

billion that was taken out for fiscal year 1971. Who, Proxmire asked, had stolen the "peace dividend"?[14]

Proxmire was referring to the funds for peacetime uses that were supposed to materialize in the federal budget once Vietnam costs declined, according to the economic planners in the Johnson administration. The amount of such funds plus new tax revenues that would be produced from an expanding population in an expanding economy were termed the "peace and growth dividend" in the report of the Cabinet Coordinating Committee on Economic Planning. If in fact military costs declined by as much as Laird had claimed, why wasn't most of the decline fully reflected in the new budget? There are two possibilities. One is that the Pentagon had deliberately overstated the costs of the war in the early years to provide an excuse for beefing up its budget. If the costs had been exaggerated, deescalation would produce far less savings than had been estimated and there would be little, if any, "peace dividend" to declare. The second possible explanation for purging the figures for Vietnam is that as the costs of the war went down, assuming they were as high as the Pentagon claimed they were, the temptation of the military to retain as much of its budget as possible proved too great to resist, and funds were simply pumped into non-Vietnam activities.

The mysterious disappearance of the "peace and growth" dividend illustrates the government's facility for hiding the military spending pea under a variety of military-program shells. Attempting to keep track of funds allocated within the Pentagon can be a futile exercise even when the funds are earmarked by Congress for a specific purpose. Until there is a vast improvement in the state of public information about these matters, it will be practically impossible for anyone outside the military establishment to follow shifts in military spending patterns as they occur. One should not expect the Pentagon to make voluntary refunds to the Treasury Department.

It is equally foolish to expect too much from *ad hoc* groups set up by the executive to study how defense spending might be reduced. The recommendations of such prestigious undertakings as the Committee on the Economic Impact of Defense and Disarmament and the Cabinet Coordinating Committee on Economic Planning for the End of Vietnam Hostilities are almost never translated into

[14] *Congressional Record,* February 10, 1970, p. S 1513.

action. In part this is because of the government's preference for studying problems rather than solving them; in part because we don't do serious postwar planning any more. The blue-ribbon study panels have become a sham whose real function may be to maintain the illusion of a government preparing for demobilization, to create hopes for "economic conversion" and "peace and growth dividends," which are more than likely to evaporate under the heat of the budgetary process.

The more promising approach is for citizens and members of Congress to question the size of the defense budget, not only by challenging major weapons systems and other programs, but also by analyzing the structure of the budget to determine whether it supports too much or too little military force to carry out the objectives assigned to it. It is possible, for example, to construct alternative defense budgets of varying dollar amounts by modifying the underlying assumptions of current military planning and changing the levels of our strategic and general purpose forces. The budget is greatly influenced by factors such as international commitments (treaties and other agreements with foreign governments), the official view of our relationship with the Soviet Union and China ("the threat") and whether, as MIT Professor William Kaufman puts it, we want to fortify the moon or become a handmaiden to the United Nations. The point is that our commitments can be changed, our assumptions can be changed, the objectives we set for the military can be changed and the ways we choose to reach these objectives can be changed.

As an illustration, it has been decided that in order to maintain a credible deterrent against the Soviet Union it is necessary to possess a strategic force capable of dealing a devastating nuclear blow in three different ways: land-based ICBMs (Minuteman), sea-based ICBMs (Polaris/Poseidon), and manned bombers (B-52s, FB-111s, and AMSA). Each of these systems is capable of killing 25 percent of the population of the Soviet Union after a successful first strike by her against us, according to the crude calculations by which such figures are derived. Each of these systems costs billions of dollars to buy and operate. The question is whether it is necessary to be able to destroy the Soviet Union once, twice or thrice. Similar questions can be raised about the decision to support a standing military force in Europe, Japan, Okinawa and Korea, about the wisdom of maintaining both land-based and sea-based (attack aircraft carriers) tactical aircraft capabilities and if so, how much of each. Obviously a multitude of issues can be examined in this manner, keeping in mind that their resolution will depend upon the degree of sanity with which we view "the threat," the commitments we get ourselves into, the objectives we specify for the defense program and other assumptions.

The budget is thus seen not as a sticky blob that grows according to some mysterious and unfathomable iron law, accessible only to military bureaucrats and military contractors. It is an instrumentality of policy that incorporates certain views about the world and ourselves; it can be adjusted upward or downward depending on which views are accepted, and it can be comprehended by the average taxpayer and the average member of Congress.

There are other techniques and one should not eschew any of them. Here, too, as in the approach to weapons procurement and military-industrial relations, it is necessary to be eclectic, to combine ideas and methods for a practical approach to a complex problem. There undoubtedly are wasteful programs that ought to be identified and removed from the budget. There are programs that become unnecessary, although they may have been necessary at one time. These programs also should be identified and removed from the budget, and the dividends of cost reductions that ought to result from their removal should be claimed as savings so that they do not fall back into the Pentagon's piggy bank. There is no substitute for constant scrutiny of military spending by persons familiar with weapons procurement.

It also should be recognized that the size of the defense budget can be changed within very wide margins without endangering our capacity to defend ourselves or the deterrence value of our forces. We can have a complete war machine with every conceivable strategic capability and with conventional forces equivalent to our highest effort in Vietnam for $100 billion, as of this writing, or we can have an economy model—one that might serve us better than the souped-up version—for $40 billion and perhaps less.[15] The question of how small the defense budget ought to be can perhaps never be answered with scientific exactitude. But analysis can help us to understand what is reasonable and necessary, provided it is per-

---

[15] See William Kaufmann's testimony in the Proxmire Committee hearings, Ninety-first Congress, first session, on "Military Budget and National Economic Priorities," Part 1, pp. 163–79.

formed outside of the Pentagon's orbit and is subjected to public scrutiny and legislative authority.

At this point the interrelation of measures to control weapons acquisitions and to drive down the costs of defense becomes clear. Any scheme of military procurement left to the devices of those who actively benefit from it will eventually become as corrupt as the contract system is today. The solution is for Congress—that is, all the members of Congress, not just a few powerful committees—and the public to assume an instrumental role in the formulation of defense policy and in the decisions regarding weapons procurement. Congress needs more complete information and the courage to use its own judgment. The people need to be assured through a variety of new institutions, public and private, that their interests, rather than those whose careers and fortunes ride on military spending, are being served. And for reforms to have any meaning the budget needs to be made small and to be kept small. *How* small is an intellectual problem that citizens must solve.

BIBLIOGRAPHY

I. **Books and Articles**

   A. Background Materials

   1. General

Angell, Norman. *The Great Illusion, A Study of the Relation of Military Power in Nations to their Economic and Social Advantage.* (New York and London: G. P. Putnam's Sons, 1911.)

Beard, Charles A. and Mary R. *The Rise of American Civilization.* Vol. I. (New York: The Macmillan Co., 1929.)

Chamberlain, John. *The Enterprising Americans: A Business History of the United States.* Harper Colophon Books ed. (New York: Harper & Row, Publishers, 1963.)

Fuller, J. F. C. *Armament and History.* (New York: Charles Scribner's Sons, 1945.)

Manchester, William. *The Arms of Krupp, 1587–1968.* (New York: Bantam Books, Inc., 1970.)

Millis, Walter. *Arms and Men, A Study in American Military History.* (New York: G. P. Putnam's Sons, 1956.)

Millis, Walter, ed. *American Military Thought.* American Heritage Series ed. (Indianapolis and New York: The Bobbs-Merrill Company, Inc. 1966.)

Nieburg, H. L. *Political Violence*. (New York: St. Martin's Press, 1969.)

Nussbaum, Frederick L. *A History of the Economic Institutions of Modern Europe*. (New York: Augustus M. Kelley Publishers, 1968.)

Renn, Ludwig. *Warfare, the Relation of War to Society*. Trans. by Edward Fitzgerald. (New York: Oxford University Press, 1939.)

Schumpeter, Joseph A. "The Sociology of Imperialisms." In *Imperialism and Social Classes*. (New York: Augustus M. Kelley, Inc., 1951.)

Smith, Adam. *The Wealth of Nations*. Modern Library ed. (New York: Random House, Inc., 1937.)

Vagts, Alfred. *A History of Militarism, Civilian and Military*. Rev. ed. (New York: Meridian Books, Inc., 1959.)

2. *Colonial Period to the Revolution*

Beard, Charles A. *An Economic Interpretation of the Constitution of the United States*. (New York: Free Press, 1965.)

Boyd, Julian P. "Silas Deane: Death by a Kindly Teacher of Treason?" *The William and Mary Quarterly*. Third Series, vol. XVI, April, July and October 1959, pp. 165–87, 319–42, 515–50.

de las Casas, Bartolome. Excerpt from "The Journal of Christopher Columbus," in *The Indian and the White Man*. Wilcomb E. Washburn, ed. Anchor Books ed. (New York: Doubleday & Company, Inc., 1964.)

Clark, Victor S. *History of Manufactures in the United States, 1607–1860*. Vol. I. (Wash., D. C.: Carnegie Institution of Washington, 1916.)

Cunliffe, Marcus. *George Washington, Man and Monument*. Mentor ed. (New York: New American Library, 1960.)

Davis, Joseph Stancliffe. *Essays in the Earlier History of American Corporations, Numbers I–III*. (New York: Russell and Russell, Inc., 1965.)

East, Robert A. *Business Enterprise in the American Revolutionary Era*. (New York: Columbia University Press, 1938.)

Ferguson, E. James. "Business, Government, and Congressional Investigation in the Revolution." *The William and Mary Quarterly*. Third Series, vol. XVI, July 1959, pp. 293–318.

Jameson, J. Franklin. *The American Revolution Considered as a Social Movement.* (Boston: Beacon Press, 1961.)

Jensen, Merrill. *The New Nation, A History of the United States During the Confederation, 1781–1789.* Caravelle ed. Vintage Books. (New York: Random House, Inc., 1950.)

Johnson, Victor Leroy. *The Administration of the American Commissariat During the Revolutionary War.* Dissertation. (Philadelphia: University of Pennsylvania, 1941.)

Josephson, Matthew. *The Robber Barons.* Harvest Book ed. (New York: Harcourt, Brace & World, Inc., 1962.)

Ketcham, Ralph, ed. *The Political Thought of Benjamin Franklin.* American Heritage Series. (Indianapolis and New York: The Bobbs-Merrill Company, Inc., 1965.)

Miller, John C. *Triumph of Freedom, 1775–1783.* (Boston: Little, Brown and Company, 1948.)

Morgan, Edmund S. and Helen M. *The Stamp Act Crisis, Prologue to Revolution.* Collier Books ed. (New York: Crowell-Collier Publishing Co., 1963.)

Morison, Samuel Eliot. *John Paul Jones, A Sailor's Biography.* (Boston, Toronto: Little, Brown and Company, 1959.)

Morris, Richard B., ed. *The Basic Ideas of Alexander Hamilton.* (New York: Pocket Books, Inc., 1957.)

Parkman, Francis. *A Half Century of Conflict.* 2 vols. (New York: Frederick Ungor Publishing Co., 1965.)

Peckham, Howard H. *The War for Independence, A Military History.* (Chicago: University of Chicago Press, 1958.)

Peckham, Howard H. *The Colonial Wars, 1689–1762.* (Chicago: University of Chicago Press, 1964.)

Putnam, Geo. Haven, compiler. *Essays of Benjamin Franklin, Political and Economic.* (New York: G. P. Putnam's Sons, 1927.)

Sawyer, Charles Winthrop. *Firearms in American History, 1600–1800.* (Norwood, Mass.: Plimpton Press, 1910.)

Schlesinger, Arthur M. *The Colonial Merchants and the American Revolution, 1763–1776.* (New York: Facsimile Library, Inc., 1939.)

Sumner, William Graham. *The Financier and the Finances of the American Revolution.* (New York: Dodd, Mead and Company, 1891.)

Thayer, Theodore. "The Army Contractors for the Niagara Campaign, 1755–1756." *The William and Mary Quarterly.* Third Series, vol. XIV, No. 1, January 1957.

Van Doren, Carl. *Benjamin Franklin*. (New York: The Viking Press, 1938.)

Ver Steeg, Clarence L. *Robert Morris, Revolutionary Financier* (Philadelphia: University of Pennsylvania Press, 1954.)

Ward, Harry M. *The Department of War, 1781–1795*. (Pittsburgh: University of Pittsburgh Press, 1962.)

Wright, Esmond. *Washington and the American Revolution*. Collier Books ed. (New York: Crowell-Collier Publishing Co., 1962.)

3. Revolution to the First World War

Andreano, Ralph, ed. *The Economic Impact of the American Civil War*. (Cambridge: Schenkman Publishing Co., Inc., 1967.)

Bruce, Robert V. *Lincoln and the Tools of War*. First ed. (Indianapolis and New York: The Bobbs-Merrill Company, Inc., 1956.)

Clark, Victor S. *History of Manufactures in the United States, 1860–1914*. Vol. II. (Washington, D. C.: Carnegie Institution of Washington, 1928.)

Green, Constance. *Eli Whitney and the Birth of American Technology*. Library of American Biography ed. (Boston: Little, Brown and Company, 1956.)

Ingersoll, L. D. *A History of the War Department of the United States*. (Washington, D. C.: Francis B. Mohun, 1880.)

LaFeber, Walter. *The New Empire: An Interpretation of American Expansion, 1860–1898*. (Ithaca: Cornell University Press, 1963.)

Larson, Henrietta M. *Jay Cooke, Private Banker*. (Cambridge: Harvard University Press, 1936.)

Nevins, Allan. *The War for the Union*. Vol. II. (New York: Charles Scribner's Sons, 1960.)

Nichols, Roy F. *The Stakes of Power, 1845–1877*. (New York: Hill and Wang, 1961.)

Oberholtzer, Ellis Paxson. *Jay Cook, Financier of the Civil War*. Vols. I and II. (Philadelphia: George W. Jacobs and Co., Publishers, 1907.)

Shannon, Fred Albert. *The Organization and Administration of the Union Army, 1861–1865*. Vols. I and II. (Cleveland: The Arthur H. Clark Co., 1928.)

Sprout, Harold and Margaret. *The Rise of American Naval Power, 1776–1918*. Fifth printing. (Princeton: Princeton University Press, 1967.)

4. First World War to Present

Barnet, Richard J. *The Economy of Death*. (New York: Atheneum, 1969.)

Baruch, Bernard M. *American Industry in the War, A Report of the War Industries Board (March 1921)*. Ed. by Richard H. Hippelheuser. (New York: Prentice-Hall, Inc., 1941.)

Baumol, William J. *Business Behavior, Value and Growth*. (New York: The Macmillan Company, 1959.)

Beard, Charles A. "The Rise of the German Navy," *The Economic Basis of Politics, and Related Writings*. Compiled by William Beard. (Magnolia, Mass.: Peter Smith.)

Campbell, Lt. Gen. Levin H. *The Industry-Ordnance Team*. (New York: McGraw-Hill, 1946.)

Catton, Bruce. *The War Lords of Washington*. (New York: Harcourt, Brace & World, Inc., 1948.)

Chayes, Abram, and Wiesner, Jerome B., eds. *ABM, An Evaluation of the Decision to Deploy an Antiballistic Missile System*. Signet Broadside ed. (New York: The New American Library, 1969.)

Coffin, Tristram. *The Passion of the Hawks, Militarism in Modern America*. (New York: The Macmillan Company, 1964.)

Committee for Economic Development. *The National Economy and the Vietnam War*. (New York: Committee for Economic Development, 1968.)

Cook, Fred J. *The Warfare State*. (New York: Collier Books, 1964.)

Eisenhower, Dwight. *The White House Years: Mandate for Change, 1953–1956*. (New York: Doubleday & Company, 1963.)

Engelbrecht, H. C., and Hanighen, F. C. *Merchants of Death, A Study of the International Armament Industry*. (New York: Dodd, Mead & Co., 1934.)

Enock, Arthur Guy. *This War Business*. (London: Bodley Head, 1951.)

Evans, Rowland, and Novak, Robert. *Lyndon B. Johnson: The Exercise of Power*. (New York: The New American Library, 1966.)

Galbraith, John Kenneth. *The New Industrial State*. (Boston: Houghton Mifflin Company, 1967.)

Gantz, Lt. Col. Kenneth F., ed. *The United States Air Force Report on the Ballistic Missile, Its Technology, Logistics, and Strategy*. (New York: Doubleday & Company, 1958.)

Janeway, Eliot. *The Economics of Crisis, War, Politics and the Dollar*. (New York: Weybright and Talley, 1968.)

Kaufmann, William W. *The McNamara Strategy.* (New York: Harper & Row, 1964.)

Keynes, John Maynard. *How To Pay for the War.* (New York: Harcourt, Brace & World, Inc., 1940.)

Kolko, Gabriel. *The Roots of American Foreign Policy: An Analysis of Power and Purpose.* (Boston: Beacon Press, 1969.)

Kolodziej, Edward A. *The Uncommon Defense and Congress, 1945–1963.* (Columbus, Ohio: Ohio State University Press, 1966.)

Lasswell, Harold D. *Politics, Who Gets What, When, How.* (New York: McGraw-Hill, 1936.)

Leuchtenburg, William E. *The Perils of Prosperity, 1914–32.* (Chicago: University of Chicago Press, 1958.)

Lewinsohn, Richard. *The Profits of War Through the Ages.* Trans. by Geoffrey Sainsbury. (New York: E. P. Dutton & Co., Inc., 1937.)

McGaffin, William, and Knoll, Erwin. *Scandal in the Pentagon, A Challenge to Democracy.* (Greenwich, Conn.: Fawcett Publications, Inc., 1969.)

Millis, Walter; Mansfield, Harvey C.; and Stein, Harold. *Arms and the State, Civil-Military Elements in National Policy.* (New York: The Twentieth Century Fund, 1958.)

Millis, Walter, ed. *The Forrestal Diaries.* (New York: The Viking Press, 1951.)

Mills, C. Wright. *The Power Elite.* (New York: Oxford University Press, 1959.)

Mollenhoff, Clark. *The Pentagon: Politics, Profits and Plunder.* (New York: G. P. Putnam's Sons, 1967.)

Mumford, Lewis. *Technics and Civilization.* (New York: Harcourt, Brace & World, Inc., 1934.)

Phelan, William D., Jr. "Nixon's 'Southern' Strategy: The Authoritarian Prescription." *The Nation,* Nov. 3, 1969.

Raushenbush, Stephen and Joan, *War Madness.* (Washington, D. C.: National Home Library Foundation, 1937.)

Riddle, Donald H. *The Truman Committee, A Study in Congressional Responsibility.* (New Brunswick, N.J.: Rutgers University Press, 1964.)

Ridgeway, James. *The Closed Corporation, American Universities in Crisis.* (New York: Random House, 1968.)

Sherrill, Robert. "The War Machine." *Playboy,* May 1970.

Staley, Eugene. *War and the Private Investor.* (Garden City, N.Y.: Doubleday Doran and Co., Inc., 1935.)

Stone, I. F. *Business as Usual, The First Year of Defense.* (New York: Modern Age Books, 1941.)

Thayer, George. *The War Business.* (New York: Simon and Shuster, 1969.)

Tobin, James. "Defense, Dollars, and Doctrines." In Wilkins, B. Hughel, and Friday, Charles B., *The Economists of the New Frontier, An Anthology.* (New York: Random House, 1963.)

Truman, Harry S. *Memoirs, Vol. I, Years of Decisions.* (Garden City, N.Y.: Doubleday & Company, Inc., 1958.)

Truman, Harry S. *Memoirs, Vol. Two, Years of Trial and Hope.* (Garden City, N.Y.: Doubleday & Co., Inc., 1956.)

B. Science and Technology

Ayres, C. E. *Science, The False Messiah.* (Indianapolis, The Bobbs-Merrill Company, 1927.)

Bronowski, J. *The Common Sense of Science.* Vintage Books ed. (New York: Random House.)

Conant, James B. *Modern Science and Modern Man.* Anchor Books ed. (New York: Columbia University Press, 1952.)

Cox, Donald W. *America's New Policy Makers, The Scientists' Rise to Power.* (Philadelphia: Chilton Company, 1964.)

Danhof, Clarence H. *Government Contracting and Technological Change.* (Washington, D. C.: Brookings Institution, 1968.)

"DOD Analyst Indicts Military Aircraft Avionics Systems." *Aerospace Daily,* August 7, 1969.

Etzioni, Amitai. *The Moon Doggle, Domestic and International Implications of the Space Race.* (New York: Doubleday & Company, Inc., 1964.)

Lapp, Ralph E. *Arms Beyond Doubt.* (New York: Cowles Book Co., 1970.)

Lapp, Ralph E. *The Weapons Culture.* (New York: W. W. Norton & Company, Inc., 1968.)

Mansfield, Edwin. *The Economics of Technological Change.* (New York: W. W. Norton & Company, Inc., 1968.)

Mansfield, Edwin. *Industrial Research and Technological Innovation: An Econometric Analysis.* (New York: W. W. Norton & Company, Inc., 1968.)

Melman, Seymour. *Our Depleted Society.* New York: Holt, Rinehart and Winston, 1965.)

Nelson, Richard R.; Peck, Merton J.; and Kalachek, Edward D. *Technology, Economic Growth and Public Policy*. A Rand Corporation and Brookings Institution Study. (Washington, D. C.: Brookings Institution, 1967.)

Nieburg, H. L. *In the Name of Science*. (Chicago: Quadrangle Books, 1966.)

Nieburg, H. L. "Social Control of Innovation." *The American Economic Review*, May 1968, pp. 666–67.

Nieburg, H. L. "R&D and the Contract State: Throwing Away the Yardstick." *Bulletin of the Atomic Scientists*, March 1966.

O'Leary, Brian. "Notes of an Ex-Astronaut—Science in Space." *The Nation*, May 4, 1970.

Orlans, Harold. *Contracting for Atoms*. (Washington, D. C.: Brookings Institution, 1967.)

Shapero, Albert. "Life Styles of Engineering." *Space/Aeronautics*, March 1969, pp. 58–65.

Snow, C. P. *Science and Government*. Mentor Book ed. (New York: New American Library, 1962.)

Snow, C. P. *The Two Cultures: And a Second Look*. Mentor Book ed. (New York: New American Library, 1964.)

Zuckerman, Sir Solly. *Scientists and War: The Impact of Science on Military and Civil Affairs*. (New York and Evanston: Harper & Row, 1967.)

C. Spending, Procurement, and Production

Adams, Walter. "The Military-Industrial Complex and the New Industrial State." *American Economic Review*, May 1968, pp. 652–65.

Anderson, Richard M. "Anguish in the Defense Industry." *Harvard Business Review*, November-December 1969, pp. 162–80.

Anthony, Robert N. *Management Accounting Principles, Revised Edition*. (Homewood, Ill.: Richard D. Irwin, Inc., 1970.)

Anthony, Robert N. "What Should 'Cost' Mean?" *Harvard Business Review*, May-June 1970.

Armacost, Michael. *The Politics of Weapons Innovation: The Thor-Jupiter Controversy*. (New York and London: Columbia University Press, 1969.)

Benoit, Emile. "The Monetary and Real Costs of National Defense." *The American Economic Review*, May 1968, pp. 398–416.

Benson, Robert S. "How the Pentagon Can Save $9,000,000,000." *The Washington Monthly,* March 1969.

Berkley, George E. "The Myth of War Profiteering." *The New Republic,* December 20, 1969.

Brownlow, Cecil. "USAF Reverting to Original C-5A Operational Format." *Aviation Week,* July 6, 1970.

Burns, Arthur F. "The Defense Sector: An Evaluation of Its Economic and Social Impact." Moskowitz lecture, New York University, 1967. Reprinted in *Congressional Record,* March 10, 1969, pp. S 2523–27.

"Congressional Informants in Trouble with Pentagon." (Washington, D. C.: *Congressional Quarterly,* January 17, 1969, pp. 133–37.)

Demaree, Allan T. "Defense Profits: The Hidden Issues." *Fortune,* August 1, 1969.

Enke, Stephen, ed. *Defense Management.* (Englewood Cliffs, N.J.: Prentice-Hall, Inc., 1967.)

Franklin, Ben A. "Federal Computers Amass Files on Suspect Citizens." *The New York Times,* June 28, 1970, p. 1.

Galbraith, John Kenneth. "How to Control the Military." *Harper's Magazine,* June 1969.

Galbraith, John Kenneth. "The Big Defense Firms Are Really Public Firms and Should Be Nationalized." *New York Times Magazine,* November 16, 1969.

Graetz, Michael J. "The Truth-in-Negotiations Act: An Examination of Defective Pricing in Government Contracts." *Virginia Law Review,* Vol. 54, no. 3 (1968), pp. 505–26.

Hersh, Seymour M. "The Military Committees." *The Washington Monthly,* April 1969.

McDonald, Donald. "Militarism in America." *The Center Magazine,* January 1970, pp. 13–33.

Melman, Seymour. *Pentagon Capitalism: The Political Economy of War.* (New York: McGraw-Hill, 1970.)

National Security and Our Individual Freedom. Committee for Economic Development, The Research and Policy Committee. (New York: Committee for Economic Development, 1949.)

Nossiter, Bernard D. "Arms Firms See Postwar Spurt, Leaders Show Little Interest in Applying Skills to Domestic Ills." *Washington Post,* December 8, 1968.

Nossiter, Bernard D. "Defense Firms Leery of Civilian Work, 'No-

Risk' Contracts Heighten Appeal of Arms Business." *Washington Post,* December 9, 1968.

Nossiter, Bernard D. "F-111 'Brain.' How Its Cost Soared." *Washington Post,* May 11, 1969.

Nossiter, Bernard D. "C-5A Limitations Data Withheld by Pentagon." *Washington Post,* August 31, 1969.

Olds, Greg. "The Military in Texas." *The Texas Observer,* February 2, 1968.

Oliver, Richard P. "Increase in Defense-Related Employment During Vietnam Buildup." *Monthly Labor Review,* vol. 93, no. 2, February 1970, pp. 3–10.

Peck, M. J., and Sherer, F. M. *The Weapons Acquisition Process: An Economic Analysis.* (Boston: Harvard Business School, 1962.)

"Pentagon Charged with Intentional Reprogramming." *Aerospace Daily,* November 26, 1969.

Perlo, Victor. *Militarism and Industry: Arms Profiteering in the Missile Age.* (New York: International Publishers Co., 1963.)

Perlo, Victor. "Arms Profiteering—It's Not a Myth." *The New Republic,* February 7, 1970.

Phillips, James. "Defense Budget Cuts of $10.8 Billion Seen Feasible." *Congressional Quarterly,* June 28, 1968, pp. 1605–10.

Proxmire, Senator William. *Report from Wasteland, America's Military-Industrial Complex.* (New York: Praeger Publishers, 1970.)

Proxmire, Senator William. "Spendthrifts for Defense," in *Peace and Arms.* Ed. by Henry M. Christman. (New York: Sheed and Ward, 1964.)

Pyle, Christopher H. "CONUS Intelligence: The Army Watches Civilian Politics." *The Washington Monthly,* January 1970.

Raymond, Jack. "Growing Threat of Our Military-Industrial Complex." *Harvard Business Review,* May-June 1968, pp. 53–64.

Roback, Herbert. "Truth in Negotiating: The Legislative Background." Paper presented to American Bar Association, Section of Public Contract Law, Honolulu, Hawaii, August 8, 1967.

Russett, Bruce M. "Who Pays for Defense?" *The American Political Science Review,* June 1969, pp. 412–26.

Scherer, F. M. *The Weapons Acquisition Process: Economic Incentives.* (Boston: Harvard Business School, 1964.)

Shoup, Gen. David M. "The New American Militarism." *The Atlantic,* April 1969.

Stone, I. F. "Nixon and the Arms Race: The Bomber Boondoggle." *New York Review of Books,* January 2, 1969.

Stubbing, Richard A. "Improving the Acquisition Process for High Risk Electronics Systems." May 3, 1968. Reprinted in *Congressional Record,* February 7, 1969, pp. S 1449–56.

"The 'Military Lobby'—Its Impact on Congress, Nation," *Congress and the Nation 1945–1965.* (Washington, D. C.: *Congressional Quarterly,* 1965, pp. 1577–84.)

von Bauer, F. Trowbridge. "Constructive Change Orders." *The Government Contractor—Briefing Papers.* (Washington, D. C.: Federal Publications, Inc., 1965.)

Watzman, Sanford. "War Profits: The Tax-Court Peephole." *The Nation,* January 27, 1969.

Weidenbaum, Murray L. "Arms and the American Economy: A Domestic Convergence Hypothesis." *American Economic Review,* May 1968, pp. 428–37.

Weidenbaum, Murray L. *Economic Impact of the Vietnam War.* (Washington, D. C.: Georgetown University Center for Strategic Studies, 1967.)

Weidenbaum, Murray L. "Defense Expenditures and the Domestic Economy." In Edwin Mansfield, ed., *Defense, Science and Public Policy.* (New York: W. W. Norton & Company, 1968.)

Weston, J. Fred, ed. *Procurement and Profit Renegotiation.* (San Francisco: Wadsworth Publishing Co., Inc., 1960.)

Wilson, Desmond Porter, Jr. *Evolution of the Attack Aircraft Carrier: A Case Study in Technology and Strategy.* Doctoral dissertation. (Cambridge, Mass.: Massachusetts Institute of Technology, February 1966.)

Zuckert, Eugene M. "The Military-Industrial Complex: A Perspective." Speech delivered before the Defense and Contract Procurement Administration Conference by the former Secretary of the Air Force. Reprinted in the *Congressional Record,* October 7, 1969, pp. E 8255–57.

II. U.S. Government Sources

A. Executive Documents and Publications

Atomic Energy Commission. *Annual Report of the United States Atomic Energy Commission for 1968.* (Washington, D. C.: U.S. Government Printing Office.)

Atomic Energy Commission. *1969 Financial Report*. (Washington, D. C.: U.S. Government Printing Office, 1969.)

Brite, George K. "Total Government Budget Outlays by Functions and Subfunctions Expressed on a Per Capita Basis and as a Percent of Total Outlays, Fiscal Years 1965 to 1970." (Washington, D. C.: Library of Congress Legislative Reference Service, 1969.)

Cabinet Coordinating Committee on Economic Planning for the End of Vietnam Hostilities. "Report to the President." In *Economic Report of the President*. (Washington, D. C.: U.S. Government Printing Office, 1969.)

Committee on the Economic Impact of Defense and Disarmament. *The Economic Impact of Defense and Disarmament*. (Washington, D. C.: U.S. Government Printing Office, 1965.)

Department of Defense, Office of the Comptroller. *Real and Personal Property of the Department of Defense, as of 30 June 1969*.

Department of the Treasury. *Statistical Appendix to Annual Report of the Secretary of the Treasury, for the Fiscal Year Ended June 30, 1969*. (Washington, D. C.: U.S. Government Printing Office, 1970.)

National Aeronautics and Space Administration. *Annual Procurement Report, Fiscal Year 1969*. Washington, D. C.: NASA.

National Science Foundation. *Research and Development in Industry, 1966*. NSF 68-20. (Washington, D. C.: Government Printing Office, 1968.)

National Science Foundation. Surveys of Science Resource Series. *Federal Funds for Research, Development and Other Scientific Activities, Fiscal Years 1967, 1968, and 1969*, NSF 68-27 (Washington, D. C.: U.S. Government Printing Office, 1968.)

Office of the Assistant Secretary of Defense (International Security Affairs), Department of Defense. *Military Assistance and Foreign Military Sales Facts*, March 1970.

Office of the Secretary of Defense, Directorate for Statistical Services. *Profit Rates on Negotiated Prime Contracts, Fiscal Year 1968*, December 10, 1968.

Office of the Secretary of Defense, Directorate for Statistical Services. *Military Prime Contract Awards by Region and State, Fiscal Years 1966, 1967, 1968*, November 12, 1968.

Office of the Secretary of Defense, Directorate for Statistical Services.

Military Prime Contract Awards and Subcontract Payments or Commitments, July 1968–June 1969, October 1, 1969.

Office of the Secretary of Defense, Directorate for Statistical Services. *Letter Contracts and Change Orders,* October 14, 1968.

Office of the Secretary of Defense, Directorate for Statistical Services. *Selected Manpower Statistics,* April 15, 1969.

Office of the Secretary of Defense, Directorate for Information Services. *100 Companies and Their Subsidiary Corporations According to Net Value of Military Prime Contract Awards, Fiscal Year 1969,* October 1969.

Renegotiation Board. *Fourteenth Annual Report of the Renegotiation Board, 1969.* Washington, D. C.

Scientific Advisory Board. *Report of the USAF Scientific Advisory Board Ad Hoc Committee on the C-5A.* (Washington, D. C.: Department of the Air Force, 1970.)

Securities and Exchange Commission. *Report of Investigation in re Lockheed Aircraft Corporation.* 2 vols., HO-423, Washington, D. C., 1970.

Turtle, Robert H. *Total Package Procurement Concept.* (Washington, D. C.: Department of the Air Force, 1966.)

U.S. Department of Commerce, Bureau of the Census. *Defense Indicators.* (Washington, D. C.: U.S. Government Printing Office, published monthly.)

War Contracts Price Adjustment Board. *Final Report of War Contracts Price Adjustment Board* (predecessor to the Renegotiation Board). Washington, D. C., May 22, 1951.

Whittaker, Phillip N., Assistant Secretary of the Air Force (Installations and Logistics). *Review of the C-5A Program.* (Washington, D. C.: Department of the Air Force, 1969.)

B. Federally Sponsored Research

Brunner, Gerti L., and Hall, George R. *Air Force Procurement Practices, 1964–1966.* (Santa Monica, Calif.: The Rand Corporation. RM-5439-PR, April 1968.)

Cross, John. *A Reappraisal of Cost Incentives in Defense Contracts.* Research Paper P-282. Institute for Defense Analysis. September 1966.

Defense Industry Profit Review. Logistics Management Institute. (Washington, D.C.: LMI Task 69-1, March 1969.)

Defense Industry Profit Review. Logistics Management Institute. (Washington, D. C.: LMI Task 66-25, November 1967.)

Evans, Capt. Stuart J.; Margulis, Harold J.; and Yoshpe, Harry B. *Procurement*. (Washington, D. C.: Industrial College of the Armed Forces, 1968.)

Fisher, Irving N. *A Reappraisal of Incentive Contracting Experience*. (Santa Monica, Calif.: The Rand Corporation. RM-5700-PR, July 1968.)

Fisher, I. N., and Hall, G. R. *Defense Profit Policy in the United States and the United Kingdom*. (Santa Monica, Calif.: The Rand Corporation. RM-5610-PR, October 1968.

Fisher, Irving M., and Hall, George R. *Risk and the Aerospace Rate of Return*. (Santa Monica, California: The Rand Corporation, December 1967.)

Greenberg, Edward. *Relationships Between R&D Contracts and Production Contracts*. Working Paper 6707, NASA Economic Research Program. (St. Louis, Mo.: Washington University, June 1967.)

Hall, George R., and Johnson, Robert E. *A Review of Air Force Procurement, 1962–1964*. (Santa Monica, Calif.: The Rand Corporation. RM-4500-PR, May 1965.)

Stockfish, J. A. *The Sociology and Politics of Military Cost-Effectiveness Analysis*. Institute for Defense Analysis. Research Paper P-535, October 1969.

Weidenbaum, Murray L. *The Military/Space Market: The Intersection of the Public and Private Sectors*. Working Paper 6712, NASA Economic Research Program. (St. Louis, Mo.: Washington University, 1967.)

C. Congressional Hearings and Reports
(arranged chronologically)

In addition to the following congressional sources, the annual hearings and reports of the House and Senate Armed Services Committees and the Defense Subcommittees of the House and Senate Appropriations Committees are storehouses of information on military procurement and related subjects.

"Report of a Special Committee of the House." *American State Papers, Military Affairs.* Vol. I, pp. 38–42. March 27, 1792.

Government Contracts. Report of the House Select Committee to Inquire into the Contracts of the Government. House Report No. 2, Parts 1 and 2. 37th Cong., 2d Sess., 1861–62.

Report of Committee on Naval Affairs on Prices of Armor for Vessels of the Navy. Senate Report No. 1453. 54th Cong., 2d Sess., 1897.

Profiteering. Letter from the Federal Trade Commission to the President of the Senate. 65th Cong., 2d Sess., 1918.

War Policies Commission Hearings. House Document No. 163. 72nd Cong., 1st Sess., 1931.

Final Recommendations of the War Policies Commission. House Document No. 264. 72nd Cong., 1st Sess., 1932.

Report of the Special Committee on Investigation of the Munitions Industry. U.S. Senate, Vols. 1–5. 74th Cong., 2d Sess., 1936.

Renegotiation of War Contracts. Report of the Special Committee to Investigate the National Defense Program. Senate Report No. 10, Part 5, 78th Cong., 1st Sess., 1943.

Concerning Faking of Inspections of Steel Plate by Carnegie-Illinois Steel Corporation. Report of the Special Committee to Investigate the National Defense Program. Senate Report No. 10, Part 7. 78th Cong., 1st Sess., 1943.

Aircraft. Report of the Special Committee to Investigate the National Defense Program. Senate Report No. 10, Part 10. 78th Cong., 1st Sess., 1943.

Transactions Between Senator Theodore G. Bilbo and Various War Contractors. Report of the Special Committee to Investigate the National Defense Program. Senate Report No. 110, Part 8. 79th Cong., 2d Sess., 1947.

Aircraft Investigations: Hughes-Kaiser Flying Boat, Hughes Photo Reconnaissance Plane, Investigations Within the Air Force. Report of the Special Committee to Investigate the National Defense Program. Senate Report No. 440, Part 3. 80th Cong., 2d Sess., 1948.

Renegotiation. Report of the Special Committee to Investigate the National Defense Program. Senate Report No. 440. 80th Cong., 2d Sess., 1948.

Economic Concentration and World War II. Report of the Smaller War Plants Corporation to the Special Committee to Study

Problems of American Small Business. U.S. Senate, Document No. 206. 79th Cong., 2d Sess., 1946.

Investigation of the Preparedness Program. Annual Report of the Preparedness Investigating Subcommittee of the Committee on Armed Services. U.S. Senate. 82nd Cong. 2d Sess., 1952.

Interim Report on Defense Mobilization: Adequacy of Air Power. Report of the Preparedness Investigating Subcommittee of the Committee on Armed Services. U.S. Senate. 82nd Cong., 2d Sess., 1952.

Interim Report on Defense Mobilization: Aircraft Procurement. Report of the Preparedness Investigating Subcommittee of the Committee on Armed Services. U.S. Senate. 82nd Cong., 2d Sess., 1952.

Report on Concentration of Defense Contracts. Report of the Preparedness Investigating Subcommittee of the Committee on Armed Services. U.S. Senate. 84th Cong., 1st Sess., 1955.

Interim Report on the Facts with Respect to Corporate Profits and Return on Net Worth of Airframe Manufactures. Report of the Preparedness Investigating Subcommittee of the Committee on Armed Services. U.S. Senate. 84th Cong., 1st Sess., 1955.

Interim Report on the Facts with Respect to Remuneration of Officers and Directors of Airframe Manufacturers. Report of the Preparedness Investigating Subcommittee of the Committee on Armed Services. U.S. Senate. 84th Cong., 2d Sess., 1956.

Major Defense Matters. Hearings before the Preparedness Investigating Subcommittee of the Committee on Armed Services, Part 2. U.S. Senate. 86th Cong. 1st Sess., 1959.

Report Pursuant to Section 4, Public Law 86–89. Report by the Committee on Armed Services. House of Representatives. 86th Cong., 2d Sess., 1960.

Hearings Pursuant to Section 4, Public Law 86–89. Hearing before the Committee on Armed Services. House of Representatives. 86th Cong., 2d Sess., 1960.

Report to the President on Government Contracting for Research and Development. Report by a Presidential task force, headed by David E. Bell, Director of the Bureau of the Budget. Senate Document No. 94. 87th Cong., 2d Sess., 1962.

Pyramiding of Profits and Costs in the Missile Procurement Program. Report of the Committee on Government Operations, Permanent Subcommittee on Investigations. U.S. Senate: Report No. 970. 88th Cong., 2d Sess., 1964.

Comptroller General Reports to Congress on Audits of Defense Contracts. Hearings before a Subcommittee of the Committee on Government Operations. House of Representatives. 89th Cong., 1st Sess., 1965.

Defense Contract Audits (Reorganization of the Defense Accounting and Auditing Division of the General Accounting Office). Report by Committee on Government Operations. House of Representatives: Report No. 1796. 89th Cong., 2d Sess., 1966.

Review of Army Procurement of Light Observation Helicopters. Hearings before the Subcommittee for Special Investigations of the Committee on Armed Services. House of Representatives. 90th Cong., 1st Sess., 1967.

Review of Army Procurement of Light Observation Helicopters. Report of the Subcommittee for Special Investigations of the Committee on Armed Services. House of Representatives. 90th Cong., 1st Sess., 1967.

Review of Defense Procurement Policies, Procedures and Practices. Hearings before the Subcommittee for Special Investigations of the Committee on Armed Services. Part 1—Introduction and Truth in Negotiations. House of Representatives. 90th Cong., 1st Sess., 1967.

Economy in Government—1967; Updated Background Material. Materials submitted to the Subcommittee on Economy in Government of the Joint Economic Committee. 90th Cong., 1st Sess., 1967.

Economy in Government Procurement and Property Management. Hearings before the Subcommittee on Economy in Government of the Joint Economic Committee. 90th Cong., 1st Sess., 1967.

The M-16 Rifle Program. Hearings before the Special Subcommittee on the M-16 Rifle Program of the Committee on Armed Services. House of Representatives. 90th Cong., 1st Sess., 1967.

The M-16 Rifle Program. Report of the Special Subcommittee on the M-16 Rifle Program of the Committee on Armed Services. House of Representatives. 90th Cong., 1st Sess., 1967.

Army Rifle Procurement and Distribution Program. Hearings before the Preparedness Investigating Subcommittee of the Committee on Armed Services. U.S. Senate. 90th Cong., 1st Sess., 1967.

Investigation of the Preparedness Program—The Army's Rifle Procurement and Distribution Program. Report by the Preparedness Investigating Subcommittee of the Committee on Armed Services. U.S. Senate. 90th Cong., 1st Sess., 1967.

Additional Procurement of M-16 Rifles. Hearings before the Special M-16 Rifle Subcommittee of the Preparedness Investigating Subcommittee of the Committee on Armed Services. U.S. Senate. 90th Cong., 2d Sess., 1968.

Additional Procurement of M-16 Rifles. Report by the Special M-16 Rifle Subcommittee of the Preparedness Investigating Subcommittee to the Committee on Armed Services. U.S. Senate. 90th Cong., 2d Sess., 1968.

Defense Contract Audits (Relationships Between Defense Contract Audit Agency and General Accounting Office). Report by the Committee on Government Operations. Report No. 1132. House of Representatives. 90th Cong., 2nd Sess., 1968.

Economy in Government Procurement and Property Management. Report of the Subcommittee on Economy in Government of the Joint Economic Committee. 90th Cong., 2d Sess., 1968.

Survey of Government Operations—Renegotiation Board. Hearing before a Subcommittee of the Committee on Government Operations. House of Representatives. 90th Cong., 2d Sess., 1968.

Report on the Renegotiation Act of 1951. Report of the Staff of the Joint Committee on Internal Revenue Taxation. 90th Cong., 2d Sess., 1968.

Extension of Renegotiation Act. Hearings before the Committee on Ways and Means. House of Representatives. 90th Cong., 2d Sess., 1968.

Renegotiation Amendments Act of 1968. Report of the Committee on Ways and Means. Report No. 1398. House of Representatives. 90th Cong., 2d Sess., 1968.

Defense Department Sponsored Foreign Affairs Research. Hearing before the Committee on Foreign Relations. U.S. Senate. 90th Cong., 2d Sess., 1968.

Competition in Defense Procurement. Hearings before the Subcommittee on Antitrust and Monopoly of the Committee on the Judiciary. U.S. Senate. 90th Cong., 2d Sess., 1968.

Amendments to the Defense Production Act. Hearings before the Committee on Banking and Currency. U.S. Senate. 90th Congress, 2d Sess., 1968.

Extension of Defense Production Act. Report of the Committee on Banking and Currency. Report No. 1322. U.S. Senate. 90th Cong., 2d Sess., 1968.

To Renew the Defense Production Act of 1950, as Amended. Hearings before the Committee on Banking and Currency. House of Representatives. 90th Cong., 2d Sess., 1968.

Review of Defense Procurement Policies, Procedures and Practices. Report of the Subcommittee for Special Investigations of the Armed Services Committee. Part 1—Truth in Negotiations. House of Representatives. 90th Cong., 2d Sess., 1968.

Military Procurement of Airborne Rocket Launchers. Hearings before a Subcommittee of the Committee on Government Operations. House of Representatives. 90th Cong., 2d Sess., 1968.

Economics of Military Procurement. Hearings before the Subcommittee on Economy in Government of the Joint Economic Committee. Parts 1 and 2. Congress of the United States. 90th Cong., 2d Sess., 1968.

The Economics of Military Procurement. Report of the Subcommittee on Economy in Government of the Joint Economic Committee. Congress of the United States. 91st Cong., 1st Sess., 1969.

Capability of GAO to Analyze and Audit Defense Expenditures. Hearings before the Subcommittee on Executive Reorganization of the Committee on Government Operations. U.S. Senate. 91st Cong., 1st Sess., 1969.

Government Procurement and Contracting. Hearings before a Subcommittee of the Committee on Government Operations. Parts 1–8. House of Representatives. 91st Cong., 1st Sess., 1969.

The Dismissal of A. Ernest Fitzgerald by the Department of the Air Force. Hearings before the Subcommittee on Economy in Government of the Joint Economic Committee. Congress of the United States. 91st Cong., 1st Sess., 1969.

Procurement of 2.75 Inch Aircraft Rocket Launchers. Hearings before a Subcommittee of the Committee on Government Operations. House of Representatives. 91st Cong., 1st Sess., 1969.

Procurement of 2.75 Inch Aircraft Rocket Launchers. Report by the Committee on Government Operations. Report No. 774. House of Representatives. 91st Cong., 1st Sess., 1969.

Review of Army Tank Program. Hearings before the Armed Services Investigating Committee of the Committee on Armed Services. House of Representatives. 91st Cong., 1st Sess., 1969.

Review of Army Tank Program. Report of the Armed Services Investigating Subcommittee of the Committee on Armed Services. House of Representatives. 91st Cong., 1st Sess., 1969.

The Efficiency and Effectiveness of Renegotiation Board Operations.

Hearing before a Subcommittee of the Committee on Government Operations. Part 1. House of Representatives. 91st Cong., 1st Sess., 1969.

The Acquisition of Weapons Systems. Hearings before the Subcommittee on Economy in Government of the Joint Economic Committee. Parts 1 and 2. Congress of the United States. 91st Cong., 1st Sess., 1969.

CVAN-70 Aircraft Carrier. Joint Hearings before the Joint Senate-House Armed Services Subcommittee of the Senate and House Armed Services Committees. 91st Cong., 2d Sess., 1970.

Extension of the Defense Production Act and Uniform Cost Accounting Standards. Hearings before the Subcommittee on Production and Stabilization of the Committee on Banking and Currency. U.S. Senate. 91st Cong., 2d Sess., 1970.

Extension of the Defense Production Act. Report of the Committee on Banking and Currency. Report No. 890. U.S. Senate. 91st Cong., 2d Sess., 1970.

Changing National Priorities. Hearings before the Subcommittee on Economy in Government of the Joint Economic Committee. 91st Cong., 2d Sess., 1970.

D. Congressional Speeches and Debates

Bennett, Sen. Wallace F.; Mondale, Sen. Walter F.; Proxmire, Sen. William; and others. "Extension of the Defense Production Act." Debate of proposed uniform accounting standards. *Congressional Record,* July 9, 1970, pp. S 10945–47, S 10952–86.

Bonner, Rep. Herbert C. "Inflationary Pressures Resulting From Military Procurement." *Congressional Record,* June 20, 1952, pp. A 4047–49.

Church, Sen. Frank. "An Insidious Assault." *Congressional Record,* June 24, 1970, pp. S 9643–53.

Ervin, Sen. Sam. "Computers and Individual Privacy." *Congressional Record,* November 10, 1969, pp. S 13980–84.

Ervin, Sen. Sam. "Computers, Data Banks, and Constitutional Rights." *Congressional Record,* February 3, 1970, pp. S 1084–91.

Fulbright, Sen. J. William. "Public Relations in the Department of Defense." *Congressional Record,* December 1, 1969, pp. S 15144–57.

Fulbright, Sen. J. William. "The Navy Public Affairs Program." *Congressional Record,* December 2, 1969, pp. S 15307–33.

Fulbright, Sen. J. William. "The Public Affairs Program of the Air Force." *Congressional Record,* December 4, 1969, pp. S 15649–74.

Fulbright, Sen. J. William. "S. 3217—Introduction of a Bill Requiring the Secretary of Defense to Submit Regular Reports With Respect to the Kinds and Amounts of Information Released for Distribution to the Public by the Department of Defense." *Congressional Record,* December 5, 1969, pp. S 15804–45.

Goldwater, Sen. Barry. "The SST." *Congressional Record,* June 18, 1970, pp. S 9327–32.

Gonzalez, Rep. Henry B. "War Profiteering Must Be Stopped." *Congressional Record,* March 14, 1966, p. 5513.

Gonzalez, Rep. Henry B. "War Profits, Inflation and Tight Money." *Congressional Record,* Sept. 28, 1966, pp. 23218–19.

Gonzalez, Rep. Henry B. "War Profiteering and Renegotiation." *Congressional Record,* December 11, 1967, pp. H 16663–67.

Gonzalez, Rep. Henry B. "The GAO on Excessive Profit Determinations of the Renegotiation Board." *Congressional Record,* July 22, 1968, pp. H 7197–202.

Harsha, Rep. William H. "Procurement Abuse Continues." *Congressional Record,* April 20, 1970, pp. H 3291–93.

Leggett, Rep. Robert L. "Military Procurement, Research and Development, and Reserve Strength Authorization, 1971." (Cost increases of ABM system and proposed amendment to reduce funds for that system.) *Congressional Record,* April 30, 1970, pp. H 3726–36.

McClellan, Sen. John. "The F-111B Plane." *Congressional Record,* August 22, 1967, pp. S 11981–86.

Moorhead, Rep. William S. "Military Procurement, Research and Development, and Reserve Strength Authorization, 1971." (Proposed amendment to delete funds for CVAN-70 nuclear attack aircraft carrier.) *Congressional Record,* May 6, 1970, pp. H 3952–60.

Olsen, Rep. Arnold. "Military Procurement, Research and Development, and Reserve Strength Authorization, 1971." (Proposed amendment to delete funds for S-3A aircraft.) *Congressional Record,* May 6, 1970, pp. H 3950–51.

Pike, Rep. Otis G. "Military Procurement, Research and Development, and Reserve Strength Authorization, 1971." (Proposed amendment to restrict the use of funds for the C-5A, S-3A and Cheyenne Helicopter aircraft, and SRAM missile.) *Congressional Record,* April 30, 1970, pp. H 3746–47.

Proxmire, Sen. William. "Use of Government-Owned Industrial Plant Equipment by Defense Contractors." *Congressional Record,* July 1, 1968, pp. S 7998–8000.

Proxmire, Sen. William. "Blank Check for the Military." *Congressional Record,* March 10, 1969, pp. S 2518–28.

Proxmire, Sen. William. "Over 2,000 Retired High Ranking Military Officers Now Employed by 100 Largest Military Contractors." *Congressional Record,* March 24, 1969, pp. S 3072–81.

Proxmire, Sen. William. "Authorization of Appropriations for Fiscal Year 1970 for Military Procurement, Research and Development, and for the Construction of Missile Test Facilities as Kwajalein Missile Range, and Reserve Component Strength." (Remarks in explanation of proposed amendment authorizing a defense profits study by the Comptroller General.) *Congressional Record,* September 17, 1969, pp. S 10743–51.

Proxmire, Sen. William. "Cost Overruns of $20.9 Billion Reported on 38 Weapons Systems." *Congressional Record,* January 21, 1970, pp. S 673–76.

Proxmire, Sen. William. "Independent Research and Development— A Billion Dollar Boondoggle." *Congressional Record,* March 2, 1970, pp. S 2748–50.

Proxmire, Sen. William. "Who Stole the Peace Dividend?" *Congressional Record,* February 10, 1970, S 1513–14.

Proxmire, Sen. William. "Defense Contracts and Lockheed Aircraft Corporation." *Congressional Record,* March 10, 1970, pp. S 3307–8.

Proxmire, Sen. William. "Lockheed Aircraft Corporation's Negotiations with the Air Force." *Congressional Record,* March 16, 1970, pp. S 3763–66.

Proxmire, Sen. William. "Fundamental Questions on Lockheed's Financial Condition Remain Unanswered." *Congressional Record,* March 31, 1970, pp. S 4690–97.

Proxmire, Sen. William. "The Electronic Battlefield." *Congressional Record,* July 6, 1970, pp. S 10545–47.

Russell, Sen. Richard. "The C-5A Aircraft Program." *Congressional Record,* July 16, 1970, pp. S 11581–83.

Schweiker, Sen. Richard S. "Better Controls Over Defense Procurement." *Congressional Record,* March 12, 1970, pp. S 3565–69.

Symington, Sen. Stuart. "Reasons Why the ABM Could Well Cost Tens of Billions of Dollars More than Currently Estimated." *Congressional Record,* March 4, 1969, pp. 2243–44.

Symington, Sen. Stuart. "Over $23 Billion Already Expended in Abandoned Missile Programs." *Congressional Record,* March 7, 1969, p. S 2464.

William, Sen. John J. "Salaries Paid in Research Projects." *Congressional Record,* April 13, 1970, pp. S 5593–95.

Young, Sen. Stephen M. "Trend Toward Militarism Must be Stopped." *Congressional Record,* March 26, 1970, pp. S 4592–93.

E. General Accounting Office Reports
(arranged chronologically)

Report on the Use of Letter Contracts by Departments of the Army, Navy, and Air Force. B-127758. November 5, 1956.

Review of Aircraft Procurement Programs in the Department of the Navy, Part I. B-133250. February 29, 1960.

Examination of the Pricing of Fuel Booster Pump Repair Kits Under Department of the Air Force Negotiated Contract AF 01(601)-20268 with Thompson Ramo Wooldridge, Inc., Cleveland, Ohio. B 133307. May 10, 1960.

Examination into the Pricing of a Subcontract for Nuclear Components Awarded by the Plant Apparatus Department of Westinghouse Electric Corporation to another Department of Westinghouse and Charged to the Navy Under a Cost-Plus-a-Fixed-Fee Contract. B-146733. July 23, 1962.

Increased Costs Incurred for Ammonium Perchlorate Purchased During 1961 for Solid-Propellant Missile Motors. B-146843. January 31, 1964.

Unclassified Summary of Findings in Classified Reports of Development, Procurement, and Deployment of an Unsatisfactory Missile System. B-146762. February 18, 1964.

Unnecessary Cost Incurred by the Government by Not Using Surplus Stockpiled Materials to Satisfy Defense Contract Needs. B-125071. April 13, 1964.

Costs Incurred for Completion of a Solid Propellant Continuous-Mix Facility for Which There Was No Planned Use. B-146897. July 31, 1964.

Uneconomical Leasing of Motor Vehicles for Use in Assembly and Checkout Operations at Minuteman Launch Sites and Avoidance of Congressional Controls Relating to Acquisition of Motor Vehicles. B-146876. October 2, 1964.

Increased Cost Resulting from Acquisition of Maintenance Trucks Produced by the Boeing Company, Seattle, Washington, for the Minuteman Intercontinental Ballistic Missile Program. B-146876. April 6, 1965.

Need for Postaward Audits to Detect Lack of Disclosure of Significant Cost or Pricing Data Available Prior to Contract Negotiation and Award. B-158193. February 23, 1966.

Review of Prices Negotiated on Selected Contracts for Ammunition and Weapons Components. B 157535. April 21, 1966.

Long-Term Leasing of Buildings and Land by Government Contractors. B-156818. September 20, 1966.

Procurement of Thrust Vector Control Nozzles for the Minuteman Missile Program. B-146876. September 30, 1966.

Need for Improving Administration of the Cost or Pricing Data Requirements of Public Law 87–653 in the Award of Prime Contracts and Subcontracts. B 39995. January 16, 1967.

Survey of Reviews of the Defense Contract Audit Agency of Contractors' Price Proposals Subject to Public Law 87–653. B-39995. February 15, 1967.

Inquiry into Practices Followed by the Department of Defense Components in Acquiring and Installing New Automatic Data Processing Equipment for Use in Computerized Management Systems. B-163074. March 13, 1968.

Review of Costs of Bidding and Related Technical Efforts Charged to Government Contracts. B-133386. March 17, 1967.

Procurement of Critically Needed Missile Fuel Under Adverse Conditions from a Sole-Source Supplier. B-157445. April 24, 1967.

Need for Compliance With the "Truth-in-Negotiations" Act of 1962 in Award of Construction Contracts. B-39995. June 19, 1967.

Procurement of Nuclear Submarine Propulsion Equipment Under Public Law 87–653. B 156313. August 31, 1967.

Improved Inventory Controls Needed for the Departments of the Army, Navy and Air Force and the Defense Supply Agency. B-146828. November 14, 1967.

Need for Improvements in Controls Over Government-Owned Property in Contractors' Plants. B-140389. November 24, 1967.

Observation on the Administration by the Office of Civil Defense of Research Study Contracts Awarded to Hudson Institute, Inc. B-133209. March 25, 1968.

Report on Certain Aspects of the Renegotiation Process and Co-ordination Between the Renegotiation Board and the Department of Defense. B-163520. June 25, 1968.

Opportunity for Savings in Space Programs by Re-evaluating Needs Before Buying Facilities. B-164027. July 3, 1968.

Need for Improvements in Price Negotiations of Defense Contracts. B-39995. August 5, 1968.

Need to Improve Management Controls Over Ammunition Development. B-157535. September 27, 1968.

Differences in Allowing Corporate Expenses as Charges to Government Contracts at Government-Owned, Contractor-Operated Plants. B-124125. November 14, 1968.

Need for Improved Guidelines in Contracting for Research with Government-Sponsored Nonprofit Contractors. B-146810. February 10, 1969.

Use of Missile Procurement Funds to Finance Research and Development Efforts. B-146876. May 7, 1969.

Evaluation of Two Proposed Methods for Enhancing Competition in Weapons Systems Procurement. B-39995. July 14, 1969.

Reasonableness of Prices Questioned for Bomb and Hand Grenade Fuses Under Three Negotiated Contracts. B-163874. July 15, 1969.

Questionable Pricing of Contracts Negotiated for Urgently Needed Bomb Bodies. B-118710. December 11, 1969.

Feasibility of Applying Uniform Cost-Accounting Standards to Negotiated Defense Contracts. B-39995 (1). January 9, 1970.

Construction of Industrial Facilities at Government-Owned Plants Without Disclosure to the Congress. B-140389. January 21, 1970.

Evaluation Needed of Cost-Effectiveness of Four More Deep Submergence Rescue Vehicles Before Purchase by the Navy. B-167325. 1970.

Status of the Acquisition of Selected Major Weapon Systems. B-163058. February 6, 1970.

Allowances for Independent Research and Development Costs in Negotiated Contracts—Issues and Alternatives. B-164912. February 16, 1970.

Feasibility of Using "Should Cost" Concepts in Government Procurement and Auditing. B-159896. May 20, 1970.

INDEX